THE HISTORIES O

A CONCISE HISTORY OF CORNWALL

Series Editor
Ned Thomas (University of Wales, Aberystwyth)

For other titles in this series, please see the University of Wales website:
www.uwp.ac.uk

THE HISTORIES OF EUROPE

A Concise History
of Cornwall

BERNARD DEACON

UNIVERSITY OF WALES PRESS
CARDIFF
2007

Published by the University of Wales Press

University of Wales Press
10 Columbus Walk
Brigantine Place
Cardiff
CF10 4UP

www.uwp.ac.uk

ISBN 978–0–7083–2032–7 (hb)
      978–0–7083–2031–0 (pb)

British Library Cataloguing-in-Publication Data.
A catalogue record for this book is available from the British Library.

Printed by Gutenberg Press Ltd, Malta

Contents

Acknowledgements

By its very nature writing a critical synthesis of this kind incurs a considerable debt of gratitude to a multitude of scholars, both living and dead. In respect of the latter, readers will recognise many of the respected Cornish historians who are referenced in the notes at the end of each chapter. Their work activated my own curiosity about Cornwall's past. In addition to those already mentioned I would like to express my thanks to colleagues who took the time to read through chapter drafts. As a modern historian who has strayed well outside his specialist period, it was particularly valuable to receive the comments of archaeologists and medieval and early modern historians such as Allen Buckley, Peter Herring, Jo Mattingly, Oliver Padel and Mark Stoyle. I doubt they will agree with everything I say but their caution may well have tempered some wilder flights of fancy. Special appreciation is due to Ronald Perry, whose observations are always incisive and invaluable. More generally, I should also acknowledge the unfailingly friendly and helpful staff at the Cornish Studies Library (now Cornwall Centre) over the years and the stimulus of colleagues and students at the Institute of Cornish Studies, notably Liz Bartlett who proof-read some early drafts. Last but not least, Penny and Merryn have patiently and uncomplainingly tolerated this and other projects.

Introduction

Cornish history is a battleground. Not in the literal sense that it is all about warfare, although we shall certainly meet some. But Cornwall's past is the focus of fiercely opposed historical perspectives. On one side a 'kernowsceptic' approach plays down Cornwall's distinctiveness and the Cornish identity and, in its more extreme form, is determined, in the words of Mark Stoyle, to 'thrust the historiography of . . . Cornwall firmly back into the box labelled "English local history", and to nail down the lid'.[1] On the other hand a 'kernowcentric' position insists Cornish history is not just English or British history writ small but is a suitable unit of study in its own right, just as are Wales or Scotland. From this perspective the Cornish language, institutions of Cornish governance such as Duchy and Stannaries and a sense of Cornishness all take on special significance. At heart, the polarities of these competing perspectives result from a debate over the contemporary Cornish identity and Cornwall's place in the British Isles. The aim of this book is to extend and transcend this debate by providing a history of Cornwall aimed at both the growing numbers of students of Cornish history at degree level and the reader who wishes to go beyond the factual details of Cornwall's past.

The most significant kernowcentric grand narrative is Philip Payton's *The Making of Modern Cornwall*, published in 1992.[2] In that volume Payton employed a centre–periphery model, arguing that Cornwall's past was ultimately structured by its peripheral relationship to the core of the English and then British state located in the south-east of the British Isles. His analysis certainly helped move the discussion of Cornish history onto a new plane. Nonetheless, it was stronger on description than explanation, tending to locate Cornwall and the Cornish people as relatively powerless in the face of the pressures of peripherality. Moreover, in its desire to emphasize the distinctiveness of Cornwall, *The Making of Modern Cornwall* underplayed differences within Cornwall.[3]

Here I present another narrative, one where Cornwall and its people are not inevitably shackled by their peripheral condition, constantly hauled back into a subservient relationship. But neither is it a story of a long and righteous struggle against English oppressors.[4] Nor, indeed, is it a Cornwall quietly integrated at an early stage into England and existing purely and simply as yet another English county: patronized, romanticized and ignored in turn by policymakers and cultural elites who reside in or look towards the metropolis of a post-Imperial Britain. Instead, I argue that in order fully to appreciate how and why Cornwall is different from (and similar to) other parts of the British Isles we must recognize a fundamental tension structuring Cornwall's past and pervading its present. Cornwall is seen by some as a Celtic country or nation, by others as an English county, and can even be imagined as both at the same time. In no other part of 'England' does this happen. It reflects the presence of two traditions influencing Cornwall over the past millennium and more; landward influences from the east, from the southern English heartland, and maritime influences from the north, south and west. These latter can appear in the form of Celtic connections with Brittany and Wales or in the links with the New World forged in the nineteenth century.

Acknowledging the presence of both traditions helps us understand Cornwall's current predicament, as a kind of halfway house between English county and Celtic nation, and the hybridity of its contemporary identity. This book takes as its other principal themes the construction, deconstruction and reconstruction of that identity over time and the tensions created by intra-Cornish differences that at times may have been as profound as those between Cornwall and other places.[5] It also attempts to restore a place for local agency in the story of Cornwall. The Cornish people are not just passively structured by anonymous forces that leave them powerless. Obviously at times global forces have wreaked great havoc, notably in the economic restructuring that followed the decline of mining in the later nineteenth and twentieth centuries. But at other times windows open up. That said, this is not a history of great men and women but of longer trends and processes.[6]

In order to understand Cornwall, therefore, one has to come to grips with its sometimes complementary but often conflicting traditions. Others have, independently, reached similar conclusions. Alan Kent echoes the analysis put forward in the following pages, describing Cornwall as an 'unresolved duality of place'. Kent calls for the need to 'work through' the 'cultural negotiations' over this duality, in order to 'understand the ironies and difficulties of being Cornish in the twentieth and twenty-first centuries'.[7] In this book I pick up on this point but suggest this is not just a problem for those of us who are Cornish in the twenty-first century. The difficulties of being 'Cornish' in any century since the ninth required people to 'work through' Cornwall's competing traditions. Another writer, the postmodernist historian James Vernon, has written of the 'ambivalent position of Cornwall in the English imagination, and of England in the Cornish imagination – of the Cornish as English, but not English'.[8] But Vernon tends to view this as a product of the modern period and is prone to under-estimate the role of the Cornish themselves in creating this ambiguous relationship. Instead, I propose that this unsettling categorization of Cornwall as 'of England but not of England' has long historical roots. Only by digging into these can both the Cornish and the English recognize Cornwall's unique place in the British Isles.

Notes

[1] Mark Stoyle, 'Re-discovering difference: the recent historiography of early modern Cornwall', in Philip Payton, *Cornish Studies Ten* (2002), p. 112.

[2] Philip Payton, *The Making of Modern Cornwall* (1992). See also the contributions to the series *Cornish Studies* published by University of Exeter Press since 1993.

[3] For the plea for a greater sensitivity to scale see Bernard Deacon, 'In search of the missing "turn": the spatial dimension and Cornish Studies', in Philip Payton (ed.), *Cornish Studies Eight* (2000), pp. 213–30.

[4] John Angarrack, *Our Future is History: Identity, Law and the Cornish Question* (2002).

[5] For a recent account of the Cornish sense of identity from an archaeological standpoint see Caradoc Peters, *The Archaeology of Cornwall* (2005).

[6] For a comprehensive modern introduction to the events of Cornwall's past see Philip Payton's *Cornwall* (2004; originally published 1996).

[7] Alan Kent, '"In some state . . .": a decade of the literature and literary studies of Cornwall', in Philip Payton (ed.) *Cornish Studies Ten* (2002), pp. 212–39.

[8] James Vernon, 'Border crossings: Cornwall and the English imagi(nation)', in Geoffrey Cubitt (ed.), *Imagining Nations* (1998), pp. 153–72.

1

British Cornwall: from west Wales to Cornwall, 500–1100

Battles loom large in the history of nations. The Norman victory at Hastings in 1066 gave the English a new legal system, ruling class and language. Bannockburn in 1314 guaranteed the continuation of an independent Scottish political identity into the eighteenth century. In contrast, the iconic battle for the Cornish ended in defeat in 838, and, unlike Hastings or Bannockburn, we know extremely little about it. We have to imagine the drizzle rolling up the river valleys from the sea away to the south, hiding the rising sun and cloaking everything in a sodden dampness. The swords, spears and shields carried by the bedraggled Cornish warrior bands almost visibly corrode as they trek eastwards. There, on the slopes of Kit Hill, a few miles west of the River Tamar, their nemesis awaits – King Egbert's royal Wessex army. Taking advantage of the fortuitous arrival of allies in the shape of a Viking 'ship army', the armed defenders of the rump of the Kingdom of Dumnonia make their final, desperate but unsuccessful bid to avoid wearing the yoke of English tyranny. But imaginations run wild, fuelled by the history of the past millennium. The month, the time of day, the weather, the numbers of participants are all lost; even the precise site, somewhere near Callington, is unknown. Nevertheless, Hingston Down was of major significance in the emergence of a Cornish people. It marked the end of a phase of resistance that had fostered a sense of identity amongst the Britons of the far south-west – the people known to the English as the 'West Welsh', the 'foreigners' of the west. In southern Britain, only Cornwall, along with Wales, was able to resist thorough 'anglo-saxonization'. It is no coincidence that Cornwall 'remains the one part of England where not all indigenous inhabitants automatically describe themselves as "English"'.[1] This chapter traces the origins of that identity and outlines what some might view as Cornwall's 'golden age', that time when it made up first part and then all of an independent British kingdom.

We can start by going further back: to the years before 600. This was a period when seaward rather than landward influences were in the ascendancy, with intensified maritime contact with Brittany, south Wales and, more indirectly, Ireland. At this time too, Britons were leaving Dumnonia for Armorica. The 'Armorican exodus' is supposed to have begun in the later 400s and by 700 Armorica had transformed itself into Brittany, with a British-speaking elite who did what the Saxons were able to do in south-eastern Britain – impose their language and culture on the local people. The consequences for Cornwall were profound. A Celtic-speaking society to the south – and Cornish and Breton languages were indistinguishable before the tenth century – placed Cornwall in a Cornubo-Armorican culture zone. Saintly links via Christian communities and pilgrims, trade exchanges, population movements and, indeed, neighbourly squabbles continued off and on for a thousand years after the Armorican exodus, maintaining an alternative point of reference for the Cornish, a reminder of what might have been. At the same time links with the eastern lowlands became more brittle with the rise of Saxon kingdoms there in the chaos that followed the departure of Roman 'order'.

Shadowy government and elusive kings

Cornwall and the west of Dumnonia were only lightly touched by Romanization. The Roman road system petered out west of Exeter, villas were virtually unknown, and Roman 'culture' only fitfully adopted. Henrietta Quinnell suggests from the archaeological evidence that the people of the west took only those Roman features that fitted local conceptions of acceptability.[2] This suggests a positive sense of identity providing a basis for cultural continuity during the fifth and sixth centuries. Such continuity meant that, unlike lowland eastern Britain, the civil infrastructure did not collapse when Roman governors left. After 410 and the departure of the Romans a native elite began to call themselves *rex* – Latin for king. These rulers oversaw the emergence of the Kingdom of Dumnonia, which may have stretched east well into present-day Somerset and Dorset. Such families, called *tyranni* (usurpers) by the British cleric Gildas, writing in the early to mid-sixth century, reoccupied Iron Age hill forts. They then imposed authority on those around them from a hill-top position literally overlooking their neighbours. Continuity of occupation at Chun in West Penwith from the fourth to sixth centuries may prove

this. Yet the actual archaeological evidence for high-status occupation of other hill fort sites is more tenuous. One after another,
obvious candidate sites at Castle an Dinas, Arallas near Truro,
Domellick (St Dennis) and Castle Dore have been discovered to have
none of the detritus associated with post-Iron Age occupation.[3]
Although, with the striking exception of Tintagel, the halls of the
British kings in Cornwall remain tantalizingly insubstantial,
shadowy kings of Dumnonia may, by the 600s, have been imposing
themselves on a decentralized network of local chieftains and rulers.
Kingship, at least before 700, was also peripatetic. Exeter, the former
Roman administrative centre, was abandoned in the fifth century
and, instead of one centre, Dumnonian royalty occupied a 'series of
seats or citadels . . . for limited periods'.[4] The king and his household
travelled around their domain, exacting tribute in terms of food and
goods as they went.

Who were these kings? Some were named in the Welsh king lists,
genealogies constructed in the ninth or tenth centuries. But these lists
are clearly in part fictitious, especially as the intent was usually to
claim descent, and therefore legitimacy, from rulers of Roman
Britain.[5] Other names can be corroborated. Two in particular take
material form. A Custennin from the Welsh genealogies could be the
Constantine mentioned by Gildas in the early 500s. Constantine was
not Gildas's favourite ruler (admittedly he was also decidedly lukewarm about the others he mentions), described as 'tyrant whelp of
the filthy lioness of Dumnonia' and accused of both adultery and the
murder of royal princes after abdicating and becoming an abbot.[6]
However, such activities were hardly unknown many hundreds of
years later among royal families and lend an air of credibility to the
account. Two generations after Constantine we meet Gerent (or
Gerrans in later Cornish). Confusingly, another Gerent is recorded as
waging war against the Wessex ruler Ine around 710 and communicating with the Wessex bishop Aldhelm a few years earlier. Which one
of these was the *Gereint rac deheu* (Geraint for the south) who turns
up in the heroic poem *Y Gododdin*, joining the Britons of Strathclyde
in an invasion of English Northumbria, and which was the Gerent
who, according to another British poem, was killed in battle against
the English at 'Llongborth', thought to be Langport in Somerset?
There are other possible kings. Some, like Tudwal, Erbin and Cato are
just names, drifting wraith-like through time. Others, like the
Dumnonian leader at the time of the battle of Hingston Down, are

unknown to us. We do not know whether he fell in battle, to be remembered in stories now long lost, or whether he was quickly forgotten, reviled by his people.

As intriguing are those names of the Dumnonian ruling elite who pop up later as folk heroes. Somewhere around 500 we glimpse a Kynwawr or Cynfawr (great hound in Old Welsh) or Cunomoros (in Latin). A Cunomorus is named on the sixth-century standing stone near Castle Dore as the 'father of Drustanus'. Drustanus is of course Tristan and, in a further twist, Charles Thomas informs us that, according to the tenth-century Breton life of St Pol just across the Channel, Cunomorus was also known as Mark.[7] King Mark is a character in the story of Tristan and Isolt which was, by the tenth century, well established in Cornish folklore, as various place name evidence suggests. It was then carried to the Continent, according to Oliver Padel Cornwall's 'most significant and best-known gift to the literary world'.[8] The inscribed stone at Castle Dore hints that these romantic literary characters of later centuries may have been real figures of the sixth. Yet, disappointingly, there is no archaeological evidence for sixth-century occupation of the nearby Castle Dore – popularly seen as Mark's palace.

But another place was linked to a popular hero. In the twelfth century Geoffrey of Monmouth placed King Arthur's conception at Tintagel. By that time Arthur was a generalized folk hero across Wales, Brittany and southern Scotland as well as Cornwall, symbolizing the lost glories of the British peoples.[9] Tellingly, he was linked to earlier narratives of kings at Tintagel. Charles Thomas suggests the place had some sort of administrative role in the Roman period, one that then made it a focal point for an emergent Dumnonian royalty keen to attach itself to the symbols of the former Roman Imperium.[10] More spectacularly, Tintagel has produced the largest known assemblage of early Byzantine pottery outside the Mediterranean world. Pottery from the eastern Mediterranean and North Africa indicates that one or more voyages were made to Tintagel sometime in the 500s, bringing wine, olive oil and foodstuffs. Thomas concludes that Tintagel was a 'centre of tribute' from the fifth to the seventh centuries – a major royal seat from which British kings exercised authority and exacted goods and services from others.[11] If Tintagel was one of the dispersed centres of royal power from the 400s to the 600s, where were the others? One candidate is St Michael's Mount.[12] Other possibilities include those places with the place-name element *lis* (court). Liskeard, Helston (*Henliston*), Arallas, Lesingey near Penzance and Helstone (as well as later Lesnewth) may have served as the administrative centres of Dumnonian Cornwall. Interestingly, these *lis* names are well spread across Cornwall, appearing in all six original Hundreds of Penwith, Kerrier, Pydar, Powder, Trigg and what became East and West Wivelshire (the original Celtic name of these last being lost). Cornish Hundreds were based on pre-Saxon administrative units, or even sub-kingdoms.[13] Analogy has been made with the Welsh *cantrefi*, literally a 'hundred homesteads', supposed to provide a hundred fighting men and it is proposed that the Cornish word for Hundred, *keverang*, carried the meaning of a muster, implying that the Cornish Hundreds were also military assembly units.[14]

Centralization

These early Hundreds may have been an organizational response to growing pressure from Wessex after 700 or they could have had broader administrative functions. David Harvey interprets them as the basic early unit of territorial exploitation, developing a surplus for the local elite, and Peter Herring suggests they played an early role in policing the use of upland commons.[15] Local government in eighth-century Cornwall could have been even more sophisticated than this. Harvey goes on to observe that the later Cornish tithings (medieval groups of ten households responsible for the conduct of its members) represent a fossilized early unit of territorial exploitation, one present before 800.[16] This was the case in the thirteenth century for all of Cornwall except, significantly, East Wivelshire and Stratton, the most easterly Hundreds where English reorganization presumably disrupted the older pattern.

By the 700s we thus have a peripatetic kingship based on centres such as Tintagel and controlling its territory through sub-kings, Hundreds and, perhaps, the proto-tithings. But around this time, there was a general process of growing royal power and centralization, one shared across English, Welsh and Scottish kingdoms alike. This was particularly noticeable in Wessex, where sub-kings were replaced by eldermen based on the later shires. Edward James asserts that 'only the peripheries remained outside [the trend to greater centralization after 700]. Cornwall, for instance'.[17] Yet, while the

Cornish Britons continued to resist incorporation into Wessex, we can discern evidence that they too shared in the general drift towards centralization after 700. Kenneth Dark points to the disuse of hill forts after the 600s, implying that sub-kings were a declining force. People were deserting their enclosed rounds for dispersed hamlets and farms – radically altering Cornwall's settlement pattern and giving us those place names beginning in *tre*, indicating a more ordered environment. And greater ecclesiastical organisation was signalled by the appearance of a Cornish bishop, Kenstec, by 833.[18] Nicholas Orme notes that later Cornish kings favoured monastic foundations at Padstow and Bodmin over others. St Petrock's monastery, based first at Padstow and then at Bodmin, and close to major communication routes both north–south across Cornwall and west–east towards Wessex, was, he suggests, close to the chief seat of later British rulers – 'probably Bodmin; a place that was central, strategic and very likely the seat of a bishop as well'.[19] Bodmin, which at the time of Domesday Book in 1086 possessed by far the best endowed Cornish religious houses, owed its exalted status to an increasingly centralized Cornish polity in the later eighth and early ninth centuries.

Life in Dumnonian Cornwall

Changing fashions in kingship had little impact on actual day-to-day life in early medieval Cornwall. Nevertheless, considerable material changes occurred. A significant reorganization of field systems paralleled the settlement shift of the early post-Roman period from rounds to trevs. By the ninth century this had produced what Herring terms a 'Cornish rural communalism', where cooperative farming was practised on strip fields associated with the small hamlets that were the usual settlement form.[20] These strips were worked under convertible or ley husbandry where two or three years of cropping would be followed by several years of sown grass, a rotation system that endured in Cornwall for almost a thousand years. The result was a mixed pastoral and arable farming economy. Cooperation on the lowlands extended into the uplands. Here, rough ground was, at this period, entirely open. It was exploited for summer grazing, for fuel (turf and furze) and for hunting wild animals. The presence of this unenclosed open upland produced a system of 'transhumance', of moving stock onto the uplands for summer grazing. Individual members of households, probably young men and women, would accompany the animals and stay on the uplands from Mayday to Halloween. Herring speculates that this practice may be connected with the popularity of festivals marking the beginning and the end of the summer grazing season.

Place-name evidence suggests that most of the 'anciently enclosed' land of medieval Cornwall was taken in by 1000, leaving one-third of land as unenclosed upland rough ground. This was not just limited to Bodmin Moor (then called Foweymoor in English or Goon Bren in Cornish), Carnmenellis, the Lizard and West Penwith. In addition there were three further large areas of upland 'waste' north of Foweymoor, around St Breock Downs and a large triangle of land in the west bounded by Goonhavern in the east, Feock in the south and Camborne to the west. Extensive areas of downland, with the now almost entirely lost lowland marshes and meadows and ancient woodlands meant that there was a 'greater visual and land use variety in the Cornish countryside' and a 'more fragmented' landscape, possibly producing distinct local material cultures.[21] This was also a landscape with few towns and limited trade. That there was some trade is implied by the kitchenware from western France that shows up in the archaeological record.[22] If kitchenware was imported then one obvious exchange would be tin. There is evidence for tin streaming at this period and some observers have concluded that the industry was 'healthy and thriving',[23] but it was probably on a relatively small scale. In general, while Cornwall from 600 to 800 was not as impoverished as Wales,[24] it did not share in the economic changes of urbanization and more vigorous market exchange that were beginning to touch England.

Nevertheless, sluggish economic change did not mean cultural conservatism. Culturally, there was both continuity and change. The archaeologists have noted changes (albeit difficult to date) in pottery as new styles of domestic equipment – of pots, platters and jars – appeared, possibly influenced by ideas from Ireland and Frisia. And ideas could be exchanged even if goods were not; new pottery fashions came into Cornwall and folk tales such as the Tristan and Isolt saga were exported. Cornwall's location at a crucial meeting place of the Atlantic seaways meant that its people were in a key position to participate in the exchange of ideas 'between the innovating centres of Ireland, France and Christian Spain'.[25] Indeed, we can isolate three broad connections shaping Cornwall and its culture in these centuries: southwards to and from Brittany, to the north to south Wales and Ireland, and a more one-way traffic from east to west from the English plains. The first and the second of these were of most significance in initiating Cornwall's Christian heritage.

The arrival of Christianity

The earliest Christian influence, no later than 450, may have been directly from Ireland and confined to the west of Cornwall and the Hayle estuary. The evidence of a gravestone from Carnsew at Hayle with an Irish name, plus an inscription bearing the first letters of the Greek *Christos* at Phillack, implies Christian practices. The later common hagiographic theme in this district of Irish saints, some-times employing bizarre modes of transportation such as leaves or stones, being oppressed by a local pagan ruler – Teudar – may recall such Irish influence. Yet, fifth-century Christianity in the west of Cornwall may equally owe its presence to the activities of early Christians in Romanized western Gaul.[26] Whichever way, it came by sea.

With more certainty, we can detect an equivalent sea-borne intru-sion further east, in the Camel-Fowey corridor. The Life of St Samson, penned in a Breton monastery in the 600s, recounts Samson's voyage to Cornwall from his Welsh monastery somewhere before 560. Landing in the Camel estuary, he refrained from visiting a monastery at Landocco in St Kew, put off by local monks ashamed by their failure to live up to Samson's expectations. Samson's band then headed southwards, on the way coming across a group of locals playing games and dancing around a menhir. Appalled by this Wicker-Man type behaviour, Samson berated the revellers before performing the predictable miracle by reviving a lad badly injured by falling off a horse. Building on this, he then went on to kill a giant serpent that had been lurking in a cave in the Fowey valley. In grati-tude the local chieftain allowed Samson to build a monastery, which Thomas believes may have been at Langurthou – Fowey – rather than the more obvious St Sampson just up the river.[27] Leaving his father in charge of this monastery Samson then departed for Brittany. This story gives us valuable information, notwithstanding the news that sixth-century Cornwall was plagued by giant serpents. The existence of the monastery at Landocco suggests that Christianity was already established by the mid-sixth century. The revellers at the standing stone imply that Christianity coexisted with more traditional religious rites and beliefs. And Samson's itinerary mirrors a larger movement of people of originally Irish descent via south Wales to Cornwall in the period from 500 to 700. Charles Thomas's detailed and fascinating investigation of the inscribed stones of this period allows him to conclude that possibly 500 to 1,000 Irish settlers from south-west Wales, already Christian and using Latin, came into Dumnonia via the Camel estuary and then spread along the river valleys to the east and south of Foweymoor across the Tamar and into south-west Devon. This was a 'land-exploiting aristocracy' whose inscribed stones, positioned as they were on some of the best land, suggest they made up an incoming elite.[28]

At first this group placed their stones on unenclosed ground, near to trackways and natural boundaries, symbols of temporal power. Gradually, however, they were more likely to be associated with later Christian sites – churches, chapels and cemeteries. Their settlement thus appears to have coincided with the consolidation of organized Christianity. In 500 Cornwall may have been 'barely Christian'.[29] By 700 it was fully Christian. Prominent in this early Christian landscape were the dispersed sites that the Cornish called *lans*, classic products of the semi-mythical 'age of the saints'. At least 140 saints have been identified in Cornwall – people such as Carantoc, Cubi, Nonn and Petroc – and 56 per cent of these were unique to Cornwall.[30] Often they gave their names to religious sites, as at Lanprobus, Lanust (St Just in Penwith) or Lansioch (St Just in Roseland). But, as Nicholas Orme reminds us, there is a 'sharp distinction between the Brittonic saints as historic people and the traditions written about them'.[31] The latter (and the first extant saint's life written in Cornwall, that of Petroc, did not appear until the mid-1000s) has helped to produce an image of a celibate, ascetic hermit living in a cave or similarly unworldly site, a holy example to his or her neighbours. Reality is more prosaic. The 'saints' in the place names could sometimes have been the founders of the church sites. Equally, they may have been important people buried there – local rulers or early clergy. Saints' lives tend to imply that virtually all saints came from across the seas. But cults travelled as well as saints. And dedications do not prove the actual movement of real people. Nonetheless, they indicate that cultural influence from Wales was important in mid and east Cornwall while there was more influence from Brittany in the south.

But the majority were actually local names. Nicholas Orme concludes that Brittany affected Cornwall, and Cornwall both Brittany and Wales, 'more than has been realised'.[32] While recent scholarship has thus restored the role of indigenous Cornish men and women in the emergence of Christianity, inter-Celtic saints' dedications are associated with the larger *lans*, which had links with religious houses overseas.

The religious landscape of Cornwall before 800 was, in Charles Thomas's words, 'pre-organised'.[33] A multitude of *lans* had emerged, enclosed communal Christian burial grounds with the later addition of (presumably) wooden religious buildings. These oval-shaped enclosures were, as the detailed work of Ann Preston-Jones reveals, more likely to be sited in the more fertile valley bottom sites and to possess an inscribed stone. They clustered particularly around the estuaries and harbours of the south coast, reflecting both the population distribution of the time and maritime links with Brittany.[34] Place name evidence suggests as many as 100 'land-owning religious communities' in eighth-century Cornwall, communities of clergy (not monks) with endowed land and presumably tithes. Later, by the eleventh century, successive appropriations and dispossessions by English and Norman overlords had reduced these to twelve 'minsters' or religious houses, with the largest being at Bodmin, St Buryan, Crantock, St Keverne and Perranzabuloe. Many of the others had by this time become parish churches with a single cleric or a cleric and curates serving a local community.

In the meantime, the Cornish church had acknowledged the administrative sway of Canterbury. Around 700 Bishop Aldhelm, abbot of Glastonbury and then bishop of Sherborne, wrote to King Gerent, pointing out the errors of the Cornish clergy in clinging to an unfashionable tonsure and the old dating of Easter.[35] Although this letter seems to have been ultimately ignored, in 833–70 Bishop Kenstec of Dinurrin, generally believed to be Bodmin, professed his obedience to Canterbury, marking a stage of incorporation of the Cornish into the English branch of the church.[36] This is sometimes seen as the imposition of a hierarchical, centrally controlled religious governing structure on a more dispersed Cornish one. But, although the Cornish church was more dispersed across the landscape, its form of government had already been converging on that of the church in England. In religion as well as politics, just as Cornish institutions began to adopt more formal structures in the eighth century, the grit around which the pearl of Cornish governance was beginning to cohere, they were swept away or fossilized – left as 'peculiarities' – by the incursion of English overlordship.

Thus in 909, when the Diocese of Crediton was established, the Cornish church was part of it. Nonetheless, in the later tenth century a Cornish diocese was established with its base at Lanaled (St Germans), and led by Bishop Conan. Lynette Olson describes St Germans at this time as 'a well established Cornish religious house near the English border rather than . . . an English outpost inside Cornwall', implying the maintenance of a recognizably Cornish religious zone well into the 900s.[37] Indeed, the literary tradition of St Germans was more Cornish than that of Bodmin despite its location nearer the eastern border. However, this distinct diocese lasted only until the 1040s when the personal ambitions of Bishop Leofric, who by this time held both Crediton and St Germans, led to a merger of the two and then a move in 1050 to Exeter.[38] Nonetheless, even at the time of Domesday in the 1080s, some of the Cornish minster churches retained special privileges. Most were free of taxation, unlike minsters in Devon, and some, such as St Buryan, Probus and Padstow, kept special rights of sanctuary. This was an echo of the separate origins of the Cornish church and 'either a privilege which originated in the pre-English period or a deliberate concession after the English Conquest'.[39] But how had that 'conquest' come about? And how far was it really a 'conquest'?

Pressure from the east

The Saxon settlement and military subjugation of the Kingdom of Dumnonia is still remarkably hazy, reconstructed mainly through the scanty details of battles recounted in the *Anglo-Saxon Chronicle* and in charters of land grants and Welsh histories. There is a danger of reading an inevitability into the process, an assumption that this was a conflict over fixed borders as in modern wars between nation-states. It is safer instead to imagine a shifting 'turbulent frontier' in the seventh to ninth centuries, one where farmers competed and quarrelled over land, where stock was grabbed, where events happened by accident as much as design. The analogy might be more the American West or the North-West frontier of British India in the nineteenth century than modern Europe. As more aggressive spirits among the

English moved west, British people were left behind for several generations in enclaves surrounded by English-controlled territory. Furthermore, we must not assume this was a one-way process. The fluid borderland between Celt and Saxon did not inexorably move westwards, with the former periodically ceding large chunks of territory to the latter. Instead there were times when the pendulum swung back, when the Britons regained territory and when the English were on the defensive.

The *Anglo-Saxon Chronicle*, with its relentless catalogue of battles between 'us' (the English) and 'them' (the Welsh, West Welsh and, later, the Vikings) may leave an over-great impression of permanent conflict and hostility between Celt and Saxon. Opinion is now swinging towards a more nuanced view of British–English relations. This mirrors a new archaeological orthodoxy that suggests, in view of the relatively small numbers of actual Germanic invaders, that the native population stayed put and did not flee to the west. Welsh kings were often found in alliance with English kingdoms; English clerics communicated with British churchmen; trade and communication took place between English and British kingdoms. King Ine of Wessex (688–726) certainly recognized that many 'Welsh' inhabited his territory and lived alongside his English subjects. On the other hand these British were also seen as different and as second-class subjects of the Wessex ruler. They had rights under Saxon law but their *wergild* (the price payable in compensation if they were killed) was only half that of their English neighbours.[40] Peaceable interludes and alliances notwithstanding, such social distinctions made by the English, the clear ethnic dividing lines suggested in the Welsh annals and the many battles between Celt and Saxon enumerated in the chronicles all indicate that the fissure between Dumnonia/Cornwall and Wessex, Briton and Saxon, was a major faultline from the seventh to ninth centuries.

In 683 the Saxons won an unnamed battle and the Britons were 'pushed to the sea'. In an over-enthusiastic and much-cited account of the English advance westwards the English local historian W. G. Hoskins placed this clash in mid-Devon and proposed that the sea concerned was the Atlantic coast of Cornwall north of St Gennys.[41] For him this explained the almost complete lack of Cornish place names north of the River Ottery. This is the only part of Cornwall which appears to have suffered a cultural obliteration similar to that in the south-west of England, where English place names were superimposed over the former British names, erasing the latter's presence from the landscape. But Hoskins may have been mistaken. For his narrative hinges on events around 710, when King Ine of Wessex made war on Gerent of Dumnonia, won a battle and made some land grants at *Linig*, near the 'River Tamer'. Hoskins placed this to the west of the Tamar near the River Lynher. This proved to his satisfaction that Devon was effectively all English by 710 and that a frontier was already established along, or even to the west of, the Tamar. There were always problems with this interpretation, one of the biggest being identifying what it was that then stopped the English from going on and colonizing the rest of Cornwall. Had this happened it is extremely unlikely that you would be reading this book now. However, Nicholas Orme cites more recent research that places Ine's land grant far to the east in Somerset, the word 'Tamer' being a misreading of the River Tone. As Orme concludes, 'this removes at a stroke the evidence that Ine had political control so far west'. Although Wessex kings were able to grant land in east and north Devon by the 720s and 730s, this does not mean that 'Gerent personally, or any of Cornwall, had fallen under Ine's control'.[42] This strongly hints that the 'sea' noted in 683 was the Bristol Channel coast of west Somerset or north Devon. It also makes a lot more sense of later events. In 722 Welsh histories record a British victory at *Hehil*. Hoskins placed this at the Camel estuary but it could be a coastal site further north, for example at Bude. But a Cornish victory over an English raiding party in the north of Cornwall hardly implies a fixed border on the Tamar at a time when small raiding bands could forage many miles into 'enemy territory'.

The geo-political context of the eighth century is particularly unclear; the *Anglo-Saxon Chronicle* merely states that in 743 and 753 King Cuthred of Wessex 'fought against the Britons', while Cynewulf, king from around 757 to 784 'often fought great battles against the Britons'.[43] Logic points to these occurring in Devon. Barbara Yorke speculates on losses and gains of territory by Wessex in Devon into the 800s. She cites a grant made by Cynewulf to Wells in east Somerset around 760–80 as compensation for a raid organized by the West Welsh.[44] And the Cornish apparently still possessed the capability and the will to raid across the countryside of north Devon as late as the 820s.[45] All this suggests that the writ of British kings still included part of modern Devon. It also implies that the visit of the English ecclesiastic Aldhelm to 'Cornwall' around 705 is evidence that Cornwall and Devon were already separate geographical concepts even before the Britons were confined to the west of the Tamar.[46] Nevertheless, Adhelm's account was also the last instance when Dumnonia was mentioned as a separate kingdom and at some point in the eighth century Dumnonia shaded into Cornwall, as the territory of the West Welsh became equated with that land west of the Tamar. On balance therefore, we can reject the traditional accounts that confine the West Welsh to the west of the Tamar from the early eighth century.[47] Instead, there was no frontier between Briton and Saxon at the Tamar until around 800.

After a British raid in 815 King Egbert of Wessex is recorded as harrying 'Cornwall from east to west'. Egbert, king of Wessex from 802, presided over an expansion of his kingdom, establishing the rule of Wessex over Kent, Surrey and Sussex, conquering for a time Mercia in the Midlands and even obtaining the submission of the Northumbrian king in 829.[48] This martial king was clearly bad news for the Cornish. Egbert's 'harrying' of 815 was probably what led to the disappearance of Cornish place names north of the Ottery. Although difficult to date, the English place names of north Cornwall are compatible with English settlement taking place after 815.[49] Unfortunately, more than a millennium has erased the details of these events. Perhaps the Cornish were forcibly expelled as punishment for earlier raids eastwards, or maybe something more grisly occurred. Evidence exists from the *Anglo-Saxon Chronicle* of a plan to massacre all the natives of the Isle of Wight by a Wessex king in order to replace them with his own people.[50] The possibility that genocidal acts are not just a phenomenon of the modern world cannot be entirely ruled out.

Whatever the fate of the British in north-east Cornwall, the period between 815 and 838 was critical for the survival of a fully independent Cornish kingdom. In 815 Egbert led his punitive campaign into Cornwall but there was a 'fuzzy' border at this time between Wessex and Cornwall, somewhere on or just to the east of the River Tamar. This is suggested by events ten years later, in 825, when the Cornish put an armed force into the field again. They were met at *Galforda*, almost certainly Galford near Lewtrenchard in west Devon. The outcome of this battle is unclear; the *Anglo-Saxon Chronicle* merely states that the 'Britons and the men of Devon' fought.[51] The significance of this laconic remark is that by this time the 'men of Devon' were regarded by the *Chronicle* as English and the ethnic dividing line approximated to the modern Cornish border. Either the Cornish continued to be dissatisfied with the status quo or they were provoked, perhaps by English settlement between the Tamar and the Lynher (indicated by a second, though less thorough-going, replacement of Cornish by English place names in that district). For, in 838, they joined with a raiding army of Vikings and the battle at Hingston Down took place. With hindsight its outcome was predictable, as confronting Egbert, victor over Mercia and conqueror of south-east England, was hardly an equal contest. After this defeat Cornish rulers were compelled to acknowledge his over-lordship and, for the first time, Wessex kings were able to dispense land in Cornwall – at Lawhitton and further west at Pawton in St Breock.

Although the English were able to exert their power within Cornwall after Hingston Down, British kings still flit elusively in and out of the historical record. For example, in a Welsh record there is a *Dumnarth rex Cerniu*, drowned in 875. Was this the King Doniert whose name can still be seen on a ninth-century stone just north of St Cleer and conveniently (though unfortunately for him) close to the Fowey River? By this time Doniert was likely to have been an under-king, paying homage to the English rulers of Wessex. John Angarrack also makes much of a line in the *Anglo-Saxon Chronicle* citing 'Hywel, king of the Cornish' as one of a bunch of kings offering allegiance to the English Athelstan in 927.[52] In fact, the refer-ence is to 'Hywel, king of the West Welsh'.[53] But there is no other reference to this ambiguous Hywel in a Cornish context, leading to the probability that the Hywel of 927 was one and the same as the Hywel of 918 who the geographically challenged *Anglo-Saxon Chronicle* records as making his submission to Athelstan's father, Edward. That Hywel was the well-known Hywel Dda, a ruler in south Wales.[54] As late as the 1000s there is a claimed 'king' Cadoc, although others term Cadoc an 'earl',[55] while the apparent presence of a 'king' Ricatus on a stone cross at Penzance dated to around 1000 has now been rejected.[56]

The construction of Cornwall

It was another century before English overlordship was clarified. Athelstan was, like Egbert, an aggressive English ruler who had, in

927, surpassed even his predecessor by bringing not only
Northumbria under his rule but, temporarily, the Welsh princes and
even King Constantine of Scotland.[57] At the height of his power, in
the 930s, according to William of Malmesbury writing in the 1120s,
he rationalized relations between the English and Cornish by recognizing the Tamar as the frontier between Cornwall and Wessex and
cleansing Exeter by 'purging it of that vile people' (the Cornish).[58]
The latter comment might be evidence that some groups of Britons
had continued to live as recognizable communities in Devon for the
couple of hundred years after the English had attained effective
control there. It also suggests that they had not been assimilated and
that Athelstan regarded Cornwall as their 'homeland territory'.

But we are left with a puzzle about the century after Hingston
Down. After Egbert's victory we might have expected the English to
press on, settle Cornwall and erase its Celtic identity as efficiently as
they had done everywhere else between Kent and Cornwall north of
the Ottery. And, a hundred years later, why did Athelstan make the
apparent concession of a homeland? Philip Payton interprets this as
an English 'accommodation' of the Cornish, stating that the 'Cornish
had to be pacified and bought off'.[59] The unequal material resources
available to Cornish and English suggest there was little the former
could have done to prevent the thorough anglicization and assimilation of Cornwall. Yet the English advance did stop in the ninth
century at or near the Tamar and this hesitation guaranteed the
survival of a 'Brittonic cultural identity in the peninsula'.[60] The
implied reason put forward by Payton is that full annexation would
have been just too much trouble. The Dumnonian British and the
Cornish had put up a stiff resistance to the English in Devon and east
Cornwall from the late seventh to the early ninth centuries. Constant
conflict over a century and a half indicates that they did not intend to
give up territory easily. This echoes Bryan Ward-Perkins's argument
that one reason the Saxon invaders came to dominate Britain culturally (in contrast to the situation in Gaul) was that 'the native British
offered exceptionally effective resistance to the Anglo-Saxon
marauders'.[61] This meant that the English could not or would not
adopt the culture of their often hostile British neighbours. Therefore,
English hesitation in pressing home their advantage after 838 may be
merely 'realpolitik'.

Another cited reason is poverty. Land in Cornwall could have been
just too poor and unappetizing for potential English settlers.

However, this appears unlikely when one considers English settlement of equally poor land in north Devon or the upland regions of the north of England. Another, strikingly different interpretation of the period from 838 to the eleventh century has emerged from archaeologists in Cornwall.[62] The starting point for this is the observation that the Romans never took over Cornwall. Instead they came to an accommodation. According to the Roman commentator Diodorus, the Cornish were particularly experienced at trade and diplomacy. As a result the Romans viewed them circumspectly, did not ravage their resources but instead tapped into some form of tribute, perhaps tin. If the Romans had the capability to annex Cornwall but not the will to do so then, the argument runs, so did Egbert and Athelstan. The Cornish were occasional irritants but not irritating enough to warrant full-scale conquest and the replacement of elites. Instead, it was the Cornish elites after 838 who displayed canny 'realpolitik', recognizing their weakness *vis-à-vis* the English and adopting a peculiarly accommodating character, acclimatizing themselves rapidly to English overlordship. Moreover, this could be done from some strength as Cornwall possessed a relatively diverse and complex economy and society with the production of a strategic metal which guaranteed the Cornish a degree of autonomy as long as that metal continued to flow. Thus, the important factor in the ninth and tenth centuries was not so much the 'accommodations' made by the early English state but the accommodating character of Cornish elites. Yet, such an interpretation looks suspiciously close to modern English stereotypes of the Cornish as a tamed, domestic 'other', a bit different and perhaps sometimes stubborn but at heart eager to please. It is also a little too convenient for Cornish self-representations as a dignified, if powerless, people to be utterly convincing. Nonetheless, it fits the facts of the period as well as any other explanation and is a useful antidote to the top–down, militaristic narrative of Cornwall's early medieval history that dominates both kernowsceptic and kernowcentric writings. Whatever the reason, there is no evidence of major Cornish unrest from the defeat of 838 until 1069.

However, there could be another, more contingent factor in the English failure to press home their advantage after 838. From the 840s Viking attacks were increasing in intensity. In the 870s Wessex was faced by a very serious Viking threat that saw, at one time, King Alfred hiding out in the Somerset marshes. Not surprisingly, the attention of Wessex's rulers after Egbert's time was riveted on this threat. They had little time for adventures in the far west when faced with the problem of their very survival. The Viking incursions were, it is claimed, a major factor in the growth of royal power and a sense of English (and Irish) identity.[63] Indirectly, the Vikings may also have saved Cornwall as a distinct cultural entity, by diverting attention and allowing virtually all of Cornwall to escape the process of colonization that occurred further east.

By Athelstan's time the Viking threat had been contained. There was then nothing to stop him turning his attention to the Cornish. However, what has been often taken as a straightforward submission of the Cornish in the 930s was more akin to a treaty. The well-known episode of 973, when Welsh and Scottish kings were supposed to have rowed the English King Edgar up and down the river Dee at Chester as a public sign of their submission is now argued to be a 'post-Conquest fictional embellishment' and more of a 'peace summit' than a humiliating submission.[64] In a similar way Athelstan's 'settlement' looks less like an imposition and more like a guarantee of cultural integrity, with the Cornish recognizing the overlordship of the Wessex dynasty in return for the concession of a homeland west of the Tamar. Cornish cultural autonomy was recognized, with the implication that westwards colonization over the Tamar should cease, and later the bishopric of St Germans respected Cornish religious identity. On their side the Cornish had to accept a degree of political and administrative integration, though in return they were, unlike the Welsh, admitted as equal subjects, with one or two exceptions, mainly financial. From this perspective, Athelstan becomes a cuddly father-figure rather than the 'warmonger, slaver and ethnic cleanser' and hammer of the Cornish as he is sometimes portrayed.[65] Athelstan apparently had a particular interest in Breton saints' cults and dabbled heavily in Breton politics.[66] He may have found the Cornish a fascinating 'other', a people who for some reason had earned a modicum of respect. As long as they acknowledged the ultimate sovereignty of the English crown, they were left with considerable autonomy within a recognized homeland. But this 'accommodation' flowed not so much from recognizing a distinct and equal people but from awareness that by the tenth century the Cornish posed no real threat to English power.

The period from 700 to 950 was thus critical for the emergence of Cornwall and the Cornish identity. Historical work on ethnicity in the early medieval period proposes that it was not, as might be expected, based on 'blood', but on power. A 'restricted ethnicity' appeared first among the ruling elites, cohering around kings and their rudimentary courts.[67] In Cornwall, the slow emergence of a more centralized political structure after 700 no doubt produced similar feelings of 'restricted ethnicity' amongst its ruling elite. What then spread this further through society was the warfare of the eighth and the early ninth centuries between the Cornish and the encroaching English. For, as in Anglo-Saxon England, warfare played a 'key role in providing new ethnic identities'.[68] Although militarily subdued and nominally subject to Wessex from the 830s, the Cornish were then left largely to their own devices for the next 200 years. During this time Cornwall lay at the border of two culture zones. In books produced in Cornwall at this time the handwriting shows English influence, whereas in contemporary Wales the influence was more from Ireland.[69] Similarly, the appearance of crosses in the late ninth century shows both English influence as well as affinities with styles in south Wales.[70] In contrast Lynette Olson has noted how the language of the St Buryan and Landochou charters of 961–3 was similar to charter material of Breton and Welsh provenance rather than those of Anglo-Saxon England and implied a continuing 'Cornish diplomatic tradition' with affinities with Brittany.[71] Clearly, Cornwall was subject to sometimes conflicting pressures from two directions after 800, from the east as well as from its Celtic neighbours.

Nonetheless, this prolonged period of relative political stability consolidated the geographical boundary of Cornwall. Oliver Padel has pointed to the clear boundary line of *tre* names near the Tamar, indicating 'a political and/or linguistic distinction at some period, probably at about the eighth to the tenth or eleventh centuries . . . in some sense a national boundary'.[72] It was precisely during this crucial period from the 830s to the 1050s that the Cornish entrenched themselves as a distinct people. But, while the English had won a right to nominal allegiance from the Cornish, this too was subject to upheaval when a new ruling elite – the Normans – arrived in 1067.

The Normans arrive

At the end of 1067 William the Conqueror marched into Cornwall 'and put down all disturbances that arose'.[73] After this he proceeded to do a relatively unusual thing. Normally, William took care to grant his followers estates in many dispersed sites, so that alternative centres of power could not arise. However, in Cornwall, like the Welsh border country and the far north of England, 'such precautions were set aside' and a single landlord was given an effectively free rein.[74] Most of Cornwall was granted to just one man, Brian fitz Eudo of Brittany. In this way Cornwall resembled a palatinate, a territory subject to the jurisdiction of a feudal lord who possessed local authority normally belonging only to the sovereign. It was clearly regarded, like the Welsh marches and northern England, as a 'vulnerable frontier'. This seems odd, given that a series of historians have sagely assured us that Cornwall had effectively become part of England by 1066. One suggestion has been that it was peculiarly vulnerable to Irish and Viking raids by sea and it is known that Viking attacks in the 980s resulted in the sacking of St Petrock's monastery at Padstow. Yet, if this were the case, the Normans were also remarkably slow to extend their defensive infrastructure – the keeps and castles of Norman power – into mid and west Cornwall, which was potentially more exposed to Viking raids.

The comparative absence of English settlement in Cornwall and their relatively superficial administrative control may have made the Normans wary. Their wariness was warranted. In the autumn of 1069 a rising occurred in Devon, as the land seizures of Norman overlords were resisted. The rebels set about besieging Exeter, symbol of Norman power, and were joined by 'hordes out of British Cornwall'.[75] The precise causes of this trek eastwards and the role taken by the Cornish are unknown but this was an early example of what, in later centuries, became something of a Cornish tradition – laying siege to Exeter. Significantly, in 1069, in stark contrast to two years earlier when they had resisted the Normans, the inhabitants of Exeter joined with them to defend their city. Rather the Normans than the Cornish! Eventually the besieged garrison broke out and drove the attackers into the arms of an arriving relief column. A 'great slaughter of the rebels' ensued, something that was also to recur in later centuries.

Norman caution when dealing with the potentially recalcitrant Cornish is indicated by the prominent role Bretons were given in the Norman settlement following 1067. Brian of Brittany and other Breton camp followers were granted a special place in Cornwall. John Carley goes further: the 'Breton settlement . . . may have strengthened the Celtic nature of Cornwall' by guaranteeing the survival of older practices and techniques.[76] However, any effect of this 'Armorican return' was to prove short-lived. In 1075 Brian was dispossessed of his lands, perhaps because of his involvement in a Breton nobles' plot against William while the king was absent in Normandy. But Cornwall still required exceptional measures. So William replaced the banished Brian with another dominant land-lord, his half-brother Robert, count of Mortain. A second, possibly more brutal and oppressive, settlement took place. The count placed a small group of Norman families as the principal sub-tenants on his 277 manors in Cornwall, kept twenty-two manors for himself and set about comprehensively exploiting this personal demesne land. In addition, he did not hesitate to plunder church lands. Furthermore, he was given the right, normally reserved to the king, to appoint his own sheriff. This 'second settlement' of Cornwall has been seen as a 'reflection of the Conqueror's concern that the governance of Cornwall and the run of the royal writ were secondary issues compared to the need to secure one more vulnerable frontier'.[77] Cornwall's continuing palatine status points to its still incomplete incorporation into the Norman state.

The snapshot evidence of the Domesday Book in 1086 certainly indicates insubstantial Norman settlement. Apart from Cardinham, Norman castles were strung along the border lands with Devon, from Poundstock and Week St Mary in the north to Trematon in the south. And unusually, Norman sub-tenants, concentrated in the east near the protection of their castles, were a minority (around a third) amongst the sub-tenants of the count of Mortain.[78] The majority of the rest possessed English names. But this does not necessarily mean they were English by origin. Oliver Padel has pointed out how there is evidence that 'in tenth century Cornwall, men with Cornish names used occasionally to take Anglo-Saxon names as well, presumably in order to make themselves respectable in the eyes of their English lords'.[79] Ethnic categories were not as rigid at this time as we might imagine. It was quite possible for the Cornish in a situation of cultural subjugation to attempt to obscure their origins.[80] And, like Norman names in England in the eleventh and twelfth centuries or celebrities' names in the twenty-first, there may have been an element of fashion in this. An unknown proportion of 'English' sub-tenants in 1086 would therefore have been Cornish. This was even more likely in those 'small settlements, with the Celtic names [that] gave to the human geography of Domesday Cornwall a character quite unlike that of . . . southern England'.[81] The lack of Norman castles in mid and west Cornwall, the concentration of Norman landlords in the east and their absence in the west, and the possibly large number of Cornish tenants all imply only partial Norman settlement.

Traditionally, eleventh-century Cornwall has been seen as extremely poor. Apart from the demesne manors of Count Robert, the vast majority of the 340 or so Domesday manors showed a fall in value over the previous twenty years. And Cornwall was a sparsely populated land. The numbers in Domesday imply a total population of only around 27,000–28,000, not that much bigger than present day Penzance or St Austell. (Around a fifth of the population were slaves, a higher proportion than further east and perhaps another indicator of Cornwall's 'frontier' status.) The uplands were virtually uninhabited; there were only two towns, Bodmin, with around 300–400 inhabitants, and Launceston; only six water mills, two of which were at Launceston, compared with eighty-one in Devon and 252 in Somerset; only five markets, again at Launceston, together with Liskeard, Trematon, Bodmin and St Germans, and this last had been 'reduced to nothing' by the granting of the new market at nearby Trematon.[82] Tin extraction and fishing were conspicuously absent. All this suggests the absence of a market economy and the prevalence of subsistence production in most of Cornwall outside the Norman/English eastern fringe and the old administrative centre of Bodmin.

Or does it? It is possible the remarkably poor state of Cornwall in the 1080s may, as in the impoverished north of England, reflect the ravages of rebellion and war and/or the appropriations of the second Norman settlement of Robert. But more likely, it indicates a defective source, with activities going on beyond manorial control and the oversight of the Norman Domesday clerks – a sort of eleventh-century black economy. For other sources such as charters mention mills; there was a mint at Launceston and slaves were worth £4, which implies a market economy.[83] It is very likely that the artificial manorial framework of the Domesday Book missed a proportion of the scattered homesteads of Cornwall, especially in the remoter and upland districts. Similarly, mills, markets and mining in Cornwall may have been beyond the touch of the tax regime, suggesting an everyday autonomy and lack of formal central oversight. Moreover, archaeological evidence contradicts Domesday, hinting at a relatively prosperous and settled land.[84]

Recently the argument has been put forward that Domesday Book conceals a lot more than a bit of fishing and tin streaming. Noting the gap between the tax assessment in Domesday and the amount of tax actually paid, John Angarrack has claimed that this 'lost tribute ... may well have been going elsewhere', to a mysterious parallel native ruler, even perhaps the enigmatic Cadoc.[85] In order to reconstruct a (strangely silent) continuing Cornish native government into the eleventh century Angarrack makes much of the issue of 'missing tribute'. However, there are problems in resorting to a ghostly native ruling elite using 'missing tribute' to finance their governmental and legal structures. For Cornwall was not the only territory underassessed in 1080. In Devon too, very similar levels of under-rating occurred. Even in Somerset there was some under-rating when compared with Dorset and Wiltshire.[86] Presumably Devonian manors were not paying tribute to a lost British ruler. The traditional explanation is that this 'missing tribute' represents what is called exempt 'fiscal demesne', a privilege whereby the owners of manors retained land tax that elsewhere went to the king. What is interesting is that the level of 'fiscal demesne', or retained land tax, was higher in Cornwall (and Devon). Even anglocentric historians admit that it may have been due to 'the previous history (of the South West) as "West Wales"'.[87] There is no 'mystery'. The 'missing tribute' in Cornwall did not go to unseen Celtic princes but into the pockets of local landlords, many of them Cornish, a few English, but the richest Norman.

Conclusion

During the centuries following the end of Roman rule in south-west Britain there was prolonged resistance to the extension of Saxon control, which slowed down markedly in the eighth century. It was hardly surprising that Dumnonia, transformed into Cornwall by 800, eventually succumbed and acknowledged the overlordship of its Wessex neighbour, at this time probably the most effective concentrated royal and ecclesiastical power in Europe. What is surprising is the fact that Cornwall survived at all as a distinct entity. That it did so was partly due to the resistance of British Celts to Saxon rule, something that fostered a feeling of identity amongst the Cornish by the eighth century. As Carew wrote seven and a half centuries after

Hingston Down, like the Welsh 'fostering a fresh sense of their expulsion long ago by the English' some of the western (i.e. Cornish-speaking) Cornish could still harbour a 'bitter repining at their [English] fellowship'.[88] That this 'repining' and the Cornish language community that contained it lingered so long was only possible because an independent British kingdom had itself survived in the west for about four centuries.

The second reason for Cornwall's survival was more due to luck. Just at the time when they came within the orbit of Wessex – in the ninth century – the latter kingdom began to face a threat to its own survival, in the shape of those erstwhile Cornish allies the Vikings. The Vikings did not save Cornwall at Hingston Down but they did play an important, albeit indirect, role in the survival of Cornwall.

A third factor shaping Cornwall's emergence was the Breton connection. Seaward links with a Celtic-speaking society provided the Cornish with cultural ties that were denied, at a similar time, to the British-speaking kingdom of Cumbria. In Cumbria, cut off from Welsh kinsmen to the south, the British language quickly died out in the ninth and tenth centuries. That Cornwall avoided a Cumbrian scenario was in part due to its Breton links and its maritime location. Breton rulers had, like the Cornish, lost their political autonomy in the 800s to their powerful eastern neighbour, but they reunified an independent Brittany (albeit on a French model) in the mid-tenth century and paid their last homage for almost 200 years to the French king. [89] Unlike their Breton cousins the Cornish had to admit their subordinate status within a larger non-British kingdom. Yet, as we have seen, Athelstan's 'settlement', though ultimately temporary, was something more than simple incorporation or annexation of Cornwall. Whether it flowed from a need to pacify the Cornish, a potentially troublesome periphery, or from a desire to reward the accommodating behaviour of a canny Cornish elite possessing valuable economic resources remains open to question.

Some outsiders, such as the anonymous Welsh cleric who wrote, in the tenth century, the *Armes Prydein* (Prophecy of Britain), could still view the Cornish as an important component of a putative pan-Celtic resistance to the English – 'and there will be reconciliation between the Cymry and the men of Dublin, the Irish of Ireland and Anglesey and Scotland, the men of Cornwall and of Strathclyde will be made welcome among us, the Britons will rise again'.[90] However, the hopes of this cleric, cherishing his dreams in some Welsh fastness, did not transpire. After the tenth century the Cornish inevitably began to be sucked into English political structures. Nevertheless, it was another five or six centuries before this political incorporation was unambiguously achieved. And transformation accompanied older cultural continuities and newer economic distinctions, as we shall see in the next chapter.

Notes

[1] Bryan Ward-Perkins, 'Why did the Anglo-Saxons not become more British?', *English Historical Review*, 150 (2000), 513–33.
[2] Henrietta Quinnell, 'A sense of identity: distinctive stone artefacts in the Roman and post-Roman periods', *Cornish Archaeology*, 32 (1993), 29–46.
[3] Ann Preston-Jones and Peter Rose, 'Medieval Cornwall', *Cornish Archaeology*, 25 (1986), 135–85.
[4] Charles Thomas, *Celtic Britain* (1986), p. 66.
[5] Ibid., pp. 66–9.
[6] Barbara Yorke, *Wessex in the Early Middle Ages* (1995), p. 15.
[7] Thomas, *Celtic Britain*, p. 70.
[8] Oliver Padel, 'The Cornish background to the Tristan stories', *Cambridge Medieval Celtic Studies*, 1 (1981), 53–81. For a summary of the Tristan and Isolt tale see Philip Payton, *Cornwall* (2004), pp. 54–5.
[9] Oliver Padel, 'Geoffrey of Monmouth and Cornwall', *Cambridge Medieval Celtic Studies*, 1 (1981), 1–27.
[10] Charles Thomas, *Tintagel: Arthur and Archaeology* (1993), p. 15.
[11] Charles Thomas, 'The context of Tintagel: a new model for the diffusion of post-Roman Mediterranean imports', *Cornish Archaeology*, 27 (1988), 7–26.
[12] Peter Herring, *St Michael's Mount, Cornwall: Reports on Archaeological Works, 1995–1998* (2000), p. 120.
[13] Kenneth Dark, *Civitas to Kingdom: British Political Continuity 300–800* (1994), p. 91.
[14] Charles Thomas, *And Shall These Mute Stones Speak? Post-Roman Inscriptions in Western Britain* (1994), p. 215.
[15] David Harvey, 'The evolution of territoriality and societal transitions', *Landscape History*, 19 (1997), 13–23; Peter Herring, 'Cornish uplands: medieval, post-medieval and modern extents', (forthcoming).
[16] Harvey, 'Evolution of territoriality', p. 17.
[17] Edward James, *Britain in the First Millennium* (2001), p. 204.
[18] Dark, *Civitas to Kingdom*, p. 233; John Davies, *The Book of Llandaff and the Norman Church in Wales* (2003), p. 11.
[19] Nicholas Orme, *The Saints of Cornwall* (2000), p. 32.
[20] Herring, 'Cornish uplands'.
[21] Ibid., I am greatly indebted to Peter Herring for the information in this and the preceding paragraph.
[22] Preston-Jones and Rose, 'Medieval Cornwall', p. 176.
[23] Ibid., p.167.
[24] Dark, *Civitas to Kingdom*, p. 233.
[25] Barry Cunliffe, *Facing the Ocean* (2001), p. 481.
[26] Thomas, *Mute Stones*, p. 199.

[27] Ibid., p. 229.

[28] Ibid., pp. 239–305.

[29] Ibid., p. 306.

[30] Orme, *Saints of Cornwall*, p. 6.

[31] Ibid., p. 19.

[32] Ibid., p. 31.

[33] Thomas, *Mute Stones*, p. 310.

[34] Ann Preston-Jones, 'Decoding Cornish churchyards', *Cornish Archaeology*, 33 (1994), 71–95.

[35] Thomas, *Mute Stones*, p. 311.

[36] Lynette Olson, *Early Monasteries in Cornwall* (1989), p. 51.

[37] Ibid., p. 66.

[38] Nicholas Orme, *Unity and Variety* (1991), p. 20.

[39] Orme, *Saints of Cornwall*, p. 10.

[40] Yorke, *Wessex in the Early Middle Ages*, p. 72.

[41] W. G. Hoskins, *The Westward Expansion of Wessex* (1960), p. 17.

[42] Orme, *Saints of Cornwall*, pp. 4–5.

[43] Dorothy Whitelock (ed.), *The Anglo-Saxon Chronicle* (1965), pp. 29–30.

[44] Yorke, *Wessex in the Early Middle Ages*, pp. 60 and 67.

[45] Whitelock, *Anglo-Saxon Chronicle*, p. 40.

[46] Orme, *Saints of Cornwall*, p. 5.

[47] For a recent example of this see Susan Pearce, *South-Western Britain in the Early Middle Ages* (2004), pp. 252–3.

[48] Yorke, *Wessex in the Early Middle Ages*, p. 94.

[49] Orjan Svensson, *Saxon Place-Names in East Cornwall* (1987), p. 146.

[50] Yorke, *Wessex in the Early Middle Ages*, p. 67.

[51] Whitelock, *Anglo-Saxon Chronicle*, p. 40.

[52] John Angarrack, *Our Future is History: Identity, Law and the Cornish Question* (2002), pp. 37 and 67.

[53] Whitelock, *Anglo-Saxon Chronicle*, p. 68.

[54] Ibid., p. 67.

[55] Angarrack, *Our Future is History*, p. 68; Philip Payton, *Cornwall* (1996), p. 91. The description of Cadoc as a 'prince of royal British blood', which Angarrack makes much of (pp. 68, 98, 122), seems to have been an invention of Richard Polwhele (*History of Cornwall*, vol 2 (1803–8), p. 22). Camden, writing in the fifteenth century, merely describes Cadoc (or Candorus) as the 'last Earl of Cornwall, of British race' (Camden, *Magna Brittania* (1610), p. 197).

[56] Charles Thomas, *Penzance Market Cross: A Cornish Wonder Re-wondered* (1999), pp. 37–8.

[57] James, *Britain in the First Millennium*, pp. 244–6.

[58] William of Malmesbury, cited ibid., p. 145.

[59] Payton, *Cornwall* (2004), p. 69.

[60] Christopher Snyder, *The Britons* (2003), p. 157.

[61] Ward-Perkins, 'Why did the Anglo-Saxons not become more British?', p. 527.

[62] Communication from Peter Herring.

[63] James, *Britain in the First Millennium*, p. 230.

[64] David Thornton, 'Edgar and the eight kings, ad 973: textus et dramatis personae', *Early Medieval Europe*, 10 (2001), 49–79.

[65] Angarrack, *Our Future is History*, p. 101.

[66] Snyder, *Britons*, p. 169.

[67] John Moreland, 'Ethnicity, power and the English', in William Frazer and Andrew Tyrrell (eds), *Social Identity in Early Medieval England* (2000), pp. 36–46.

[68] Barbara Yorke, 'Political and ethnic identity: a case study of Anglo-Saxon practice', in Frazer and Tyrrell, *Social Identity*, p. 89.

[69] N. H. Webb, 'Early medieval Welsh book-production', Ph.D. thesis, University of London (1989).

[70] Preston-Jones and Rose, 'Medieval Cornwall', p. 158.

[71] Olson, *Early Monasteries*, pp. 64 and 84.

[72] Oliver Padel, 'Place-names', in Roger Kain and William Ravenhill (eds), *The Historical Atlas of South West England* (1999), pp. 88–9.

[73] Orderic Vitalis, cited in John Carley, 'The Norman Conquest of Devon and Cornwall', M.Litt. thesis, Oxford University (1989), p. 14.

[74] Ian Soulsby, *The Cornwall Domesday* (1988), p. vii.

[75] Carley, 'Norman Conquest', pp. 21–2.

[76] Ibid., p. 195.

[77] Ibid., p. 71.

[78] Soulsby, *Cornwall Domesday*, p. 14.

[79] Padel, 'Geoffrey of Monmouth and Cornwall', p. 2.

[80] See also Ward-Perkins, 'Why did the Anglo-Saxons not become more British?', p. 525.

[81] H. C. Darby and R. Welldon Finn, *The Domesday Geography of South West England* (1967), p. 345.

[82] Soulsby, *Cornwall Domesday*, p. 8.

[83] Communication from Oliver Padel.

[84] Communication from Peter Herring.

[85] Angarrack, *Our Future is History*, pp. 93 and 122.

[86] Darby and Finn, *Domesday Geography of SW England*, p. 349.

[87] Ibid., p. 311.

[88] Richard Carew, *Survey of Cornwall* (1811, originally published 1602), p. 184.

[89] Snyder, *Britons*, pp. 153–6.

[90] Cited in Ann Williams, *Kingship and Government in Pre-Conquest England c.500–1066* (1999), p. 126.

2

Medieval Cornwall: distinctiveness and dependence, 1100–1495

Historians of Cornwall tend to pass rapidly over the three or four centuries after 1100 in order to arrive at the more interesting events of the sixteenth and seventeenth centuries. As a result there are few links from the medieval period back to periods of independence or forward to the phase of resistance.[1] Moreover, despite a growing literature on the identity of peoples in the medieval British Isles,[2] there is no work on the medieval Cornish identity. This is a pity as processes that came to fruition in the Tudor period had their genesis in earlier centuries. Medieval Cornwall was influenced by two external institutions – the crown in England and the church in Rome. The tension between these institutions produced a space in which, while political and administrative integration deepened, cultural differences were maintained. This chapter begins by exploring the enduring compact forged between Cornwall and the Crown, the repercussions of which echo down through the centuries, and then discusses how the economy of Cornwall changed, with a noticeable hinge around 1349 accompanying the Black Death. The waning and waxing of the Cornish identity is then reviewed. Finally, the role of the church is examined, noting the way it opened up Cornwall to wider European influences but at the same time protected Cornish language communities.

Crown and duchy: from 'accommodation' to colonization

As late as the early 1500s the audience for the saint's play *Beunans Meriasek*, based in and around Camborne, was being invited to imagine a Cornish-speaking Cornwall from the Lands End to the River Tamar, although the linguistic reality was by this time very different. The duke of Cornwall states:

Me ew duk in oll Kernow
Indella ytho ow thays
Hag uhel arluth in pow
A tamer the pen an wlays

I am duke in all of Cornwall
as was my father
and high lord in the country
from Tamar to Lands End

Narratives of a unified Cornish-speaking Cornwall, with its rulers
located at Tintagel, that symbol of political power stretching back to
pre-Conquest times, bore more than a hint of memories of political
independence. The extent of such memories has triggered a heated
debate. On the one hand kernowcentrics argue that Cornwall was
granted political institutions of 'accommodation' by the English state
in this period, recognizing and formalizing a status of semi-
independence. Some reconstruct the duchy of Cornwall as the
continuation of a shadowy governing structure tracing its roots back
directly to the independent rulers of eighth-century Cornwall.[3]
Meanwhile, the kernowsceptic side responds by pointing to
Cornwall's political integration into England and to the gradual
application of the institutions of the English state, particularly in the
thirteenth century.[4] The king's courts were being held by the end of
that century, Cornwall was divided into Hundreds as were English
counties, Cornish MPs sat in the House of Commons and the law
applied was English law. In all these matters Cornwall clearly differed
from Wales.

But political fusion accompanied a set of 'peculiarities'. As early as
the second half of the tenth century, frankpledge was imposed on
Cornwall, as it was across England south of the Humber. The adult
male population (excluding landlords, clergy and the mentally handi-
capped) was made 'collectively responsible for apprehending and
bringing before a court any of their number accused of crime'.[5] It was
administered via tithings, units that by the end of the thirteenth
century were regarded as an actual piece of land rather than the original association of ten persons. However, as we have seen, in
Cornwall tithings (and Hundreds) may have been units in the English
chain of command but had much older roots, back to earlier British
forms of government of the 700s or 800s. Although the superficial
form was 'English', the details of administrative institutions often
bore the imprint of Cornwall's non-English roots. By the twelfth

century tithings and frankpledge had been joined by the more obvious novelty of sheriffs. Even so, an early sheriff of Cornwall was involved in an obscure feud with some Norman landowners. Somewhere between 1100 and 1129, possibly at Trereife near Penzance, several Normans were killed by locals. As Oliver Padel points out, this episode was widely known outside Cornwall at the time and may have been an 'anti-Norman rebellion'.[6] Some Cornish landowners at least were clearly not yet entirely reconciled to Norman overlordship. Because of events like this the power granted by the monarch in the eleventh century first to Brian of Brittany and then to Robert of Mortain was confirmed in the troubled years of the 1140s.

The landing of Empress Matilda in Sussex in 1139 and her effort to reclaim the crown from King Stephen triggered civil war over the succession to the English throne. William Fitz Richard of Cardinham, the major Cornish-based landlord of the time, joined the rebellion early in 1140 and 'an energetic and ferocious campaign' ensued. There then occurred a counter campaign by King Stephen and his local supporters, but after a royal defeat far to the east at the battle of Lincoln, Cornwall remained in the hands of the rebels until the later 1140s.[7] Political uncertainties at the heart of the English ruling class and the core of the English state provided opportunities on the periphery. The Scottish King David was able at this time to claim overlordship over Cumbria and Northumberland and back this up by temporarily occupying England as far south as Preston. Meanwhile, in Wales native princes re-established their control over border areas. But, in stark contrast to Scotland and Wales, there was no popular unrest in Cornwall and no hint of an attempt to restore native rulers in the place of the Anglo-Normans. By the twelfth century it seems there was no indigenous source of power left in Cornwall strong enough to reassert their claims and take advantage of a time when the power of the English state was weakened. Cornwall's defeat by Egbert, the settlement of Athelstan and the land redistribution of the Normans had resulted in the effective disappearance of its native ruling class. By the mid-twelfth century there were no families in Cornwall with either the aspirations or ability to recreate a British polity.

Or did Cornwall already have a native administration, with its own parallel law codes and system of government, coexisting with Anglo-Norman structures, just as Welsh princes coexisted with Norman landlords in Wales? This at least is the argument of John Angarrack.[8] For him a separate British jurisdiction continued, bridging the period of semi-autonomy before 1066 and the formation of the Stannary courts (which provided a legal framework for mining) around 1200. Stannary law was built on the foundation of this 'Cornish legal system', while the later duchy of Cornwall in 1337 took over the powers of a system of indigenous government that had descended almost intact from the days of Dumnonia. While this is an ingenious attempt to build legitimacy for Stannary institutions, at present there is no corroborating evidence for the existence of a coherent (and strangely mute) Cornish jurisdiction. There is no reason to assume that Stannary law emerged out of the British law of the period before 936. It is just as possible it was a new framework, codifying the customary practices of tin streaming, as had happened in other mining districts of the British Isles such as the Forest of Dean, Derbyshire and the Mendips.

Other new constructions were the castles hastily thrown up in response to the troubles of the 1140s, for example at Truro, and the creation or recreation of the earls of Cornwall. And not just one earl but two. King Stephen created Alan of Brittany as earl a few months after Reginald de Dunstanville had been made earl by Robert of Gloucester.[9] Eventually, the local dominance of Matilda's supporters resulted in Reginald's confirmation. He wielded considerable power. Mark Page points out how, in Reginald's time from 1140 to 1175, no Cornish accounts were presented at the exchequer at Westminster, royal officers were excluded from Cornwall and the earl possessed the right to pardon outlaws.[10] Such powers amounted to de facto palatine status for Cornwall. However, the power balance between earls and crown changed during the thirteenth century, especially after 1272. In 1227 Henry III's brother Richard was made earl of Cornwall. Richard, the most powerful magnate among the English ruling class, retained considerable powers. These included the right to appoint the sheriffs (seized back from local knights who had paid the king for the right to elect their own sheriff), the profits of county courts and all but one of the Hundred courts, feudal incidents such as wardship (administering the estates of a deceased tenant if the heir was under age), arranging marriages of such heirs, relief (fees paid by incoming tenants or by purchasers of freeholds), the rights to a half share of wrecks at sea and the chattels of convicted felons and, last but very definitely not least, the profits of the stannaries.[11] As a result Cornwall contributed from a third to a half of the earls' income in the thirteenth century.[12]

Yet, the thirteenth-century earldom did not enjoy the palatine status of its twelfth-century predecessor. For example, Cornish sheriffs gradually began to present accounts at the exchequer. This happened six times during the earldom of Richard, between 1227 and 1272, but fourteen times in the years from 1272 to 1300.[13] Furthermore, all the nine taxes of Edward I's reign (1272–1307) were paid by Cornish taxpayers (although the tinners were a significant exception). Royal justice, albeit infrequent, was dispensed when the king's courts periodically descended upon Cornwall and by the late 1250s Cornwall was part of an assize circuit. Page argues that local landowners looked to the king for justice and not to the earls, while a high number of Cornish cases were brought before the royal courts at Westminster.[14] Also by this time, Cornwall was represented in Parliament by two knights and burgesses from six towns. In all these aspects – taxation, justice, representation – Cornwall by 1300 resembled English shire counties. However, the presence of the earls in the thirteenth century followed by the creation of the Duchy of Cornwall in 1337 guaranteed that integration remained 'administratively peculiar'.[15] Cornwall was still not a 'standard county' in 1284 and 1302 in relation to the king's eyre courts of itinerant justices (early versions of assize courts). Instead, it retained 'peculiar' customs and practices.[16]

What the earls, first Richard and then his son Edmund (earl from 1272 to 1300) did succeed in doing was to build a more efficient mechanism for generating income from their Cornish possessions. In 1198, tin mining was placed under a royal warden, William de Wrotham, who 'improved' stannary procedures, introduced more stringent codes and increased the level of taxes.[17] This ensured that the earls were well placed to reap the benefits of rising tin production. In the 1230s, Earl Richard acquired Tintagel and had built a castle there by 1245. This grandiose status symbol (already ruinous by the 1330s) stood as a reminder to people of his authority through occupying such a symbolic site, one with renewed connotations of power after the 1130s when the Arthurian romances of Geoffrey of Monmouth were popularized. Castle building, extravagant deer parks and the wholesale granting and confirming of borough status were also visible statements of the power of the earls.

More tangibly, Earl Edmund in the 1280s and 1290s shifted the administrative capital of Cornwall away from Launceston, almost within throwing distance of the Tamar and reassuringly close to

England. From this base, clinging to the very edge of Cornish territory, the tentacles of Anglo-Norman power had gradually stretched
themselves westwards. The port and stannary town of Lostwithiel
was now chosen as the location for the administrative headquarters
of the stannaries, later known as the Duchy Palace. Before this, Earl
Richard had, in 1268–70, bought up and dispersed the estates of the
two most powerful local families, the Valletorts and Cardinhams.[18]
As a result, their castles at Trematon and Restormel fell into the earls'
hands. The circular keep at Restormel provided a political counter-
part to the economic power of the stannaries, much of which flowed
through the nearby town of Lostwithiel.

All this ensured the political dominance of the earls, albeit one
tempered by ultimate royal control. The local knightly class was
clearly subordinate to the absentee earls. Cornwall was 'subject to the
ducal claims of two largely absentee lords [king and earl], who were
too distant for the men of [the county] to enjoy many ties of
patronage and allegiance'.[19] It suffered the disadvantages of remote
government without any of the advantages of patronage and protection, 'primarily an asset to be exploited and very little of the wealth
extracted from it was returned'.[20] Cornwall had become little more
than the ground over which competing external landed interests
squabbled. This was perhaps most evident in the feud in the 1270s
between Bishop Bronescombe of Exeter and the young Earl
Edmund. During this time the bishop's deer park near Truro, St Allen
church and his borough of Penryn were all subject to attacks by the
earl's officers.[21] The bishop in turn retaliated by wholesale excommu-
nications. Anglo-Norman colonization led to colonialism, as
earldom and diocese siphoned Cornish wealth off into southern
England.

The Duchy of Cornwall

In 1300 Earl Edmund died leaving no heir and after a confused
period the earldom was re-branded in 1337 as a Duchy with its
revenues earmarked for the eldest son of the monarch. This finally
neutered the potentially troublesome and independent earldom.
Nonetheless, there has always been a tendency among Cornish historians to view the duchy as a symbol of Cornish autonomy, following
A. L. Rowse's characterization of it as 'a little government of its

own'.[22] Some even see it as 'a Celtic survival'.[23] This is an over-romantic view, resulting from an excessive focus on the modern linkage of nation and state. The probability that the Cornish made up a cultural nation without a distinct political leadership or institutions is somehow unacceptable. The Duchy of Cornwall therefore stands in for missing independent political leaders. Those wishing to emphasize the duchy's independence have seized on the claim made by its attorney General in 1855 that, after the duchy charters of 1337/8, the crown 'entirely denuded itself of every remnant of seignory and territorial domination' in Cornwall, handing sovereignty over to the duchy.[24] The duchy's lawyers produced a mass of supporting evidence, partly based on the Duchy charters and partly made up of assertions about 'ancient constitutions'. However, we need to be a little more critical of this source. In 1855–7 the duchy lawyers were presenting the best legal case they could to gain the right to wrecks in Cornwall. This is not the same as fourteenth-century evidence for how people saw the distinction between crown and duchy or how those powers were exercised in practice. Sometimes, the duchy lawyers were just plain wrong, as when they claimed that the duchy's rights were 'more extensive even than had ever been enjoyed by the earls'.[25] They were not. Earl Reginald in the twelfth century enjoyed far wider powers than the later duke of Cornwall.

We must not be distracted by the smoke and mirrors trickery of nineteenth-century lawyers. Instead, the duchy can be interpreted rather differently. While its lawyers in the 1850s made a great deal of its 'independence' from the crown, the duchy owed its very existence to the crown and the duke was the heir to the crown. Disputes between duchy and crown in the nineteenth century were more akin to a family squabble than a dispute between two clearly separate governing institutions. Indeed, because of the lack of an heir the duchy was actually in crown hands for seventy-one of the 120 years from 1377 to 1497. And kings appear to have disposed, disrupted and restored the duchy at will in the late medieval period.[26] Rather than a 'Celtic survival' the duchy is a permanent reminder of Cornwall's former quasi-palatine status of the eleventh and twelfth centuries. Norman and Angevin kings granted the earls considerable leeway in order to maintain ultimate control over this vulnerable frontier. But as Cornwall was slowly integrated into the administrative structure of medieval England the power of the independent earls became an anachronism and was whittled away. The duchy was the concluding step in this process, an attenuated rump of palatine status kept safely within the family. It certainly had its 'mini-government' but that government was an arm of royal government.

However, the formation of the duchy did have a series of unintended longer term consequences that helped to shape Cornish identity. By providing a locally visible system of government it created a 'Cornish' pole of allegiance. Cornishness became associated with and allied not to the crown directly but to its offspring, the duchy. Furthermore, this could give material meaning to folk memories of independent Cornish rulers reproduced in the Cornish language plays. In a more concrete fashion, by guaranteeing the independence of the stannaries, the main source of its income, the duchy maintained a social group – the tinners – free from feudal ties and with a reputation for turbulence. Indeed, we can view the Duchy as an institutional device for containing the stannaries, making them safe for royal exploitation. This is evident in the duchy charters, which were as much about drawing limits around existing customary stannary freedoms as about granting 'concessions' to tinners.[27] But it was always a perilous tightrope to walk, guaranteeing the independence of stannary courts (and therefore maintaining tin production and profits) yet on the other hand not allowing too much freedom to what was, in effect, a potentially alternative jurisdiction. Despite these contradictions, the duchy was seen by 1500 as the guarantor of Cornish 'traditional' rights and customs, liberties more bound up by this time with the tinning industry than memories of a British past, the latter restricted to the Cornish-speaking culture zone. Cornish identity had become, by the 1480s, inextricably bound up with the future of the royal family and a very important link in the chain of Cornish history had been forged – one that produced that Cornish blend of conservatism and dependence (on the English crown) on the one hand and rebelliousness and independence on the other.

Economic and demographic growth

Economically, while the duchy of Cornwall was a machine for siphoning profits from Cornwall into royal coffers in the south-east of England, a brutal statement of Cornwall's dependent position, it also sowed some of the seeds of later industrialization, building on the prodigious growth of the Cornish economy in the twelfth and thirteenth centuries. If we are to believe Domesday Book, when the Normans arrived Cornwall had more in common with the remaining territories of the Celtic princes of Wales and Ireland than it did with England. However, by the 1340s Cornwall had converged with England. The driving forces of this were, as elsewhere, a steady growth of population and the beginnings of urbanization, but in Cornwall this growth had an extra dimension in the role of the tin trade. Just as political association did not mean an end to administrative 'peculiarities', so economic expansion and integration into wider markets accompanied and produced its own 'peculiarities'.

In the 250 years between Domesday Book and Black Death the population of the British Isles more than doubled.[28] By the early 1300s Cornwall's population was around 80,000 or higher and its population density had overtaken that of Devon.[29] Moreover, its growth rate was higher than the vast majority of English counties. Hatcher concludes there was 'evidence of prodigious colonisation . . . an expansion of settlement comparable with that achieved by the great colonising counties of the north of England'.[30] Just as in England, where the regions with the greatest growth were the most sparsely settled in 1086, so in Cornwall Penwith grew at a much faster rate than east Cornwall.[31] During the long decades of population growth settlements crept further into the previously unpopulated uplands and nibbled away at former open grazing land.[32] Farms had appeared high up on Foweymoor by 1241; Fernacre Farm was recorded at 900 feet above sea level in the lee of Rough Tor, indicating that the limit of settlement had been reached. The spread of farms well into the uplands was a symptom of population pressure in the lowlands where the number of families eventually outstripped the number of holdings, leading to a process of land sub-division. By the 1300s many holdings were no more than ten English acres in extent, or even smaller on good land.[33]

John Hatcher suggests a strong link between this colonization and the expansion of tin production. At times of greatest population pressure there may have been up to 8,000 persons engaged in some way with tinning, either working in the streamworks or buying, selling or transporting tin, with perhaps as much as 10–15 per cent of the Cornish population involved in tin production.[34] The volatility of production suggests that people moved in and out of tinning relatively easily, combining it with other ways of making an income. Stannary customs were 'expansionist' and 'egalitarian', allowing easy

entry into tinning and enabling its rapid growth to meet new demand
as uses were found for tin in the production of pewterware, roofing,
glazing, bells, organs and artillery.[35] In the thirteenth century the tax
on Cornish tin was far higher than that imposed on tin from Devon,
perhaps an echo of the different rights given to English and British
subjects by ninth-century Wessex kings. But in return for imposing
this massive coinage duty – up to 20 per cent of the price – the
monarch confirmed special freedoms for tinners. At the same time
they were placed under the warden of the stannaries and his officers,
to some extent outside the jurisdiction of the sheriff and local officials. In 1201 King John's Charter removed tinners from villeinage
(from the services and fines owed by unfree tenants) and guaranteed
their freedom to bound land for tin. In 1305 Edward I's Charter of
Liberties gave tinners freedom from general taxation, tolls and
market dues, although at the same time placing them under the jurisdiction of itinerant assize judges in the event of serious offences. In
1402, Henry IV confirmed these rights.[36] Royal policy thus produced
a local mining community that lived to some extent outside the
normal bonds of patronage and dependence, but, as its boundaries
with the rest of Cornish society were porous, this independence
spilled over and coloured that general society.

More people meant more markets and more markets more towns.
Towns in medieval Cornwall were of two types. Some, for example
Bodmin, Liskeard and Helston, emerged organically out of eleventh-
century settlements. But most were deliberately fostered by landlords.
Camelford, Grampound and Tintagel were planted by the earls of
Cornwall. Others owed their existence to lesser lords, who established
towns for profit, conferring various rights on the townsfolk to run
their own affairs outside manorial control in the hope that markets
would flourish and spiralling urban rents line their pockets. Thus
Truro was the speculative venture of Richard de Lucy, lord of
Kenwyn manor.[37] Situated at the head of a large estuary and at the
focus of land routes, it was a success, once another landlord's speculation at Newham, just down the river, had been seen off. However, by
the late fourteenth century even Truro was 'much impoverished',[38]
partly the result of the establishment by the bishop of Exeter of
Penryn, better placed to capture the growing coastal trade of the thirteenth century. While the number of boroughs has led to later
medieval Cornwall being described as 'one of the most densely
urbanised counties',[39] even the largest were extremely small by

modern standards. In the early fourteenth century the biggest Cornish town was only home to around 1,300 people and most had only 500 inhabitants. Less than 10 per cent of the population was urban at this time. Nevertheless, this should be seen in perspective. Cornwall's largest town in 1377, Bodmin, was only just under half the size of Exeter, one of England's major provincial towns.

Demographic growth, towns and tinning had all played their part in producing a dynamic society by the early fourteenth century. Another aspect of this dynamism was that 'nowhere in medieval England did a land market operate so freely, so competitively, so regularly and on so large a scale'.[40] This was the result of the introduction, sometime in the thirteenth century, of conventionary tenancies, fixed seven-year leases of land. In 1337 the duchy initiated regular accession courts at the end of the term of these leases, when they were put up for offer again and the rent adjusted in line with the demand for land. The result, by the middle of the fourteenth century, was a high turnover of holdings; in the duchy manor of Helston in Kerrier only 22 per cent of the tenants of 1337 were still in possession in 1347 and on all duchy of Cornwall lands less than half the land was in the hands of the same family after ten years.[41] As Fox and Padel state, 'the idea of unchanging, medieval rural societies, full of family communities with a distant past, should perhaps be abandoned'.[42] Nowhere was this more the case than fourteenth-century Cornwall, a relatively egalitarian and mobile society, with 'remarkably few traces of a peasant aristocracy' in the 1330s and 1340s.[43] A revolution in tenure had taken place, as colonization of the wastes and tin mining speeded up the process of converting unfree into free tenancies. True, unfree tenancies could be found even after the Black Death, for example at Liskeard and Stoke Climsland in 1382 where unfree tenants were still liable to forfeit all their belongings to their lord on their death.[44] But this was unusual. The absence of demesne farming (direct farming by the landlord), the use of conventionary tenancies, the light or obsolete labour services owed by tenants have all led John Hatcher to conclude that fourteenth-century Cornwall was 'non-manorial', only lightly touched by the feudal superstructure of medieval England.[45] In its social structure, fourteenth-century Cornwall was diverging from the experience of medieval England, gradually shrugging off the feudal shackles fastened temporarily onto it in the eleventh and twelfth centuries. And then the Black Death struck.

Plague, stagnation and diversification

In 1348 a ship from the Continent brought its deadly cargo of plague
into harbour in Dorset. Within a year the disease had spread through
southern England and into Cornwall, producing a mortality rate of
between 30 and 45 per cent.[46] The plague then returned periodically;
the 1360/2 outbreak in Cornwall was perhaps as virulent as that of
1349/50. The numbers of new clergy instituted by the bishop of
Exeter provide a clue to the numbers dying. In the twelve months
from March 1349, when the plague struck, eighty-five new clergy
were instituted in Cornwall, compared with an annual average of just
4.2 over the previous ten years.[47] The short-term effects of the plague
were catastrophic. Tin production virtually collapsed, there was a
drop in fish catches and the populations of the towns shrank. A
quarter or more of holdings on duchy manors fell vacant and landlords were forced to reduce or even remit rents.[48]

Nevertheless, in the medium rather than short term there was a
remarkably rapid recovery. The driving forces of the earlier growth –
tinning and towns – bore the immediate brunt of the economic
contraction. In contrast agricultural activity remained buoyant and
vacancies on duchy manors, especially in the east and north of
Cornwall, were negligible as early as 1351. This has been taken as
indicating the presence of a considerable body of landless labourers
before 1349, who swiftly occupied holdings left vacant. The balance
of activity shifted from the more marginal tinning to the more
dependable farming. Moreover, the Black Death, acting on an
already mobile society, produced what was a virtual revolution in
the composition of tenants, as many died, some of the survivors
took the opportunity to move on to better land, and a large proportion of the formerly landless were able to gain a tenancy.

Over the longer term declining levels of population in the century
or more after the Black Death had more profound effects. A dramatic
switch from arable farming to pasture land and rough grazing on the
edges of the uplands reversed the reclamations of the previous 200
years. Cereal cultivation was concentrated on the better coastal lands,
particularly those south of the central spine of Cornwall, and there
was a gradual shift away from the coarser oat grains that had been
widely used in medieval Cornwall for baking and brewing. Cornish
ale brewed with oats was given a bad name by Andrew Borde when
he observed as late as the 1540s that it was 'like wash as pigs had

wrestled in'.[49] But change was in the air much earlier than this. Records of mills at St Columb show that wheaten bread and barley-brewed beer were replacing oats as early as the 1460s. Indeed, when compared with other places, Cornish farming on the lowlands seems relatively productive in the fifteenth century and certainly not backward.[50] But everywhere falling numbers of people led to shrinking settlements in the period from 1350 to the late 1400s. Hamlets shrank to single farms, while some small settlements of one or two farms disappeared altogether. In Helston in Kerrier, taking in a large proportion of the parish of Wendron situated amongst the less hospitable uplands, the forty-five inhabited sites of the early 1300s were reduced to just thirty-one by the late 1400s. Areas like this would have the 'wrecked appearance of single farmsteads . . . and deserted tofts and messuages resulting from total abandonment of farmhouses and farmland'.[51]

Meanwhile the basic patterns of rural society persisted. Fox and Padel have characterized the medieval Cornish hamlet as a 'body of shareholders', where the tenants periodically reallocated land in the intermingled unenclosed town fields amongst themselves in order to share out their rent burden. The 'rules and rhythms of these settlements were determined not by lords but by small groups of farming families conforming by custom to established practices', even though there was considerable mobility in and out of such communities.[52] But, during the fifteenth century this endearing picture of a peasant democracy began to be modified. The turnover of holdings was reduced, at least on duchy lands, and declining competition for land by the mid-1400s tipped power back from landlord to tenant. The majority of holdings were more likely to be renewed by the 1420s than change hands and in 1441 on some manors longer fourteen or twenty-one-year leases were introduced,[53] a step from market-sensitive conventionary leases towards the copyhold leases held on three lives that were to dominate Cornish tenancy arrangements for another 300–400 years. Yet there was still almost complete turnover on some of the Arundell manors in the late fifteenth century. Fox and Padel explain this by reference to the role of mining and the prevalence of service in husbandry, when young men (and women) spent periods of time working as living-in farm servants, a practice that persisted well into the later nineteenth century. Mining boosted savings and living-in husbandry led to mobility, the combined result of which was an increased likelihood of movement to take up a more promising holding elsewhere.[54] Moreover, for the enterprising farmer, the late medieval period presented opportunities even if he stayed put. Landlords could be persuaded to subsidize the repair of buildings and sluggish demand for land always meant there was a chance of taking on more holdings. This resulted in the second important change of the fifteenth century, the rise of a 'small group of kulaks' who were busily engrossing holdings.[55] After the 1370s there was a progressive increase in the number of tenants farming more than one holding,[56] a recognizably modern class of farmers, more concerned with producing food for the market than sustaining the household.

While social changes triggered by population decline led to the slow emergence of a farming elite, the effects on tinning operated in the opposite direction. Earlier, in the thirteenth century, tin merchants and dealers had a strong hold over the industry. Because of the length of time between coinages and the lack of capital held by labouring tinners, dealers in London and merchants in Cornwall financed the industry, advancing money to labouring tinners and charging interest on it. In the early 1300s between a third and two-thirds of all the tin presented for coinage was registered in the names of just ten persons, powerful evidence for a small class of merchant tinners who owned tin streamworks, dealt in tin and controlled tin exports. These merchants lived in the towns and tapped the capital of the gentry, clergy and, after 1337, duchy officials who were keen to take their slice of the tin profits. The most important merchant at the turn of the fourteenth century was Gerard de Villiers of Lostwithiel.[57] A few miles to the north and a few decades later the Blake family of Bodmin were also leading tin merchants and frequent suers for unpaid debts, indicating their role as money lenders to tinners.[58]

However, merchants such as these, or 'Abraham the Tinner', reputed to employ 300 men in 1357 in seven streamworks on Foweymoor, faded away after the 1350s.[59] In response to a petition from the commons of Cornwall in 1376, Parliament agreed that the definition of 'tinner' should be confined to manual workers in tin works and their privileges restricted to them.[60] While this was largely ignored, it indicated that working tinners possessed a new-found confidence after the Black Death. An increase in the numbers presenting small amounts of tin for coinage and a 'great reduction' in the activity of leading merchants in the fifteenth century mark a levelling of the inequalities of the first half of the fourteenth century.[61] The tin industry became more egalitarian as labourers'

wages rose and credit became more easily available. The great dispar-
ities of wealth of the thirteenth and early fourteenth centuries, when
there was a small number of very wealthy merchants and a mass of
impoverished working tinners, diminished. By the later fifteenth
century the mining community was more independent and more self-
confident than it had been 200 years previously. As the pendulum
swung away from the merchants towards working tinners, production
slowly shifted westwards towards the Penwith and Kerrier
Stannaries,[62] resulting in a shift in the coinages. For a period in the
early fifteenth century Lostwithiel had been the only coinage town.
But by the 1460s the westward drift of production was recognized in
the renewed use of Truro as a coinage town and, in 1492, Helston was
added to the list.[63] As mining orientated itself towards the west a
divergence opened up from the 1420s in the economic fortunes of east
and west Cornwall. As tin production fell in the first half of the
fifteenth century, land rents also fell in the west but held up in the
east.[64]

Cultural distinctiveness

East and west Cornwall may have been drifting apart economically
during the 1400s but was this echoed culturally? In the 'first English
Empire' of the Angevin kings, from the 1100s to 1300s, there were
two broadly differing culture zones in the British Isles.[65] In the south-
east corner of England lay the English heartland, with its feudal and
hierarchical social pyramid. Here, the countryside was intensively
farmed, with classic open fields and nucleated villages occupied by a
tenantry bound to their landlords by a series of intricate customary
obligations. It was different in a large swathe of Ireland and in north
and west Wales, where native princes still ruled and power was
counted more by the number of men and women controlled than
land owned or feudal dues paid. But there was also a 'large intermediate area' between these poles of 'sweet civility and barbarous
rudeness'.[66] And places could shift from one culture zone to another.
Cornwall was such a place. Yet it remained fundamentally different
from those counties carved out of Saxon kingdoms, as it was a
conquered British province. Before the arrival of the Normans in
1066 the Cornish had clearly been regarded as a distinct ethnic
group.[67] But in the post-1066 period ethnic boundaries were fluid and

shifting, as the rapid assimilation of Norman identity by Englishness seems to prove.[68] How far were the Cornish still a distinguishable people?

Reconstructing group mythologies in Cornwall is difficult as a vast amount of orally transmitted evidence was lost with the decline of Cornish as a spoken language from the sixteenth century. Only tantalizing hints remain. Nicholas Orme notes how, as late as the fifteenth century, folklore about Cornish saints gave them an Irish context and not an English one, 'indicating consciousness of a separate Cornish heritage'.[69] The Breton and Welsh origins of some Cornish saints and the high number of local saints distinguished medieval Cornwall from English counties. Furthermore, Oliver Padel has established the existence of a body of Arthurian folk legends in Cornwall before the works of Geoffrey of Monmouth in the twelfth century.[70] Evidence for this comes from 1113, when a group of French canons from Laon journeyed through Cornwall. At Bodmin, the clerics, expressing scepticism about the reality of Arthur, were assailed by an irate local who caused a disturbance at the priory by insisting that Arthur would return. For Padel this was an example of 'strong national feeling when [Arthur] was mocked by outsiders'.[71] However, this and the saints' cults seem to point as much to wider 'British' rememberings as to a specifically Cornish national identity. It has become unfashionable to stress a historic inter-Celtic identity in recent years but the Cornish in the medieval period retained an identity (albeit hazy and shifting) that looked seaward towards Wales, Ireland and Brittany as much as landward towards their political overlords in England.

Furthermore, the works of Geoffrey of Monmouth made Cornish writers of the later twelfth century reflect on their sense of British belonging. For Hugh Thomas, Cornwall was 'one area . . . where [Geoffrey's *Historia Regum Britannie*] did help to sustain an existing British identity'. John of Cornwall, who wrote a version of the prophecies of Merlin, 'spoke of the devastation by the inhabitants of Devonshire "among us"', from which Thomas concludes he had a sense of being a Briton, distinct from the English.[72] While Geoffrey of Monmouth's work did little to dent a burgeoning English identity – in fact his 'Matter of Britain' was swiftly co-opted into the 'Matter of England' – 'only in Cornwall, where there were linguistic and perhaps other cultural features that made British identity and a connection to Geoffrey's past believable, did Geoffrey have any influence on identity, by shoring up and reshaping an ethnic identity that

already existed'.[73] The words 'shoring up and reshaping' are important as they suggest that late twelfth-century elites in and from
Cornwall began to reidentify themselves with a British ancestry that
had been relatively inarticulate since the tenth century. It may be no
coincidence that this rearticulation, with its greater sense of pride and
confidence in ancestry, also coincided with the development of strong
anti-Celtic stereotypes in twelfth-century England. Perhaps in the
later 1100s cultural and ethnic boundaries were being drawn more
sharply, reinforcing a sense of Cornishness.

A sense of inter-Celtic connections coexisted with an awareness of
the Cornish as one of the named peoples of Britain. In his eulogy to
the military might of King Edward I, written around 1300, Pierre de
Langtoft wrote, for example, that:

> Now are all the islanders joined together,
> And Albany reunited to the royalties
> Of which Edward is pronounced lord.
> Cornwall and Wales are in his power,
> And Ireland the great at his will.
> There is neither King nor Prince of all the countries
> Except King Edward who had thus united them.[74]

Cornwall was still being seen here as one of the 'countries' of the
British Isles. In addition, its people continued to be distinguished
from the English. Rulers, secular and religious, addressed their
peoples in greetings clauses. Thus in 1173 a charter was addressed at
Truro to the barons of Cornwall and to 'all men both Cornish and
English'.[75] In the 1150s Earl Reginald addressed all his men, 'French,
English and Welsh (i.e. Cornish)'.[76] The common use of 'Cornubiae',
'le Cornwaleys', 'of Cornwall' as the surname of people in England
in the thirteenth century may be seen as a mark of identity, although
the same process worked for parts of England, such as Devonshire
and Kent.[77] But in those places 'William the Englishman', who quarrelled with, and mortally wounded, 'Fabian the ploughman in a field
at Connerton', would not have been described as such. The source for
this also reveals the multi-ethnic composition of thirteenth-century
Cornwall with Gascons and Welshmen also figuring in the court
records.[78]

Nevertheless, as in more modern times, Cornwall and the Cornish
could also be ignored, especially as we move into the fourteenth
century. Thus, in the 1350s Ranulph Higden's account of the seven

peoples of Britain failed to mention the Cornish. While the Cornish could still be regarded as one of the peoples of Britain as late as 1603,[79] it seems that they began to be increasingly vulnerable to omission in the 1300s. This may reflect R. R. Davies's observation that, from the late eleventh to the late fourteenth century, there was a noticeable reduction in the numbers of identifiable peoples in the British Isles.[80] The complexity of the twelfth and thirteenth centuries gradually gave way to the four peoples – English, Scots, Irish and Welsh – of the 1400s. Davies links this to a growing sense of nationality amongst the English, Scots, Welsh and Irish. As the space for identifiable peoples shrank, smaller and more marginal groups lost visibility. As the Cornish never comprised more than 2 per cent of the population of the British Isles at the most, they were always likely candidates for oversight, whether deliberate or accidental.

Language: distinction and division

In 1342 the Archdeacon of Cornwall rather despairingly begged the Bishop to accept his resignation as 'the folk of these parts are quite extraordinary, being of a rebellious temper, and obdurate in the face of attempts to teach and correct'.[81] Such communication problems reflected differing cultural practices. For example, Cornish naming customs were different. Oliver Padel points out how some Cornish people's second names remained fluid well into the sixteenth century.[82] This was much later than in neighbouring Devon where surnames were generally being passed on from parents to children by the fourteenth century. In contrast, the Cornish resembled the Welsh, whose hereditary surnames only crystallized during the sixteenth and seventeenth centuries. But Padel's work on surnames also suggests two qualifications. First, in fourteenth- and fifteenth-century Cornwall, the Welsh pattern of fluid names coexisted with an English pattern of fixed hereditary surnames. This reminds us of medieval Cornwall's intermediate cultural positioning, poised between and overlapping 'Celtic' patterns to the north and English practice to the east. Second, three-part names, where men took their surnames from their father and grandfather's Christian names, were confined almost entirely to the four western Hundreds and were absent from Cornwall east of the Camel–Fowey line.[83] Distinctiveness was therefore most marked in Cornish-speaking mid and west Cornwall, whereas in east

Cornwall naming customs approximated more closely to the English norm. This west–east division has also been discovered by Orme in relation to saints' cults and dedications.[84] Parishes that bordered on Devon celebrated fewer British saints and more international and English saints. The Cornish language was therefore the key factor in reproducing cultural distinctiveness.

In the tenth century Cornish was spoken across the vast majority of Cornwall. The first major surviving written work in the language outside place names was the *Vocabularium Cornicum*, a list of a thousand words with Cornish and Latin equivalents, compiled in the twelfth century. After that we have to wait almost another 200 years for direct traces of the language, either in the form of testimony about the state of Cornish or in the production of the first of the medieval dramas – both of which date from the fourteenth century.

What was the state of Cornish in those intervening two centuries? There are indirect hints of its presence. James Whetter notes that Richard of Cornwall, recommended to become a prebend in a Franciscan school at Oxford around 1247, was described as 'lacking in command of the English tongue, presumably because English was his second language'.[85] Statements about Cornish in the fourteenth century provide more information about the linguistic balance.[86] In 1336 a sermon by Bishop Grandisson of Exeter at St Buryan was translated from Latin into Cornish by the rector of St Just, as we might expect in this far western location. Three years later, in 1339, a licence was granted to a curate of St Merryn, part of his duties being to preach in Cornish. This suggests the district west of the Camel estuary was Cornish-speaking. In 1354/5 a Franciscan friar was appointed at Truro for those who knew Cornish and another at Bodmin for those who knew Cornish and English. This was a revealing distinction. It might show that the Truro district was Cornish-speaking but that both Cornish and English could be found within reach of Bodmin. More intriguingly, in 1349 the death rate from plague was so high that it was reported no chaplain could be found suitable for the parish of Minster since none could speak Cornish. This was well to the north of the Camel. However, this plea was actually written from the monastery at Tywardreath and there may be doubts about it.[87] But even if we accept the evidence for Cornish still being spoken in a remote part of north Cornwall, it remains the only non-place-name evidence for Cornish east of the Camel–Fowey line in the fourteenth century or later.

The common model assumes that the English language gradually replaced Cornish. Speculative lines on maps that purport to mark language 'boundaries' add to the impression of a progressive westwards retreat of the Cornish language.[88] But they need to be taken with a pinch of salt for two reasons. First, linguistic borders are not neat lines. Instead the real picture was much more confused, with islands of speakers of one language surrounded by the other language and with the small towns even in the west having more English (and French and Flemish) speakers than the surrounding countryside. A cursory glance at twentieth-century maps of Welsh speakers or a linguistic map of modern eastern Europe indicates that language communities on the ground co-mingle in confusing ways and that these patterns persist for a considerable amount of time. The second reason for not imagining a steady westwards retreat of Cornish is that this runs contrary to the actual experience of the Welsh and Irish languages in the medieval period. In both those societies at certain times English-speaking areas reverted to being Celtic-speaking. In the fourteenth century there were 'substantial gains' for Welsh in south Wales while in Ireland the first wave of Anglo-Norman settlers were in large measure Gaelicized in the later medieval period. [89] In similar fashion Nicholas Williams argues for a 're-Celticised' east Cornwall during the twelfth and thirteenth centuries.[90]

However, this seems to run counter to the evidence of both place names and family name formation in thirteenth- and fourteenth-century east Cornwall. In his synthesis of the historical geography of Cornish, Matthew Spriggs finds 'the evidence [for the period before 1300] difficult to interpret', although Julyan Holmes has argued strongly that Cornish was still spoken as far east as St Kew and Looe in 1400.[91] Yet the pattern of family names in east Cornwall contradicts this, with a lack of Cornish language elements in fourteenth- and fifteenth-century surnames. My own conclusion is that the Cornish language rapidly retreated from most of east Cornwall in the 200 years after 1100. This may be connected in some way with the extension of Norman power in Cornwall and its concentration in the east or with the growth of population that occurred from the eleventh to the mid-fourteenth century. But a relatively rapid phase of language loss was then followed by a period of stabilization as a boundary between predominantly Cornish-speaking districts to the west and English districts to the east was established and maintained for perhaps 200 years from 1300–50 onwards near the eastern boundary of Pydar and Powder Hundreds. This stabilization created Cornwall's own shorter lived version of the division in south-west Wales between English/Flemish- and Welsh-speaking areas or the boundary between Breton and Gallo in Brittany. It was linked to changes in the church and to the emergence of a religious literature in Cornish.

Religious change and language maintenance

In terms of religious practice medieval Cornwall was part of a wider European culture zone. In the rise of saints' cults and guilds, in the emergence of a new monasticism from the eleventh century, in changing fashions in services, in the growing practice in the thirteenth century of making endowments to pay for chantry priests who would say prayers for the dead, Cornwall shared in more global changes. Cornish men and women, like good Christians elsewhere, took part in pilgrimages, locally to places such as the chapel of Our Lady in the Park at Liskeard or St Day's chapel at Gwennap, and to the 'premier Cornish shrine' of St Michael's Mount.[92] But sometimes wider processes took on a unique, local flavour. Thus it was with the founding of collegiate churches, a cheaper form of monasticism. In 1265 the Bishop of Exeter founded Glasney College at Penryn.[93] Together with changing attitudes towards the use of vernacular languages in religion, this place played a major part in the emergence of a Cornish literature. In the same century, changing ideas in Europe about the best way to disseminate the gospel led to a growth of preaching and teaching. The work of the friars, who went amongst the people to preach, put a greater emphasis on local languages instead of Latin. Thus, in the thirteenth century there was a flowering and Europeanization of Welsh religious literature.[94] And in 1311 the making of the feast of Corpus Christi into an official holy day led to the emergence of mystery plays written in English.[95] It was later in the fourteenth century that the first surviving Cornish play, the *Poem of the Passion*, appeared, written in order to be performed at public, open-air performances. In this way the Cornish language emerged above the horizon of literacy, taking advantage of wider changes in religious fashion. This coincided with a period, after the high point of English power in 1300, when English dominance in the British Isles faltered and space again opened up for the non-English cultures of Britain to reassert themselves.[96] It was in these years, from 1350 to 1500, that Williams's 'recelticization', if it occurred, should be sought. It is just possible that the stabilization of the linguistic geography and the higher status granted to Cornish by its use in religious drama and its patronage by the church may have accompanied a 'celticizing' of the small market towns, early centres of English speakers, that had sprung up in mid and west Cornwall between 1100 and 1300.

In the late 1300s the three plays of the Ordinalia were composed. As Brian Murdoch notes, 'there has been some readiness to accept glib comments on an expected rusticity in the works'.[97] In contrast his detailed study of the Cornish dramas convinced him that they possessed real literary merit, the Ordinalia cycle marking the 'high point of medieval Cornish literature, the point at which Cornish merges most fully into the literature of medieval Europe'. [98] These plays stood apart from the English cycles in many respects and indicate the emergence of a distinct Cornish literary tradition, although one within the mainstream of European literature. Murdoch's conclusions contrast with those of a Welsh scholar, Brynley Roberts, who argues that 'lacking any institution which could nurture it and ensure the continuation of its language and context over a long period, the literary tradition had declined and died by the fourteenth and fifteenth centuries'.[99] While some of Roberts's summary of the Cornish dramas is misleading, notably in his assertion that the plays are 'full of unadopted English borrowings', he does make the observation that the register of literary conventions in the plays is far more limited than in contemporary Welsh medieval writings, suggesting in turn that the literary ability of Cornish was relatively restricted. This point reminds us that there is no evidence for translations of the gospel or other prose religious texts from this period and no non-religious writings. The plays were a means to instruct people in the tenets of Christianity and in this way they were instrumental for an external organization, the church, rather than emerging organically out of Cornish culture. Unlike the situation in Wales, the disappearance of a Cornish-speaking ruling elite had removed an institutional prop for Cornish literature. In the fourteenth and fifteenth centuries religious literature was therefore grafted onto the language, part of the creation of a new literary tradition. The political defeat and incorporation (however ambiguous) of Cornwall in the ninth to eleventh centuries had stifled the emergence of a separate Cornish literary tradition. Cornish had survived as the language of the people but the secular elite that could have nurtured it did not exist. When a more confident landed class began to reappear after 1200 its top echelons were anglicized. Although lesser gentry in the west spoke Cornish well into the sixteenth century – Chynoweth presents a case of two western landowners speaking Cornish amongst themselves in a courtroom in 1579[100] – there was no unbroken chain back to a period of British rulers, in contrast to Wales. The absence of support from a native elite or of institutional support outside the church meant, therefore, that the Cornish language was always vulnerable, dependent on changes in religious practices and policies which inevitably originated outside Cornwall.

Fifteenth-century Cornwall: divisions and diversification

By the fifteenth century Cornish was restricted to mid and west Cornwall, although there it fostered a distinct sense of ethnic identity, with its own naming customs, oral folklore, musical traditions and memories of former times. The linguistically unified Cornwall of the tenth century had given way to a land of two vernacular languages: English, spreading from the east, and Cornish, kept alive by Cornwall's seaward links to Brittany and to European religious culture. And in the 1400s this cultural division was increasingly over-laid by economic divisions. The geographical divergence can be seen when the tax assessments of the early sixteenth century are compared with those of the fourteenth century. Over this period, reversing the pattern before the Black Death, it was the Hundreds of East and West, in the east of Cornwall, that grew fastest.

Although Cornish wool had been exported as early as the twelfth century,[101] its quality was not highly regarded. Nevertheless, the export of cloth from Cornish ports seems to have increased markedly in the first forty years of the fifteenth century, before being eclipsed by the much greater growth of cloth production in Devon. Henderson noted as many as sixty tucking mills in medieval Cornwall, which suggests widespread cloth manufacture.[102] The impact of this expanding textile manufacturing was felt mainly in the east, where Cornish farmers were boosted by growing demand for food and maybe for wool from across the border. For Hatcher, this helps to explain the divergence in economic fortunes within Cornwall over the fifteenth century.[103] As rents in western manors declined, accompanied by a slow collapse of tin production, rent incomes held up in the east. Growing distinctions between east and west were mirrored by growing diversification. In fifteenth-century Cornwall the structure of the economy was 'fundamentally different from the economies of many . . . English counties; it was complex and diverse, with a high industrial and commercial content'.[104] Tinning was not the only industrial occupation that stimulated demand. Stone and slate quarrying were also present, but it was maritime related activity that was growing the fastest.

Cornish ports were well placed to benefit from an increase in shipping. Trade with Europe – in particular with Brittany and western France – was long-standing. Merchants from Helston, Bodmin and Truro had been selling tin in Bordeaux and La Rochelle as early as 1265.[105] To this can be added the coastal trade from Cornwall to the centres of pewter manufacture via Southampton and London.[106] Tin was still the staple Cornish export in the late fifteenth century, along with fish, leather and cloth, the latter trade by this time concentrated in a multitude of voyages to and from Brittany.[107] Carrying pilgrims on the route to Santiago de Compostella as well as the demands of war and periodic opportunities for privateering all helped boost the fortunes of those with easy access to the sea. Ports like Lostwithiel and Truro, tucked safely in their estuaries, gave way in the 1400s to the newer ports of Fowey, Penryn, Padstow and Mounts Bay. Keeping these ports and the seamen who visited them supplied with food and materials helped maintain the fortunes of nearby farms. Fish had become an important component of overall trade, with the western ports of Marazion, Penzance and St Ives, together with Fowey, pre-eminent. A fish-curing industry developed as men sailed to the fishing grounds off southern Ireland and even as far as Iceland. In the late fifteenth century deep sea fishing was joined by inshore seine pilchard fishing, as Cornish traders met a rising demand for fish from England and from Mediterranean countries.[108]

Overall, Cornwall was one of the fastest growing places in the British Isles in the fifteenth century, along with Devon and a group of counties surrounding London.[109] Outstanding increases in relative wealth in the 150 years after the Black Death is evidence that it did not succumb to economic decline during this period of population contraction. Cornwall's diversified late medieval economy was in addition cause and effect of an extensive rebuilding beginning in the fifteenth century and continuing into the sixteenth. This included churches, such as St Ives (1410–34), Callington (1430s) and Bodmin (1469–72), with new stained-glass windows put into churches at places like St Neot and St Kew; bridges and quays, as at Looe (1411–36) and Wadebridge (1468); and rural housing, where the medieval long house, in which people shared the building with their cattle, began to be phased out during the 1400s.[110] This fifteenth-century rebuilding and the greater vitality of Cornwall's economy was no doubt the underlying factor in the migration of men from Brittany to Cornwall. Subsidy lists of the 1520s reveal a high proportion of 'aliens' in Cornish parishes, particularly those of the west and the south coast. But in mid and west Cornwall these economic migrants attracted by higher wages were hardly culturally alien. Breton would have been close enough to Cornish at this time to be mutually intelligible and the wave of Breton migrants may well have helped to reinforce the Cornish language from the mid-1400s onwards.

The Duchy had postponed the growth of a great magnate class in Cornwall. Nevertheless, the relative lack of royal interest in the duchy from the late fourteenth century allowed a 'growth of magnate influence' in the fifteenth century.[111] At first some of these, like the Courtenays, earls of Devon, were absentees, but others were home-grown. The Arundells of Lanherne, Bodrugans and Colshulls were major gentry families of the fifteenth century. As that century proceeded they competed for influence with other older families such as the Bassets and St Aubyns and upwardly mobile upstarts such as the Edgcumbes, Grenvilles and Treffrys. Consequently, in the fifteenth century there was considerable instability within this gentry class. Feuds and violent clashes were not uncommon, with many men gaining experience in fighting during the long wars in France. Gentry families acted in some respects like warlords and violence was a well established instrument of politics. As James Whetter concludes, 'gangs run by the landholding families appear to have been commonplace at this time'.[112] Tyldesley noted that gentry violence was a striking feature of Cornwall in the period from 1377 to 1422,[113] reflecting a turbulent society, one made even more so by the volatility injected by the tin industry. For example, in 1343 'gang warfare' was reported between tinners while tin merchants regularly used armed retainers to back up their legal rights.[114] Later, in 1465 about 100 persons in the pay of various gentlemen attacked a St Columb merchant, Richard Tomyow, and took off a large amount of tin.[115]

Nonetheless, although Rowse described this situation as 'feudal anarchy'[116] the gentry remained subject, albeit intermittently, to royal justice.

Ambitious families and the possibility of wealth through trading opportunities and the tin industry combined to produce a tempestuous society in the fifteenth century, one where people were quick to resort to violence. If we add to this the role of the duchy and the continued use of a vernacular language that marked the population off from their governing classes we can begin to discern the ingredients for the dramatic risings that took place in the period from 1497 to 1549. A. L. Rowse wrote that Cornwall had lain 'quiet, it might be almost be said dormant, throughout most of the Middle Ages, a small conquered country on the remotest outskirts of Europe, held in possession by its Anglo-Norman feudal class'.[117] Conquered and exploited it certainly was and, when viewed from Westminister, it may have been remote but, as we have seen in this chapter, Cornwall was hardly 'dormant' during the Middle Ages.

Conclusion

Cornwall had entered the Norman era accommodated or accommodating, its people spared the full rigours of anglicization and retaining a considerable measure of autonomy. However, this compromise was shattered by the arrival of the Normans. In the century after 1066 they imposed their rule, first on the far east of Cornwall, the original Saxon pale. Relations between the native population and their political overlords may have worsened, with hazy reports of conflict in 1069 and the early twelfth century. But the parachuting of a Norman landed class and the more direct rule of the early earls was the harbinger of a more vigorous integration into the structures of the English state, a process that had gone a long way by the late 1200s. Simultaneously, in the context of Norman expansionism, the English language supplanted Cornish in the east. However, in the late twelfth and the thirteenth centuries there was a renewed Cornish self-confidence, as Geoffrey of Monmouth's Arthurian romance legitimated the British origins of the indigenous landed class and restored a sense of pride. A reasserted Cornish identity in the thirteenth century coincided with changes in religious practice. Most importantly, the church began to preach the gospel through vernacular languages. This fortuitously counteracted the growing landward influences associated with political integration and built on Cornwall's seaward links, given form by saints' cults and pilgrimages and trading links that looked southwards to Brittany and Spain. The production of miracle cycles and saints' plays in the Cornish language and its use by the church was one factor helping to stabilize the language frontier for 200 years at the eastern edge of Pydar and Powder Hundreds. During this time it more than held its own, propped up by the church even though political expropriation had led to the loss of lay patronage several centuries earlier.

However, the cultural stabilization of the Cornish language community in the period after 1300–50 began to widen cultural differences within Cornwall as the east came under more English influence. Pressures pulling east and west apart were exacerbated by economic change in the fifteenth century as tinning moved westwards and east Cornwall enjoyed the spin-offs from a growing cloth industry across the Tamar. The trans-Cornwall institution of the duchy to some extent ameliorated this, offering a potential pole of allegiance for Cornishness and locking Cornwall both east and west into a close relationship with the crown. In particular the compact between crown and tinners resulted in a tradition of cherished independence for the latter in return for a steady flow of revenue to the former. Though spilling over into the rest of society the westwards shift of tinning meant that this 'independence' coloured the west of Cornwall more than the east. These developments may have produced a sense of 'communal cultural defensiveness' in the west by the later fifteenth century.[118]

But all Cornwall benefited from a diversified economy and the appearance of new economic opportunities in the 1400s. These also helped to create a more vigorous gentry class, replacing many of the old Anglo-Norman families and occupying the social landscape between peasantry and duchy. It was the attitude of the gentry that was soon to prove critical as the late medieval compromise between landward and seaward, English and Celtic, influences began to splinter in the late fifteenth century, before shattering completely in the sixteenth.

Notes

[1] For an early attempt at an overview see L. E. Elliot-Binns, *Medieval Cornwall* (1955). For a more recent synthesis see Philip Payton, *Cornwall* (1996/2004), chap. 5.

[2] See R. R. Davies, *The First English Empire: Power and Identities in the British Isles 1093–1343* (2000); William Frazer, 'Identities in early medieval Britain', in William Frazer and Andrew Tyrrell (eds), *Social Identities in Early Medieval Britain* (2000).

[3] Philip Payton, *The Making of Modern Cornwall* (1992), p. 47; John Angarrack, *Our Future is History: Identity, Law and the Cornish Question* (2002), chaps 6 and 7.

[4] Adrian Hastings, *The Construction of Nationhood: Ethnicity, Religion and Nationalism* (1997), p. 44; Barbara Harvey (ed.), *The Twelfth and Thirteenth Centuries 1066–c1280* (2001), p. 253.

[5] P. A. S. Pool, 'The Tithings of Cornwall', *Journal of the Royal Institution of Cornwall* (1981), 275–335.

[6] Oliver Padel, 'Geoffrey of Monmouth and Cornwall', *Cambridge Medieval Celtic Studies*, 8 (1984), 1–27.

[7] David Crouch, *The Reign of King Stephen 1135–1154* (2000), p. 115.

[8] Angarrack, *Our Future is History*, pp. 122–3.

[9] Crouch, *The Reign of King Stephen*, p. 115.

[10] Mark Page, 'Royal and comital government and the local community in thirteenth-century Cornwall', D.Phil. thesis, Oxford University (1995), p. 43.

[11] Ibid., pp. 42–3.

[12] Ibid., p. 74.

[13] Ibid., pp. 15–16.

[14] Ibid., pp. 15–17 and 46.

[15] Ibid., p. 10.

[16] G. D. G. Hall, 'Three courts of the hundred of Penwith', in C. A. F. Meekings (ed.), *Medieval Legal Records* (1978), pp. 170–7.

[17] John Hatcher, *English Tin Production and Trade before 1500* (1973), p. 20.

[18] Page, 'Royal and Comital Government', p. 85.

[19] Ibid., p. 161.

[20] Ibid., p. 74.

[21] Ibid., p. 36.

[22] A. L. Rowse, *Tudor Cornwall* (1941), p. 82.

[23] Payton, *Making of Modern Cornwall*, p. 26.

[24] Ibid., p. 66; Angarrack, *Our Future is History*, p. 197.

[25] Payton, *Making of Modern Cornwall*, p. 66.

[26] John Hatcher, *Rural Economy and Society in the Duchy of Cornwall 1300–1500* (1970), p. 7.

[27] As argued by Angarrack, *Our Future is History*, p. 127.

[28] John Hatcher and Mark Bailey, *Modelling the Middle Ages: The History and Theory of England's Economic Development* (2001), pp. 30–1.

[29] John Hatcher, 'New settlement: South West England', in H. E. Hallam (ed.), *The Agrarian History of England and Wales*, vol. 2, *1042–1350*, (1986), p. 235.

[30] Ibid., p. 236.

[31] H. C. Darby, R. E. Glasscock, J. Sheail and G. R. Versey, 'The changing geographical distribution of wealth in England: 1086–1334–1525', *Journal of Historical Geography*, 5 (1979), 247–62.

[32] John Hatcher, in footnote to Peter Hull (ed.), *Caption of Seisin of the Duchy of Cornwall, 1337* (1971), p. lxviii.

[33] Hatcher, *Rural Economy*, p. 25.

[34] Hatcher, *English Tin Production*, p. 47.

[35] Ibid., pp. 14–15, 26, 48.

[36] Allen Buckley, *Medieval Cornish Stannary Charters* (2001), pp. 5–7; Hatcher, *English Tin Production* p. 48.

[37] Charles Henderson, *Records of the Borough of Truro before 1300* (1929), p. 6.

[38] Cited in J. G. Pounds, 'The historical geography of Cornwall', Ph.D. thesis, University of London (1945), p. 158.

[39] Page, 'Royal and Comital Government', p. 72.

[40] John Hatcher, 'Non-manorialism in medieval Cornwall', *Agricultural History Review*, 18 (1970), 1–16.

[41] Hatcher, *Rural Economy*, p. 98.

[42] H. S. A. Fox and Oliver Padel, *The Cornish Lands of the Arundells of Lanherne, Fourteenth to Sixteenth Centuries*, (2000), p. cxx.

[43] Hatcher, *Rural Economy*, p. 100.

[44] H. S. A. Fox, in Edward Miller (ed.), *The Agrarian History of England and Wales*, vol. 3, *1348–1500* (1991), p. 765.

[45] Hatcher, 'Non-manorialism'.

[46] John Hatcher, *Plague, Population and the English Economy 1348–1530* (1977), p. 250.

[47] Hatcher, *Rural Economy*, p. 102.

[48] Fox, *Agrarian History*, p. 722.

[49] Cited in Alan Kent (ed.), *Looking at the Mermaid: A Reader in Cornish Literature 900–1900* (2000), p. 265.

[50] Fox, *Agrarian History*, pp. 307–9.

[51] Ibid., pp. 168; Fox and Padel, *Cornish Lands of the Arundells*, p. cix.

[52] Fox and Padel, *Cornish Lands of the Arundells*, pp. xci–xciii.

[53] Hatcher, *Rural Economy*, p. 120.

[54] Fox and Padel, *Cornish Lands of the Arundells*, pp. cxvii–cxviii.

[55] Fox, *Agrarian History*, p. 724.

[56] Hatcher, *Rural Economy*, p. 139.

[57] Hatcher, *English Tin Production*, p. 79.

[58] Ibid., p. 80.

[59] Ibid., p. 62.

[60] Ibid., p. 63.

[61] Ibid., p. 69.

[62] Sandy Gerrard, *The Early British Tin Industry* (2000), pp. 58–9.

[63] Hatcher, *English Tin Production*, p. 77.

[64] Hatcher, *Rural Economy*, p. 161.

[65] Davies, *First English Empire*, p. 110.

[66] Ibid., p. 110.

[67] Hugh Thomas, *The English and the Normans: Ethnic Hostility, Assimilation and Identity 1066–c.1220* (2003), p. 27.

[68] Ibid., pp. 47–50.

[69] Nicholas Orme, *The Saints of Cornwall* (2000), p. 44.

[70] Oliver Padel, 'Geoffrey of Monmouth'.

[71] Oliver Padel, *Arthur in Medieval Welsh Literature* (2000), p. 122.

[72] Thomas, *English and Normans*, p. 353.

[73] Ibid., p. 355.

[74] Cited in R. R. Davies, *The British Isles 1100–1500: Comparison, Contrasts and Connections* (1988), p. 26.

[75] Henderson, *Records of the Borough of Truro*, p. 9.

[76] Peter Hull (ed.), *The Cartulary of Launceston Priory* (1987), pp. 9 and 17.

[77] James Whetter, *Cornwall in the Thirteenth Century: A Study in Social and Economic History* (1998), p. 221; Page, 'Royal and comital government, p. 14.

[78] P. A. S. Pool, 'The Tithings of Cornwall', p. 278.

[79] Mark Stoyle, *West Britons: Cornish Identities and the Early Modern British State* (2002), p. 33.

[80] R. R. Davies, 'The peoples of Britain and Ireland 1100–1400: 1. Identities', *Transactions of the Royal Historical Society*, 6/4 (1994), 1–20.

[81] Cited in Payton, *Making of Modern Cornwall*, p. 56.

[82] Fox and Padel, *Cornish Lands of the Arundells*, pp. cxxiv–cxxxiv.

[83] This argument is expanded in Bernard Deacon, *The Cornish Family* (2004), chap. 3.

[84] Orme, *Saints of Cornwall*, p. 45.

[85] Whetter, *Cornwall in the Thirteenth Century*, p. 222.

[86] Much of the evidence in this paragraph is cited in Martyn Wakelin, *Language and History in Cornwall* (1975), pp. 88–9.

[87] Personal communication from Oliver Padel.

[88] Ken George, 'How many people spoke Cornish traditionally?', *Cornish Studies*, 14 (1986), 67–70.

[89] Davies, *First English Empire*, p. 181.

[90] Nicholas Williams, *Cornish Today: An Examination of the Revived Language* (1995).

[91] Matthew Spriggs, 'Where Cornish was spoken and when: a provisional synthesis', in Philip Payton (ed.), *Cornish Studies Eleven* (2003), pp. 228–69 and Julyan Holmes, 'On the track of Cornish in a bilingual country', in Payton, *Cornish Studies Eleven*, pp. 270–90.

[92] Christopher Holdsworth, 'From 1050 to 1307', and Nicholas Orme, 'The Later Middle Ages and the Reformation', in Nicholas Orme (ed.), *Unity and Variety* (1991), pp. 29–30 and 55–64.

[93] Orme, 'Later Middle Ages and Reformation', p. 55.

[94] Brian Golding, 'The Church and Christian Life', in Harvey, *Twelfth and Thirteenth Centuries*, p. 148.

[95] Norman Davies, *The Isles; A History* (1999), p. 426.

[96] Davies, *First English Empire*, pp. 187–8.

[97] Brian Murdoch, *Cornish Literature* (1993), p. 6.

[98] Ibid., p. 41.

[99] Brynley Roberts, 'The Celtic languages of Britain', in Geraint Jenkins (ed.), *The Welsh Language before the Industrial Revolution* (1997), p. 412.

[100] John Chynoweth, *Tudor Cornwall* (2002), p. 286.

[101] John Hatcher, 'Farming techniques – south west England', in Miller, *Agrarian History of England and Wales*, p. 398.

[102] Cited in Ian Soulsby, *A History of Cornwall* (1986), p. 49.

[103] John Hatcher, 'A diversified economy: later medieval Cornwall', *Economic History Review*, 22 (1969), 208–27.

[104] Hatcher, *Rural Economy*, p. 35.

[105] Hatcher, *English Tin Production*, p. 23.

[106] Ibid., p. 136.

[107] Rowse, *Tudor Cornwall*, p. 73.

[108] Maryanne Kowaleski, 'The expansion of the south-western fisheries in late medieval England', *Economic History Review*, 53 (2000), 429–54.

[109] R. S. Schofield, 'The geographical distribution of wealth in England, 1334–1649', *Economic History Review*, 18 (1965), 483–510.

[110] Fox, *Agrarian History*, p. 734.

[111] James Whetter, *The Bodrugans: A Study of a Cornish Medieval Knightly Family* (1995), p. 92.

[112] James Whetter, *Cornish People in the Fifteenth Century* (1999), p. 109.

[113] C. J. Tydesley, 'The crown and the local communities in Devon and Cornwall from 1377 to 1422', Ph.D. thesis, Exeter University (1978), p. 25.

[114] Hatcher, *English Tin Production*, pp. 86–7.

[115] Whetter, *The Bodrugans*, p. 153.

[116] Rowse, *Tudor Cornwall*, p. 101.

[117] Ibid., p. 101.

[118] Stoyle, *West Britons*, p. 20.

3

Rebellious Cornwall: the turbulent centuries, 1495–1648

When the Tudors arrived the Celtic countries met their nemesis. In Ireland attempts to impose English law and the English tenurial system on the Gaelic lords from the 1540s were unsuccessful and produced, after the 1560s, a series of rebellions on the one hand and multiplying schemes for plantations on the other, sowing bitter seeds for the dismal seventeenth century. In Scotland, the battle of Flodden in 1513 was a disastrous defeat for the Scots, who lost 10,000 men, as well as the cream of their nobility and their king.[1] Thereafter Scotland, though retaining its independence, lay in uneasy anticipation of the next English incursion. The Acts of Union of 1536 and 1543 imposed county administration on Wales and Welsh law and rules of tenure were finally abolished. And it was not just Tudor monarchs who were honing their new-found centralizing powers. Across the Channel France effectively exerted its governorship over the duchy of Brittany in 1491 and this was ratified by a formal treaty of union in 1532.

It is tempting to see Cornwall in the same light. Like the Gaelic lords the Cornish resisted incorporation. Like them they ultimately lost. Like the Welsh their Celtic language gave rise to a religious conservatism. But unlike Welsh, the Cornish language entered into a fatal decline in the Tudor period. For some historians duchy and stannaries still provided Cornwall with a 'certain aura (and indeed reality) of territorial semi-independence'.[2] And Cornwall could still be described as comprising one of the four parts of Britain. According to Polydore Vergil, writing in the 1530s, there were Englishmen, Scots, Welshmen and Cornish people, 'which all differ among themselves, either in tongue, either in manners, or else in laws and ordinances'.[3] But, within a hundred years Cornwall had 'become English'.[4] The most overt marker of cultural difference – the Cornish language – was in terminal decline, a decline that some have also applied to the Cornish identity.[5] Yet paradoxes remain. Philip Payton views the Tudor era as 'pivotal in the creation of modern Cornwall', a time when the intrusion of the

Tudor state 'undermined the very fabric of what we may call "Celtic-Catholic" Cornwall'. But he also notes the Charter of Pardon of 1508, when Henry VII restored the rights of the temporarily suspended stannaries and went further, granting the Stannary Parliament the right of legislative veto, a 'powerful reaffirmation of Cornwall's distinctive place within the state' and 'a curious contrast' with Tudor centralization. [6] Furthermore, the Tudor period saw Cornwall's parliamentary representation rocket from fourteen to forty-four MPs. By 1584 Cornwall elected almost 10 per cent of the House of Commons, even though it contained only around 2 per cent of the population of the kingdom, making it grossly over-represented.[7] Tensions between narratives of 'final integration' and 'continued accommodation' are not the end of the story. There was also an apparent contrast between a readiness to take up arms to resist the actions of the state on the one hand and an exaggerated loyalty to the crown on the other.

When, in 1485, Henry Tudor returned from exile in Brittany to triumph over the Yorkist King Richard III, Cornwall occupied an ambiguous position: part English, part Celtic. Its Cornish-language culture succoured memories of distant British rulers and coexisted with a duchy presence that echoed the autonomy of the twelfth-century earls; its stannary courts protected the cherished customary liberties of the tinners. By the end of the Tudor period this ambiguity was much diminished, the duchy moribund and in the process of being centralized and, more crucially, the Cornish language in headlong retreat, abandoned by the gentry, ignored by the new (county) elite and despised by the social climbers. The medieval balance of crown and church had been shattered by the religious Reformation of the sixteenth century. The church was first brought firmly under the control of the crown and then an extra dimension was added. By the seventeenth century Parliament was contesting with the king his right to steer the realm. Such high political manoeuvrings were bad news for what remained of Cornish autonomy. As the crown established its supremacy over the church, seaward influences fell away and landward pressures intensified. Connections with Brittany and the wider European continent were severed. Moreover, as Parliament learnt to flex its muscles, the intimate relations of Cornwall and crown, formalized in the fourteenth century, became of less value.

For most of the period from 1485 to 1648 Cornish people peaceably went about their affairs, ultimately accepting the changes brought about in government and church.

However, at several points, they also most emphatically resisted those changes. Cornwall was home to a series of risings, six in all in 1497, 1548–9, 1642 and 1648, and several other rumours of risings during these same centuries. Mark Stoyle has brilliantly succeeded in restoring a voice to the losers in this process, to 'those who sought to perpetuate the Cornish sense of difference' rather than to undermine or suppress it.[8] He did this by arguing that a sense of ethnic identity underpinned Cornish 'politico-religious behaviour' over this period. The risings punctuating these centuries were the visible manifestations of a 'conviction that their separate cultural identity was under attack',[9] the points when forbearance finally cracked and resistance took on a physical form.

The historical battleground

Kernowcentrics view the transition period from the medieval to the modern worlds as the heroic last stand of the Cornish people, who were dragged kicking and screaming into the English state, with the latter using a considerable amount of force in the process.[10] In contrast, Kernowsceptics play down the cultural distinctiveness of early modern Cornwall and slot Cornwall into a wider 'regional' framework.[11] However, both interpretations adopt an unduly black and white model – of Cornwall as either Celtic duchy or English county. Neither perspective is able to escape the distortions caused by seeing the period through the prism of modern English and Cornish nationalisms. I want to propose here that the changes of the Tudor period were neither as extensive nor as traumatic as has sometimes been made out. After all, a sense of Cornish identity did survive the seventeenth century and the Cornish language lived on until the very end of the eighteenth, though confined to the social and geographical margins. In the fifteenth century, as we have seen, Cornwall was already a hybrid territory of English and non-English influences, of both landward (to the east) and seaward (to the south) connections. The precise balance of this mix changed and landward links became, for a time, dominant, but hybridity survived the seventeenth century wars – just – and enough of non-English Cornwall remained to serve as the launch pad for a modern rediscovery and reassertion of Cornwall's non-Englishness.

Stoyle's book *West Britons* is tellingly subtitled *Cornish Identities and the British State*, correctly implying that more than one identity coexisted in sixteenth- and seventeenth-century Cornwall. However, it nevertheless focuses on just one identity, the ethnic Cornish identity. There was certainly an identity rooted in the Cornish language. But there was also a political identity of loyalty to English crown and kingdom, or that less articulated ethnic identity of those who had, in east Cornwall, spoken English for generations. And there were other types of identity, most notably religious. Understanding Cornwall in this period is not just a simple question therefore of tracking the decline of one (ethnic) identity. As I have already argued, medieval Cornwall was a place where different identities shared the same social terrain. Rather than the either/or dichotomy inherent in the idea of a Cornish 'people' in addition to 'English', 'Welsh' and 'Scottish' peoples, it may be more fruitful, if more difficult, to imagine a series of layered, or 'nested' identities, involving attachments to locality, to ethnic group, to institutions, to territories and to kingdoms.[12] In the early modern period the borders between these shifted and reformed. Cornish ethnicity indubitably played a key role as one of these identities but it always coexisted with other identities: religious, territorial or status. Furthermore, the basis of ethnic identity was itself transformed in these years, from language to territory. The identities of late medieval Cornwall (religious and ethnic) dissolved, but out of the embers there emerged new, more modern identities. To outline this process I intend to focus on the risings of 1497 and 1549, before moving on to reject the thesis of a continuum between the events of 1497/1549 and the 1640s. I also review four identities present in early modern Cornwall: ethnic, religious, status and political, before summarizing Cornish involvement in the civil wars of the seventeenth century.

The 1497 risings

In the early years of Henry VII's reign the embers of Yorkist resistance smouldered on. Scottish dalliance with Perkin Warbeck helped to trigger off war with Henry VII's England in 1496, when Henry was not universally popular, feared more than loved.[13] In Cornwall anger at the level of taxes needed for a far-away war was compounded by popular disaffection over the suspension of the stannaries in 1496, following disputes over stricter rules on tin bounding and tin coinage.

Discontent came to a head in May 1497 in the far west and found its mouthpiece in a St Keverne blacksmith, Michael Angove. Here, a tradition of lawlessness and direct action was well entrenched and a Cornish-speaking population was less amenable to control by an anglicized gentry class, many of whom were absent. The insurrectionary flames soon spread and the rising found its second major leader at Bodmin, where Thomas Flamank, a lawyer in the town's leading family, provided its intellectual justification. The Cornish force then did something unusual for localized tax protestors. They struck directly across the heart of southern England towards London, picking up in Somerset Lord Audley, who gave a veneer of magnate support. The tax rebels' demands found a sympathetic audience in south-west England, where new wealth resented the tax demands. But, as no rebellion in this period could fail to have a dynastic element, the rising was viewed by the landed elites as the last gasp of the Wars of the Roses that had riven the aristocracy of England since the mid-fifteenth century.[14] Indeed, fifteenth-century Cornish gentry rivalries smacked of the squabbles of the English magnates. Henry Bodrugan's colourful career as the leading Cornish Yorkist of the 1470s and 80s – a combination of political fixer and local warlord – was eventually brought to an end in 1487, when the former Lancastrian rebel of 1483, Richard Edgcumbe of Cotehele, was given power to arrest him for stirring up 'sedition'.[15] After a skirmish at his home near Mevagissey, Bodrugan was forced to leap from a cliff and set sail for Ireland, cursing the Edgcumbes for posterity as he left. Bodrugan's disinheritance may have become a 'focus of resentment'; James Whetter, for one, argues that his reputation for extortion was overdrawn by his Tudor opponents and that in contrast he enjoyed considerable local support.[16] Whatever the truth of the matter, several of the participants in 1497 had family or other connections with Bodrugan. On the other hand, in a percipient analysis of the 1497 revolts Lucy Rhymer concludes there is little evidence for active Yorkist involvement until after Blackheath.[17]

The insurgents marched on unopposed to Kent, hoping to gain support. In this they were disappointed but the contemporary account, the *Great Chronicle* of London, reported that the rebels were 'favoured' by the people of the territories they passed through, and paid well for their supplies.[18] This source also reported that the rebel force was 15,000 strong, although desertions had reduced it to 9,000 or 10,000 by the time it encamped at Blackheath to the south-

east of London. There Angove and Flamank's force was easily
defeated, with the loss of some 200 lives according to the *Chronicle*.
The rising failed because, ultimately, enough nobles rallied to the
king. However, 'it seems odd that no peer was able to block their
march – or even to try to do so – before they got to London'.[19] The
nobility sat on the fence until the last moment possible. While their
neutrality allowed Angove and Flamank to strike at the heart of the
English state, it did not provide the material support necessary for
their victory. The disparity between the Cornish and royal armies at
Blackheath was painfully obvious, the former lacking well-armoured
men, artillery and cavalry.[20] Lord Audley was beheaded while
Angove and Flamank suffered the fate of being hung, drawn and
quartered. It was when being drawn through the streets of the City to
Tyburn that Angove is reported to have declaimed that he would have
a 'fame perpetual and a name immortal',[21] which, if true, implies
considerable bilingual ability. But it was only the Cornish Revival of
later centuries that restored a place in history to Angove.

Henry's intention was to send the bodies of Angove and Flamank
back to Cornwall for public display as a terrible warning of the
consequences of treason – a normal piece of ritual accompanying
fifteenth-century rebellions. But, hearing of the continued 'unquiet
and boiling' disaffection in Cornwall in the summer of 1497,[22] this
was not deemed the wisest course of action. Indeed, only three people
were executed after the Angove rising and the other rebels received
pardons.[23] It would have been difficult, in that disturbed summer, for
the king's men to exact retribution in Cornwall itself. For, within two
months of the defeat at Blackheath, the Yorkist pretender Perkin
Warbeck had landed in the far west, at Sennen Cove. Cornish discontent allowed them to be co-opted more explicitly into Warbeck's
project. His supporters quickly seized St Michael's Mount and
marched to Bodmin, where he was proclaimed King Richard IV, ironically at the same town that had prematurely declared Henry VII king
in 1483.[24] This second rising grew to include possibly 6,000 or 7,000
men and among them four minor gentry; John Nankivell of St
Columb, Walter Tripcony of Manaccan, Humphrey Calwodeley of
Helland and William Barrett from St Mabyn. Adopting more traditional tactics than Angove and Flamank, they set about besieging
Exeter but were repulsed after brief hand-to-hand fighting in the
cramped streets of the town.[25] This time the gentry in Devon and
Somerset, aware of events at Blackheath, rallied to King Henry and

actively opposed the insurgents. Meanwhile, the rebels, uncertain about their strategy, moved away from Exeter and into a military cul-de-sac near Taunton. Here their 'royal' leader Warbeck deserted them and fled to the coast. The rebels surrendered; some leaders were hung and most of the others pardoned, any with material resources having to buy their pardons. In this way Henry VII had extracted £14,000 in fines by 1507.[26]

Rowse's view that Cornwall was 'impoverished' and exhausted by the process of retribution and remained 'quiet for half a century' has been an influential one.[27] But the notion of a cowed and humiliated Cornwall in the generation or two after 1497 has been challenged by Philip Payton, who draws attention to the play *Bewnans Meriasek*.[28] Written sometime between 1465 and 1504, its villain is a King Teudar, a figure familiar from local folklore, linked to the persecution of early Irish Christian missionaries in west Cornwall. A villain named Teudar must have had 'political overtones' after 1497.[29] Rather than languishing in defeat, Cornwall seethed with active resentment. By the 1530s another outlet for this resentment had appeared.

The 1548/1549 risings

This time religious reform was the backdrop to conflict. The 'Reformation Parliament' of 1533–6 formally separated the Church of England from Rome by the Act of Supremacy in 1534. Potential opposition from the nobility and gentry was bought off by the device of dissolving the monasteries and selling their estates. In Cornwall the Killigrews of Arwenack, the Prideaux family, the Grenvilles and Godolphins all became major buyers of monastic property, a clutch of estates also fell into the hands of the duchy and even the stubbornly Catholic Arundell family of Lanherne was a purchaser of monastic land.[30] Cornish monasteries had become lax, even corrupt, and their problems did not arouse general sympathy. Their dissolution went off relatively quietly with one exception. In 1537 news reached William Godolphin, the government's main supporter in west Cornwall, that a man named Carpysacke had commissioned 'a painting of a banner of Christ, with his wounds abroad and a banner in his hand',[31] echoing the Pilgrimage of Grace in northern England in 1536, a revolt against the religious changes being imposed from

London. Goldolphin had him arrested, brought to trial and executed. The alacrity with which Godolphin acted suggests that the local gentry were tied tightly into the 'networks of governance' of Thomas Cromwell, Henry's principal minister, loyal to the crown and willing to take efficient action locally to quell unrest.[32] But Cromwell fell from power in 1540 and thereafter perhaps local government became less efficient.

To exercise royal supremacy over the church was one thing, to initiate far-reaching liturgical change was another step altogether. Pent-up demands for a less Catholic liturgy, regarded as semi-treasonable while Henry was alive, burst forth on his death in 1547. His successor, the young Edward VI, allowed Thomas Cranmer, arch-bishop of Canterbury, to revise the Anglican service, encourage the newly available English-language versions of the Bible to be read, and write a Book of Common Prayer in 1549. Faith in God's mercy was now all that was needed; the old religious practices, where people prayed for the dead and did penance in this world for the next, were jettisoned by the reformers. All the ways in which people atoned for their sins, and their forebears' sins – the chantry prayers, the saints' cults, the icons and images – began to be frowned upon as mere superstition. No longer of spiritual value, the financial worth of church possessions – plate, vestments, bells, ornaments – began to be assessed by government-appointed commissioners. In Cornwall the archdeacon, William Body, played a leading role in this. Body was no unworldly cleric. In 1537, he had bought the archdeaconry of Cornwall for a period of thirty-five years.[33] In 1540 he decided to exercise his rights and collect in person the archdeacon's dues from the clergy of Cornwall, meeting at St Stephen's church, across the valley from Launceston. However, he was there confronted by John Harris, prebendary of Glasney. There was a scuffle, daggers were half-drawn and the archdeacon ended up being dragged unceremoni-ously out while the church doors were locked against him.[34] This was followed in 1547 by a somewhat obscure 'hostile demonstration' against Body's visitation, purportedly at Penryn, but involving protesters from Penwith Hundred.

All this was happening against a backcloth of 'dearth and infla-tion'.[35] Prices of food and drink were rising fast, something felt the most by those who were dependent on wages for all or a proportion of their income. Such people would include tinners. And there may have been another, hitherto unnoticed, reason for the willingness to take the considerable step of rebellion in 1548 and 1549. The year 1547 saw a very serious mortality crisis. Burial registers from parishes across Cornwall indicate that over 10 per cent, perhaps as many as 15 per cent, of the population perished. In Camborne and St Columb the reason for this devastating mortality was clear – plague. Nothing like these levels of mortality were to be experienced again. Such a massive demographic crisis must have had a profound effect. Perhaps people connected this sudden revisitation of the plague with the changes in religion, upsetting customary ways of interceding with the Almighty. In consequence, they felt they had less to lose from rebellion.

For the Regency Council ruling England 1548 was a troubled year generally. Inconclusive war with Scotland was compounded by a series of riots during the summer. In the midst of this the government ordered that all religious images be removed. William Body arrived at Helston to oversee this in early April 1548, his arrival coinciding with the Easter processions and rituals being suppressed by the new order. The focus of growing local anger, on 5 April he was murdered.[36] The men indicted for his killing included William Kylter, a small farmer of Constantine, and Martin Jeffrey, a clergyman from St Keverne. The rebels came from a district that stretched from Perranzabuloe in the north, through Redruth and Gwennap to Grade and Ruan in the south.[37] The majority of those indicted – fifteen – were from the turbulent parish of St Keverne. For a week or two the normal process of law broke down. But the gentry of east Cornwall, led by Sir Richard Edgcumbe, swiftly raised men to quell the rebellion and aid their beleaguered western counterparts. Parishes in the east, including St Veep, Morval, Lanteglos by Fowey, St Winnow, Boconnoc, Stratton and Launceston, sent men to resist the 'commotion in the west part'. By 23 April the rebellion, which involved around 3,000 people, was quashed and several of the ringleaders were later hung, drawn and quartered.

This did little to prevent a much more serious and protracted rising a year later. It began in June 1549 at the traditional insurgents' rallying point of Bodmin, although it is likely that there had been considerable unrest for weeks, or even months, previously. A few days after the Cornish began to assemble, the people of Sampford Courtenay in Devon rose in rebellion, though Cornwall provided the 'most steadfast leaders' and 'remained the power base of the rebellion'.[38] The news from Sampford Courtenay encouraged the Cornish to march eastwards, with 'banners unfurled, swords, shields, clubs, cannon, halberts, lances and other arms, offensive and defensive, armed and in warlike manner'. They carried before them the 'pyx or consecrated host borne under a canoply, with crosses, banners, candlesticks, holy bread and water'.[39] Being less affected by the new religious ideas sweeping across western Europe, it is likely the rising began in Cornish-speaking west Cornwall. A greater attachment to saints' cults fuelled anxiety about religious change, and this was further exacerbated as the changes threatened to entrench the conquerors' tongue at the heart of the church in the guise of the English Prayer Book. In mid and west Cornwall, ethnic and linguistic identities thus overlapped with religious identities. But the latter may have been the 'first-order' identities of this period,[40] as early demands for a Cornish liturgy were soon swamped by conservative religious interests, indicating the constituency for the rising spread well beyond the Cornish-speaking community. Religious unrest also accompanied hostility to the gentry and tensions within the local gentry class. On their way eastwards the rebels seized Sir Richard Grenville and imprisoned him at Launceston, while other gentry were besieged and captured at St Michael's Mount. Anti-gentry feeling was also reflected in a demand for a limit on the number of servants employed.[41] Meanwhile, those gentry keenest to support the religious changes emanating from the centre – the Godolphins in the west and the Grenvilles in the east – were challenged by supporters of the out of favour Lanherne Arundells. Intra-gentry conflicts meshed with religious disputes and, in a temporary breakdown of local government, the rebels were able to secure the whole of Cornwall.

The Cornish eventually linked up with the Devonians at Crediton, then moved east and by 24 June had virtually surrounded Exeter. Lord John Russell, the president of the short-lived Council of the West, was sent from London but, lacking local support, kept his distance to the east of Honiton. The rebels laid siege to Exeter for over a month yet the rebels failed to take it, a somewhat surprising outcome when we are told that 'within, there were a great many sympathizers with the rebels' cause'.[42] Perhaps the townsfolk feared the possibility of looting; perhaps there was an ancient distrust of the ethnically different Cornish. Ultimately, German, Italian, and later Welsh mercenaries were obtained for Russell's force and provisions paid for by merchants in Bristol and Somerset. By late July he was confident enough to move against the Prayer Book army, which was defeated at Fenny Bridges and then at Clyst Heath in close-quarters fighting. The siege of Exeter was lifted. In what has been described as the 'fiercest fighting seen in southern England during the sixteenth century'[43] the Cornish and their Devonian allies were pushed westwards. That their morale was not easily broken can be seen in the regrouping at Sampford Courtenay, but they were again defeated on 17 August, after which the remnants of the Cornish force fled back across the Tamar, where their leader, Humphrey Arundell, gave himself up in the streets of Launceston.

In the absence of a more generalized rising, the financial and military resources of the state had outweighed those of the rebels. But the Cornish leaders may also have made two tactical errors. By besieging Exeter rather than, as Angove and Flamank had done in 1497, heading eastwards, they lost the advantage of surprise and were unable to capitalize on indecision in the government camp, which was faced by sporadic problems over a wide area of England. Second, by easing the siege of Exeter to launch an unsuccessful pre-emptive attack on Russell's force in late July they lost the chance of taking the town. Rowse suggests Exeter was on the very brink of collapse through shortage of food.[44] Perhaps another week would have led to its relatively bloodless fall. The resources then available to the Cornish army and the symbolic impact of the fall of one of Tudor England's largest towns just might have unnerved the government and given heart to its opponents in other places.

Ethnic identity

When explaining these risings, Kernowcentrics place Cornishness at the centre. Noting that support for 1497 came from 'smaller landed families which stood on the border between gentry and yeomanry', Rowse went on to suggest that 'these sprang from the Cornish people themselves, and had Cornish names . . . it may not be fanciful to suggest a common element of Cornishry, of that resentment of a conquered people against the English'.[45] Philip Payton has also noted that after 1485 a 'British project' took on a renewed lease of life when Henry VII stressed his Welsh antecedents and named his first son Arthur.[46] What were courtly romances in London tapped into deeper hopes and memories in Wales and Cornwall, where the myth of Arthur as a returning popular saviour still circulated, with Henry's court astrologer indicating in his almanac for 1500 that the Cornish still expected Arthur's imminent return.[47] The discovery of a new Cornish saint's play with an Arthurian theme – *Bewnans Ke* – dated to just around this time, reinforces this theme.[48] If Henry Tudor's British project roused expectations among the Cornish, then his failure to deliver and his suspension of stannary rights in 1496 were even more galling. The attack on tinners' liberties was perhaps especially threatening to local cultural identity and it has been claimed that tinners 'formed the bulk of the rebel forces in 1497'.[49] The revolts of 1497 can in this light be read as a reaction to dashed expectations and threats to local customs.

It has been even easier to read 1549 as resistance to Tudor attacks on Cornish 'difference'. The role of the Cornish language and the early demand for a Cornish liturgy is central to kernowcentric explanations of 1549. However, this request was dropped from the final list of demands and reduced to an afterthought.[50] Although it was overshadowed by the religious agenda, opposition to the English Prayer Book on linguistic grounds is central to Mark Stoyle's view that the protection of their culture lay at the heart of the Cornish insurrection, exacerbated by a gap between gentry and commons. However, the thesis that ethnic anxieties and anti-English resentment linked the risings of 1497, 1549 and 1642 has its own problems. First, neither Angove's rising of 1497 nor the Prayer Book rising in 1549 were by any means entirely Cornish affairs. While beginning in Cornwall they both gained active support in Devon and Somerset. According to Rowse Devon parishes paid almost as much in fines after 1497 as did Cornish.[51] Furthermore, both risings gained considerable support within Cornwall from the English-speaking east. While in 1497 eleven of the fourteen rebels named in Parliament for treason did hail from Cornish-speaking districts, in 1549 both the gentry leaders of the Cornish force lived in east Cornwall.[52] The seriousness of the 1549 rising lay in the fact that, unlike 1548, it was not restricted solely to Cornish-speaking west Cornwall but drew in support from the east too as well as from over the border in England. However, if these revolts were principally fuelled by resentment of the English, we should surely have expected them to recruit overwhelmingly from the western, Cornish-speaking parts of Cornwall.

Or would we? It is unclear whether Mark Stoyle's *ethnie* comprised the Cornish-speaking Cornish only, those he convincingly argues possessed the characteristics of a separate people,[53] or stretched to

encompass the east Cornish. Stoyle asserts that the ordinary inhabitants of English-speaking districts of Cornwall 'clearly felt a greater
identification with their western brethren than with the English
proper'.[54] But little evidence is provided to support this claim, other
than a sense of 'county' loyalty (surely more likely at this period
among gentry than commons), a high degree of inter-marriage
(although this would take place on a locality scale rather than a
Cornwall-wide scale), and a mass participation in mining. Yet the
centre of tin mining by this time lay to the west, in Penwith and
Kerrier Hundreds. Moreover, the Dartmoor tin industry gained its
second lease of life in the late fifteenth century and reached a peak in
the period from 1515 to 1530 when it produced around a quarter of
all the tin from Cornwall and Devon.[55] Devon's production remained
significant into the 1590s, serving to blur the 'differentiation' that
Stoyle claims to find in the sixteenth century.

If anything, the experience of 1549 produced a sense of common
Cornishness rather than reflected it. Norden noted that the Cornish
in the late sixteenth century harboured 'a kind of concealed envy
against the English, whom they affect with a desire of revenge for
their fathers' sake'.[56] This oft-cited comment surely implies that there
was a generalized desire for revenge for the barbarities committed
against their fathers (and grandfathers). When Norden wrote of
'fathers' he literally meant their fathers. The 1549 rising had produced
a shared antipathy on the part of both Cornish- and English-
speaking Cornish people towards the victors of that contest. But, this
response was deeper and different in intensity for the 'western people'
who, according to Carew, fostered 'a fresh memory of their expulsion
long ago by the English'.[57] There, the disaster of 1549 added its own
quota to historical memories of Britishness and the Arthurian folk-
myth. Nevertheless, Mark Stoyle himself admits that the 'desire on
the part of many ordinary Cornish people to "revenge" themselves
upon the English and strike a blow in defence of the old Cornish
culture' was 'vague' and 'inchoate'.[58] It was 'vague'and 'inchoate'
because no one has uncovered an explicit call for political self-
determination for the Cornish in this period. But that would be very
unlikely as nationalism, in the sense of the demand for an independent system of government based on a distinct people, lay in the
future for most societies.

Kernowsceptic historians tend to play down the presence of the
language in the early sixteenth century. In a recent survey of the late

medieval period Ralph Griffiths asserts that Cornish had 'gradually retreated west of the River Tamar until by 1500, it was spoken only in the far west and had not produced a written literature for some time'.[59] This is wrong on all three counts. First, the language did not 'gradually' retreat but held its own for up to 200 years before the mid-sixteenth century. Second, it was not spoken 'only in the far west' and, third, the saints' plays *Bewnans Meriasek* and *Bewnans Ke* have both been dated to the end of the fifteenth century, as has the miracle play *Gwreans an Bys*. Griffiths claims that Truro was a 'linguistic borderland' in 1500 and Cooper asserts that Cornish was only spoken 'west of Truro', in a few 'pockets of land . . . isolated from the rest of the county'.[60] But such claims hardly square with the evidence that 'Cornish was in use in St Columb [fifteen miles east of Truro] in the mid-16th century'.[61] Later, in the 1580s, some fishermen at Gorran 'could not well speak or understand English', while in 1595 Cornish could still be heard at nearby St Ewe, also just west of St Austell.[62] Evidence from people's second names indicates that Cornish-language nicknames and occupational names were still widely deployed in Pydar and Powder Hundreds in the 1540s almost up to the Camel–Fowey line.[63] Both literary and name evidence therefore strongly suggests that mid-Cornwall was Cornish-speaking well into the mid-sixteenth century. What then happened was that English, already spoken in parts of this district, expanded at the expense of Cornish. Rather than a westwards movement, however, we should imagine a thinning out of Cornish speaking in Pydar and Powder in the two generations between the 1540s and the 1590s. By 1600 the language frontier did lie nearer Truro and then the thinning out process took place over the next century in Penwith and Kerrier Hundreds, until by 1700 Cornish was confined to a strip of coastal parishes between Lizard Point and St Ives.

There were obvious reasons for the decline of Cornish. First, the Reformation had cut links with Brittany. Cornwall's export trade in the sixteenth century had been directed towards Brittany and economic links were reinforced by the migration in the late 1400s of considerable numbers of Bretons to Cornwall. In some maritime parishes in the west they made up as much as a quarter of house-holders in the 1520s tax lists. Breton union with France, coinciding as it did with Henry VIII's break with Rome, ultimately broke the cultural connections between peoples who spoke similar languages and from this point on the Breton and Cornish languages diverged.

Second, it was no coincidence that mid-Cornwall was home to the majority of Cornwall's main recusant Catholic gentry. The growing pressure on such families after the 1560s may also have increased pressure on the Cornish language, associated with Catholicism by its role in the 1549 rising. Stoyle points out how the Prayer Book Rebellion turned linguistic diversity into a contested issue, tainting the language with sedition. He compares the fate of Cornish with that of Welsh; as the Welsh people accepted the Reformation relatively quietly their language was not seen as a threat. In contrast, it was Cornish attempts to resist the Reformation that 'eventually sealed the fate of the Cornish language'. [64] The Cornish had perhaps forgotten the lessons of the tenth and eleventh centuries when tactical acquiescence safeguarded their culture. But there was another contrast between the Cornish and Welsh languages. By the sixteenth century Cornish had no gentry patrons. In Wales, the support of landlords ensured the survival of a bardic tradition. Religious reformers in England and Wales also backed the production of a Welsh Bible which, intended to help the understanding of English services, had the unforeseen result of helping to create literacy in the Welsh language. However, in Cornwall, there was insufficient support for the publication of a Cornish Bible, whether from local gentry or religious reformers.

Some Cornish nationalist writers have argued that there was a more short-term cause for the decline of Cornish. For them the 'Prayer Book War' brought about the 'final extermination' of the Cornish language as the result of mortality approaching genocidal rates.[65] It is true that the estimated Cornish casualties in 1549 were far higher than in 1497, amounting to perhaps as many as 10 per cent of adult men, a similar proportion to that of Frenchmen who died in the killing fields of the First World War, but over a far shorter period.[66] But other evidence for demographic and economic dislocation is less clear cut. Tin production fell by 30 per cent from 1547 to 1549 (unfortunately the figure for 1548 is missing) but it had almost recovered its 1547 level by 1553.[67] Yet tin production also fell by more than 30 per cent in the space of a single year in 1568 and again in 1570. The economic effects of 1549, though visible, were not unique. Furthermore, populations can revive very rapidly even from such disasters as 1547 and 1549. While large numbers of Cornish speakers died in the period 1547–9, this was not the critical factor in the loss of the language.

With lukewarm support from their own gentry and already geographically marginalized, Cornish did not need active suppression by the state. A recent study of Tudor attitudes to Cornish, Welsh and Irish concludes that 'there is no evidence that the Tudor governments wanted to suppress the Cornish language'.[68] Stoyle concludes there was 'no great animosity towards the Cornish language in the 1530s' while Cooper notes the injunctions of Bishop Veysey in 1538 for Cornish to be used where English was not understood.[69] The decline of Cornish was more an unintended consequence of religious reform than deliberate repression. Thus, as late as 1560 permission was given for the use of Welsh and Cornish for the Prayer Book and there is evidence of Cornish being used in church services throughout the sixteenth and into the seventeenth century for the Lord's Prayer, Apostles Creed and the Ten Commandments. Brennan concludes that Cornish receded 'not because of hostility from England, but because of economic factors such as increased commercial links and the increased importance of ports consequent upon naval developments and the war with Spain'.[70] Add to these the failure to translate the Bible into Cornish, the suppression of the mystery and saints' plays for religious reasons and the severing of links with Brittany and the decline of Cornish was a foregone conclusion. Moreover, its decline meant that the foundations for a Cornish ethnic identity clearly separate from the English were steadily undercut. That identity, in the medieval period tolerated by the English, was now equated with rebelliousness and had become a 'stigmatised identity'.[71] This increased its vulnerability.

Religious identity

Religious grievances were the thread linking the 1548 and 1549 risings.[72] Both the rebels' proclamation at Helston in 1548 and, a year later, the first eight articles of those assembled at Bodmin were explicitly religious.[73] Frances Rose-Troup linked religious conservatism to distance from London – 'the greater the distance from London the more intense their opposition to the changes – in Cornwall, as well as Yorkshire'.[74] More recent commentators agree this rising was primarily religious in motivation and the involvement of many priests, including the vicar of St Thomas, just outside Exeter, a Penryn man, is taken as supporting evidence. Priests at Pillaton,

Poundstock, St Cleer, St Veep, St Neot, Gulval, St Keverne and Lelant were among those punished after the rising.[75] Edwards repeats the consensus that 'in the south western rebellion grievances were mainly religious'.[76] The general culture of saint veneration in Cornwall, one that to some extent survived the defeat of the 1549 rising,[77] could have heightened the shock of the attack on traditional religious practices.

But what happened when the defence of the old religion failed? Clearly the religious identity of the Cornish changed markedly between 1549 and 1642. The estimated 15 per cent of Cornish gentry who did not embrace Protestantism came under intense scrutiny.[78] The most prominent, the Arundells of Lanherne, soon lost all influence in local government, sealing a process that had already begun before 1549. Sir John Arundell, arrested during the rising and sent to the Tower of London but then released by the Catholic Queen Mary, came under increasing surveillance after her reign and particularly when pressure on Catholics was increased in the 1570s. In 1584 he was consigned to the Tower and died there in 1590. An earlier martyr for the old religion was Francis Tregian of Golden, near Probus. Tregian was arrested in 1577, together with a missionary priest trained in exile at Douai, Cuthbert Mayne.[79] Both were executed. Tristram Winslade, a member of the wealthiest family to support the 1549 rising, ended up going abroad and joining the Spanish Armada fleet in 1588. By the 1590s, around eighty recusant gentry, around a fifth of all Cornish gentry, were either dead, in prison or in exile. The majority, on the contrary, outwardly conformed to the rapid changes in religious fashion. Others, a minority but including sheriffs such as Francis Buller, Piers Edgcumbe, Anthony Rous and Thomas St Aubyn, whole-heartedly embraced the new Calvinist doctrines and could be classed as Puritans.

It is difficult to gauge popular reaction to the persecution of the recusant gentry and their priests. There was little hint of any potential unrest in the 1570s. Maybe the commons had been cowed into submission. Or perhaps they were largely indifferent. Yet Mark Stoyle argues that

> many Cornish people contrived to resist this process [of Protestantism]. They did so, not by refusing to become Protestants, but by becoming Protestants of a very traditional kind, largely unaffected by the Puritanism that suffused the reformed faith throughout much of England. By 1600 or thereabouts the Cornish had thus managed to reinvent a distinctive religious identity for themselves.[80]

By the 1640s, a 'conservative "Anglicanism" was seen as an integral part of [Cornish] national identity' and, when this faith was threatened by a Puritan-dominated Parliament, religious anxiety merged with ethnic factors to produce Cornish royalism.[81] In making this observation Stoyle compares Cornwall with Scotland and Ireland where, similarly, resistance to English religion played a large part. However, the Scots were fighting to preserve a Presbyterian church with no bishops, and the Irish were defending Catholicism. The Cornish, on the other hand, were fighting for the Church of England and for the very Prayer Book they had opposed in 1549. This difference cannot easily be glossed over. It remains unclear exactly how far this was a 'distinctive' religious identity. If the Anglican liturgy had become bound up with Cornish perceptions of identity, then we must expect the former to have influenced the latter. And the pulpits of Anglican churches after the Reformation echoed to prayers for the monarch and exhortations to obedience in the homilies read out by the clergy. Moreover, the shrinking basis of the Cornish language meant that it provided an ever less effective immunity from the drip feed of royal propaganda that issued forth from the pulpits. Such propaganda, together with state-encouraged celebrations of royal vital events and foreign policy successes, played its part in producing an imagined English Protestant nation. As the Cornish-language community shrank from the mid-sixteenth century onwards the vacuum produced was promptly filled by English nationalism. Cornwall by the 1640s was a different place from the Cornwall of the 1540s, let alone the 1490s. It was not only its gentry who were anglicized but large numbers of the common people, exposed to a virulent nationalism. But that nationalism was not Cornish; it was English.

Royalist identity

The Anglican pulpits were not the only places reproducing a Cornish royalist tradition. A conservative religious identity that looked eastwards found a fertile soil in communities which already believed in a special link between (English) crown and (Cornish) gentry and commons. The presence of the duchy of Cornwall and absence of nobility had ensured that, earlier than elsewhere, self-reliant gentry looked to the monarch, rather than to nobles' service.[82] The extension of Tudor local government produced new positions of influence such as magistrates and lords lieutenants, although it may be significant that none of the first three sixteenth-century lords lieutenant were actually based in Cornwall. It has been claimed that the gentry who undertook the government of their local areas increasingly viewed themselves within a 'maturing' English imagination after the 1550s.[83] Certainly, there seems to have been little reluctance on the part of the gentry to adopt this self-image. Not that this was confined to Cornwall. Philip Jenkins has argued that, in Wales too, local elites enthusiastically integrated themselves into an English national polity, developing a political ideology of 'Britishness' expressed through loyalty to the Tudor and Stuart dynasties and their associated pageantry, propaganda and mythology. Even speaking the Welsh language was 'an act of loyalism rather than dissidence', for the Welsh saw the church and monarchy as 'thoroughly Welsh' with the crown encouraging this through the person of the prince of Wales.[84] The contrast with Cornwall lay in the fact that, while adopting English political and religious institutions, the Welsh gentry remained keen supporters of the Welsh language and its culture. In sixteenth century Cornwall most gentry were already anglicized culturally, thereby providing no counterbalance to the royalist myth. The Welsh also viewed themselves as 'British' rather than 'English'. In Cornwall, while there were some in the seventeenth century who called themselves 'ancient Britons',[85] there was also a readiness to adopt the label 'English'.

Yet, just as Tudor and Stuart monarchs took care to flatter Welsh sentiment, so they cultivated Cornish opinion, by offering the Cornish gentry a special place at the heart of the English state. This was spectacularly illustrated by the fifteen new parliamentary boroughs created between 1529 and 1584. Active lobbying by Cornish gentry for fuller participation in the Tudor state has been cited as a factor in this growth.[86] For some this development was 'testimony to its [Cornwall's] assimilation'.[87] For others it was evidence of 'a new mechanism of constitutional accommodation', giving the Cornish gentry a 'distinctive role of its own in the affairs of state'.[88] But those MPs did not have to be Cornish. In fact over two-thirds of the MPs for the new borough seats were outsiders.[89] So if this was 'constitutional accommodation' it was oddly indirect at this stage. While ambitious Cornish gentry scrambled for the new posts created by expanded county government, in the 1500s the perks of its older medieval status were still available. One echo of the greater recognition afforded to Cornwall as a separate province in earlier times and a sign of that special relationship between Cornish gentry and crown was the excessively large number of Cornishmen at court in London. In the 1510s 13 per cent of courtiers were Cornish gentry.[90] This over-representation continued throughout the reign of Elizabeth I.

Another echo was the duchy of Cornwall. Yet the lack of a male royal heir from 1547 to 1603 meant that the duchy reverted to the crown and became a de facto department of the exchequer.[91] Haslam has argued that the Elizabethan duchy in consequence suffered 'benign neglect' through to the 1570s, when the crown began selling off those Cornish estates acquired from the monasteries in the 1530s. By 1603 the duchy was an 'administrative backwater, surviving only because it had been in part forgotten'.[92] Yet benign neglect and administrative backwaters may have been very welcome to both Cornish tenants and local gentry. The absence of a ducal household with its retinue of hangers on all avidly seeking posts and sinecures meant more of the loot could be shared around amongst the gentry in Cornwall.[93] Indeed, the survival of the duchy might seem anomalous in an English state that set about eradicating local peculiarities with relish after the 1530s, the Acts of Union with Wales or the abolition of the earldom of Chester being prime examples. But the reasons the duchy did not attract the attention of the reformers were twofold. First, it posed no potential threat to central power. Any lingering connection with independent British rulers was long forgotten and, even in the troubled 1540s, none of the insurgents looked to the duchy or to any legal rights it might theoretically have possessed as an alternative source of sovereignty. Second, it channelled money into royal coffers, providing about 5 per cent of crown income in the 1540s. In addition, the duchy acted to bolster loyalty to the crown. Cooper has argued that the duchy's role in paying for coastal forts from the 1510s onwards was particularly important in fostering a popular allegiance through protecting the people,[94] although this argument looks thin given that duchy protection did not prevent Spanish raids on Penryn in 1568, and the Scillies, Mounts Bay, Cawsand Bay and Falmouth in the 1590s.

In the 1600s things began to change. The financial demands of the Stuart princes Henry, and then Charles, were prodigious. In 1610 Prince Henry's household spent £18,000 a year on his houses, £10,000 on his food and £3,000 on his wardrobe.[95] This was enough to maintain approximately 6,000 to 12,000 Cornish families for a year, or between a third and two-thirds of the whole population! To feed this voracious appetite, the Prince's Council, moribund since the death of Prince Arthur in 1502, was reconstructed in 1611. By this time the duchy was not regarded as a territorial fief but as a convenient source of cash. To exploit it more efficiently the Council carried through a 'fiscal feudalism', tightening up the demands on duchy tenants, increasing rent revenues and making more use of the duchy's political machine. From the point of view of Prince Charles, this was highly successful.[96] Of course, from the point of view of both duchy tenant and duchy office-seeker it was decidedly unwelcome. From the Cornish perspective, the 'revitalized' Stuart duchy was control imposed from London. Far from being an antidote to centralization the duchy had become, by the 1630s, its agent.

Given the squeeze on duchy tenants Cornish support for the crown in the Civil Wars becomes more surprising. But the critical factor here was not so much the Duchy but the stannaries. Anne Duffin argues that the sway of the Duchy was in fact weakened in 1640, on the eve of the Civil Wars, by the rival interests of the stannaries.[97] The strength of popular royalism in the west rested more upon stannaries than duchy. The former protected an independent occupational group, one not tied to the gentry through deference. In the sixteenth century the miners' customary laws and liberties were passed on in an oral culture that relied heavily on the memory of the older members of their communities. This memory may by this time have included the belief that the crown was the creator, rather than the arbiter, of their liberties.[98] Stannary law might have had its roots in the period before the twelfth century but, half a millennium later, the overt royal symbolism of coinage days and coinage halls had reinforced a 'firmer partnership' with the crown.[99] Non-interference in stannary courts and the granting of a convocation in 1508 seemed to leave the tinners with considerable self-government, although we should note that no general convocation of tinners actually met before 1588. And then eleven of the twenty-four stannators were knights and gentlemen, indicating that the industry was well on its way to being controlled by the merchant and landed classes. Whatever the reason, the Stannary Convocation did not attempt to use its new-found powers, perhaps evidence that the bargain between tinners and monarchs was relatively stable in the sixteenth century. Meanwhile, the gentry, horrified and embarrassed by the taint of disloyalty that clung to them after

1549, embraced the royal connection with growing enthusiasm, attracted even more so by growing prospects of positions and power.

Status identity

Economically, the sixteenth century was a period of price inflation which swung the balance of economic advantage away from the common people and back towards the gentry and landowners. Inflation was in large part caused by a rise of population and the number of people in Cornwall revived from the post-plague low of around 60,000 or so to 90,000 by 1640.[100] These extra mouths began to stretch the resources available to feed them. Cornwall, admitted Richard Carew in the 1590s, had its fair share and more of the poor.[101] He went on to qualify this by stating that few places 'own fewer' of their poor, claiming that many vagabonds in Cornwall were Irish. But the numbers of Cornish poor who were arrested in Devon in the late sixteenth and early seventeenth centuries and sent back to their home parishes suggests Carew understated indigenous poverty.[102] Evidence for the economic state of Cornwall in the late sixteenth century is hard to come by, although the output of tin fell after the 1540s and was stagnant from the 1550s right through to the 1630s. Given that the population rose by 50 per cent during these same years the tin industry was not helping to feed the extra mouths. On the other hand farmers began to respond to higher food prices. The open fields of lowland medieval Cornwall, which had already disappeared east of Bodmin–Lostwithiel by the later 1500s, began to be enclosed in the west also where, during the seventeenth century, agricultural techniques began to catch up those of the east.[103]

If farmers gained from rising prices, then landlords could ratchet up rents to maintain their income. By the 1600s, amongst the increasingly numerous gentry class, there was considerable jostling. Only three families – the Arundells of Trerice, the Godolphins of Godolphin, and the Trevanions of St Michael Caerhayes – appear in lists of the eight richest gentry families in both the 1540s and 1641.[104] Some families had disappeared entirely, extinct in the male line; some had left; some had fallen foul of the political changes of the sixteenth century; others had just not been able to take full advantage of new economic opportunities. At the same time a third of the gentry of the 1600s had only established themselves as such in the Elizabethan period.[105] Such social mobility perhaps owed a lot to the presence of the tin industry in Cornwall. Thus Piers Edgcumbe, head of one of Cornwall's wealthiest families in the 1500s, lost £4,000 in failed mining ventures after the 1560s. At the same time Richard Lanyon of Gwinear, who died in 1592, was reputed to have made £4,000 in just four years, enabling his family to make the transition from yeomen to gentry.[106] But a general growth in trading opportunities was a more important factor in the rise of the Cornish gentry. The Boscawens were tin traders in Truro in the early sixteenth century, with their acceptance onto the justices' bench in 1547 heralding their arrival; the Rashleighs were merchants from Devon who settled in Fowey somewhere between 1520 and 1540 and made their money from trade and privateering expeditions against the Spanish. In 1600 their new house at Menabilly signalled their transition from merchants to greater gentry. Of Cornwall's two peers in 1641, the Mohuns of Boconnoc had been an established and rising family in the sixteenth century, but the Robartes of Lanhydrock were altogether more recent. Richard Roberts was another Truro merchant, trading in wood and furze among other things, who left £5,000 to his son John in 1593. John made his fortune by lending to tin producers and his son, another Richard, could change the family name to the more affected Robartes, purchase a knighthood for £12,000 in 1616, buy the Lanhydrock estate in 1620 and still have £10,000 left over to spend on a baronage in 1625.[107]

The growth of trading opportunities along the south coast, the stagnation of mining, the convergence of Cornish agriculture, and perhaps a worsening problem of destitution across Cornwall all helped to scale down earlier economic distinctions between east and west. Simultaneously the difficulties faced by the Cornish language after the 1540s also worked to diminish intra-Cornish difference and were making it potentially easier for Cornwall to be imagined in the seventeenth century as a single territory with a homogeneous people.

The British wars of the 1640s

The summer of 1642 found Parliament and the king manoeuvring for support. In south-east Cornwall the Puritan gentry, linked to 'godly' networks that stretched eastwards across the Tamar, came out in support of Parliament. Sir John Eliot had gone from St Germans to

the 1629 Parliament to denounce the forced loans through which
Charles I was raising money and the threat to Protestant liberties
posed by the return to more traditional church rites. Eliot led a
faction that included other east Cornish gentry, such as William
Coryton of Pentillie, Sir Richard Buller and Sir Alexander Carew,
son of the historian, Richard Carew of Antony. They were joined in
1642 by some western gentry – including Nicholas Boscawen of
Tregothnan and John St Aubyn of Clowance as well as one of
Cornwall's two peers, Lord Robartes of Lanhydrock. On the other
side was ranged Cornwall's other peer – Mohun of Boconnoc, as well
as most of the older families – Francis and Sidney Godolphin, Sir
Richard Vyvyan, John Arundell of Trerice and Francis Basset. Until
late September of 1642 both sides were actively attempting to recruit
in Cornwall and the greater gentry seemed evenly split in their allegiance. And yet, suddenly, on 6 October Buller's parliamentary force
retreated from Launceston and took refuge in Plymouth. Cornwall
was almost the only 'county' entirely held by the king's supporters.
Mark Stoyle claims that at least 10,000 men had turned out at the
posse comitatus (the county call to arms) and notes contemporary
reports that 'all the west part' had come out for the king. Anne Duffin
also notes the 'thousands who turned out' to support the royalist, and
non-Cornish, commander Ralph Hopton against Buller and the
parliamentarians in September 1642.[108] Therefore, 'October 1642 did
not see a contest between two well-matched groups, but the rout of a
small body of Roundhead gentlemen and their retainers by a vast,
and somewhat unruly, Royalist mob'.[109] This was 'another revolt',
part of Cornwall's 'long tradition of rebelliousness'.[110]

   In January 1643 a parliamentary army entered south-east
Cornwall. They were met by Hopton's royalists at Braddock Down,
halfway between Lostwithiel and Liskeard. The parliamentarians
lost heart after a charge led by Bevill Grenville, from Stowe in the far
north of Cornwall, and fled back to Saltash. Not for the first time,
the Cornish infantry defeated a better equipped force. In early 1643 a
second parliamentarian army entered Cornwall. This too was
defeated, even more spectacularly, at the Battle of Stamford Hill, just
north of Stratton, in May, despite holding a distinct advantage in
terms of better ground and outnumbering Hopton's army by two to
one.[111] The Cornish force, at almost 4,000, then marched eastwards,
eventually playing an important part in the victories at Lansdown,
near Bath, and Roundway Down, north of Devizes, in July. Late that

same month the royalists laid siege to Bristol and, in a desperate
attack on England's second city, took it. But these victories came at a
terrible cost for the Cornish contingent. Their leaders were killed in
action – Sidney Godolphin in Devon, Bevill Grenville at Lansdown,
Sir Nicholas Slanning and John Trevanion at Bristol. Furthermore,
Coate mentions 200 Cornish foot killed and 300 wounded at
Lansdown, while at Bristol perhaps as many as 500 lost their lives in
the assault on the city ramparts. The royalist victories of Lansdown
and Bristol marked the high point of the royalist war effort but the
effective end 'of the Cornish army as a fighting unit'.[112]

During the spring and summer of 1644 the parliamentary military
commander, the earl of Essex, gradually marched his army into the
west of England. Encouraged by Robartes, he decided to deal a
strategic blow to the king by occupying Cornwall, the heartland of
royalism. However, Essex was not only opposed by Cornish forces
hastily raised by Francis Basset and the brother of Bevill Grenville,
Sir Richard Grenville, who had changed sides in early 1644. In his
rear, King Charles himself had decided to pursue the parliamentarians westwards. In the light of this, the decision to cross the Tamar
was not the wisest. As Essex moved further west he discovered the
people were almost uniformly hostile. Local men flocked to join the
king's pursuing army and the parliamentarians were forced into a cul-
de-sac in the hills between Lostwithiel and Fowey. Trapped, Essex's
cavalry managed to make a desperate escape eastwards, while Essex
himself recognized the inevitable and fled by boat. His army was
allowed to leave Cornwall and, harassed by the local populace,
humiliated, demoralized and bedraggled, the invading force trudged
back across a rain-sodden east Cornish countryside. Only a sixth of
the soldiers who left Fowey eventually arrived in the safer pastures of
Dorset.[113]

With the departure of Essex's army Cornwall was again solid for
the king. Yet the royalists were unable to take advantage of this as
events turned against them in the north and midlands of England.
Instead of joining the march east with the King's army, many
Cornish soldiers remained behind, to enlist with Grenville, who was
laying siege to Plymouth. By the end of the year he had some 5,000
men under arms.[114] But, despite possessing this large force, Grenville
was still unable to take Plymouth. And in March 1645 he reluctantly
conceded to the king's orders and marched the bulk of his men east to
join in the siege of Taunton. Once there, however, Grenville himself

was quickly wounded, leaving the Cornish forces 'leaderless and demoralised' and under the overall command of the heavy-drinking Lord George Goring, for whom Grenville had little regard. Sapped by casualties in the fighting around Taunton and, some claimed, encouraged by Grenville, the Cornish steadily deserted, so that by June only 600 of the original 3,000 remained at Taunton.[115]

Meanwhile, as the royalist generals argued, the parliamentary side had radically reorganized their own military leadership. In early 1645 the New Model Army, led by Sir Thomas Fairfax and Oliver Cromwell, established the conditions for eventual victory. In June 1645 this army won the decisive Battle of Naseby in Leicestershire. In September Bristol fell to Fairfax and the New Model Army turned its attention to one of the last remaining redoubts of royalism – the west of England and Cornwall. In the meantime Grenville, by now recovered from his wounds, had regained control of the New Cornish Tertia. In these circumstances, with Fairfax approaching, Grenville came up with an innovative proposal. He advised Prince Charles to sue with Parliament for peace, on condition that Parliament respected the autonomy of those areas still controlled by royalist forces – Cornwall and west Devon. The prince could live off the revenue of the duchy of Cornwall. This is one of biggest 'what ifs' of Cornish history. What if the prince had accepted Grenville's proposal and what if (admittedly extremely unlikely) Parliament had agreed. Cornwall, albeit a 'greater' Cornwall including parts of Devon, would have been autonomous of the English state with its own institutions of government. It all rapidly became academic. The Prince's Council rejected Grenville's scheme and had him arrested. Soon after this, Fairfax resumed the offensive. With the removal of the one commander who retained a strong personal following, the die was cast. In February 1646 the royalists were defeated at Torrington. By the end of that month Fairfax had crossed into Cornwall near Stratton. With local support melting away – helped by the disciplined behaviour of the parliamentarians – Hopton surrendered at Tresillian Bridge, near Truro, on 12 March. A month later the royalist garrison at St Michaels Mount gave up the fight. That left just Pendennis Castle – the last place on 'mainland' Britain to resist parliament – to hold out until 17 August. Fittingly Cornish forces were amongst the last to give up the King's cause.

Conclusion

Were the events of the 1540s and 1640s connected? Cornish ethnicity before the Civil Wars fundamentally rested on the Cornish language and the culture contained within it. But this was increasingly confined from the 1540s onwards to a shrinking western heartland. While resentment within that culture no doubt still played a part in the 1640s, it was by this time a very marginal part, as the Gear Rout of 1648, restricted to a pitifully small number of rebels in the far west, might suggest.[116] However, the 1648 rising should not distract our attention from two more novel aspects of the Civil Wars. First, the fierce hostility directed towards Essex's parliamentary army in 1644 indicates that the population of Cornwall east of Lostwithiel was as royalist as that of the west. But this was a district where the 'old culture' based on the Cornish language had long been replaced by an English-speaking culture, perhaps for as long as 350 years. Cornish royalism did not therefore correlate simply with the geography of the Cornish language. Second, Stoyle recounts the growing depth of hatred for the Cornish on the part of parliamentary pamphleteers, reacting against the humiliating defeat of Essex's army in 1644. In this pamphlet war the Cornish were constructed as the 'other', a united group opposed to the parliamentary cause. Stereotypes were created, exaggerating the 'difference' of the Cornish and minimizing divisions within Cornwall. But this 'difference' and the identity that accompanied it did not rest on the 'old culture'. On the contrary, the level of pamphleteering had injected a qualitatively new dimension to the situation, one hardly present in 1549, let alone 1497. The growing literacy inherent in this explosion of publication was creating a new sense of identity as much as merely reflecting an old one.

What did tie the hundred years from the 1540s to the 1640s together was Cornish loyalty to the crown. The special relationship of the Cornish gentry families with the crown, the presence of the duchy and more particularly the stannaries, plus the adoption of a conservative Anglican religious identity, conspired together to guarantee Cornish royalism in the Civil Wars of the seventeenth century. But these years also contained the germ of a new sense of Cornish identity, one potentially more political than cultural. Here, Richard Grenville's scheme of 1645 'to establish a semi-independent Cornish state' takes on new meaning. For Stoyle, Grenville was playing the nationalist card and appealing to 'particularist sentiment', 'the old Cornish desire for autonomy' and the 'old Cornish dream of a national revival'.[117] For him these aspirations had lain under the surface since 1497, just needing Grenville's proposal to be reignited. Or had they? In contrast, Grenville's scheme can be read as a very novel one. He was appealing to Cornish sentiment and to a residual loyalty to the duchy for a new purpose, to establish Cornish autonomy. If he really was acting like some kind of seventeenth-century Slobodan Milosevic this is surely more reminiscent of modern than sixteenth-century politics. For where were the explicit demands for autonomy or semi-independence in 1497 or 1549? The leaders of those risings had appealed to established institutions, and couched their petitions in a legalistic and conservative language.[118] The demands of 1645 look more like a new development than a reassertion of old demands.

So instead of viewing the 1640s as the end of a long period of cultural resistance they can be seen as the beginning of a new, more modern sense of Cornish identity, one based on territory rather than language. Print literacy helped to create a view of 'Cornwall' as a distinct unit, one less differentiated between east and west. Now all Cornish people, both Cornish- and English-speaking, could imagine themselves as 'Cornish'. These new imaginations and a new sense of 'Cornishness' for a short period in the mid-seventeenth century combined with a residual Cornish-speaking ethnicity in the west. Earlier, culture had been more important than territory. Later, in the eighteenth century, territory became more important than culture. But crucially, with the emergence of ideas of shared territory as markers of Cornwall and the Cornish, a sense of Cornishness was sustained despite the decay of the Cornish language. Moreover, while the cultural underpinnings of a distinct Cornish ethnicity were indeed entering into a twilight phase in the 1640s other developments in the economic sphere were about to come to fruition and, as we shall see in the next chapter, in the long run these led to a revived sense of Cornish 'difference' and a renewed sense of Cornish confidence.

Notes

[1] Susan Brigden, *New Worlds, Lost Worlds: The Rule of the Tudors, 1485–1603* (2001), p. 105.

[2] Philip Payton, *The Making of Modern Cornwall* (1992), p. 57.

[3] Polydore Vergil, cited in Mark Stoyle, *West Britons: Cornish Identities and the Early Modern British State* (2002), p. 31.

[4] Adrian Hastings, *The Construction of Nationhood: Ethnicity, Religion and Nationalism* (1997), p. 67.

[5] Mark Stoyle, 'Cornish Rebellions, 1497–1648', *History Today*, 47/5 (1997), 22–28.

[6] Philip Payton, *Cornwall: A History* (2004), pp. 131, 115.

[7] John Chynoweth, *Tudor Cornwall* (2002), p. 268.

[8] Stoyle, *West Britons*, p. 182.

[9] Ibid., p. 4.

[10] John Angarrack, *Our Future is History: Identity, Law and the Cornish Question* (2002), pp. 171–89.

[11] Ian Arthurson, '. . . "as able we be to depose him" . . . rebellion in the South West 1497', in Simon Parker (ed.), *Cornwall Marches On! Keskerdh Kernow 500* (1998), pp. 22–8; J. P. D. Cooper, *Propaganda and the Tudor State: Political Culture in the Westcountry* (2003).

[12] See C. S. L. Davies, 'Review of *West Britons*', *English Historical Review*, 68 (2003), 913–15.

[13] Brigden, *New Worlds*, pp. 28–9.

[14] Ian Arthurson, *The Perkin Warbeck Conspiracy 1491–99* (1994).

[15] James Whetter, *The Bodrugans: A Study of a Cornish Medieval Knightly Family* (1995), pp. 173–8.

[16] Ibid., p. 176.

[17] Lucy Rhymer, 'The rebellions of 1497 reconsidered', BA dissertation, University of Durham (2003), p. 21.

[18] Chynoweth, *Tudor Cornwall*, p. 209.

[19] C. S. L. Davies, *Peace, Print and Protestantism 1450–1558* (1977), p. 102.

[20] A. L. Rowse, *Tudor Cornwall* (1941), p. 126.

[21] Ibid., pp. 127–8.

[22] Cited in Chynoweth, *Tudor Cornwall*, p. 210.

[23] Rowse, *Tudor Cornwall*, pp. 127–8.

[24] Ian Arthurson and Nicholas Kingwell, 'The proclamation of Henry Tudor as King of England, 3 November 1483', *Historical Research*, 63 (1990), 100–6.

[25] Rowse, *Tudor Cornwall*, pp. 131–2.

[26] Chynoweth, *Tudor Cornwall*, p. 211.

[27] Rowse, *Tudor Cornwall*, p. 140. See also Julian Cornwall, *The Revolt of the Peasantry 1549* (1977), p. 47.

[28] Philip Payton, '"a . . . concealed envy against the English': a note on the aftermath of the 1497 rebellions in Cornwall', in Philip Payton (ed.), *Cornish Studies One* (1993), pp. 4–13.

[29] Cooper, *Propaganda*, p. 81.

[30] Chynoweth, *Tudor Cornwall*, p. 129.

[31] Frances Rose-Troup, *The Western Rebellion of 1549* (1913), p. 49.

[32] Mary Robertson, '"The art of the possible": Thomas Cromwell's management of west country government', *Historical Journal*, 32 (1989), 793–816.

[33] Rowse, *Tudor Cornwall*, p. 149.

[34] Ibid., p. 158.

[35] Mark Nicholls, *A History of the Modern British Isles 1529–1603: The Two Kingdoms* (1999), p. 124.

[36] For accounts of this rising see Rose-Troup, *Western Rebellion*, pp. 75ff, and Ian Arthurson, 'Fear and loathing in west Cornwall: seven new letters on the 1548 rising', *Journal of the Royal Institution of Cornwall* (2000), 68–95.

[37] Arthurson, 'Fear and loathing'.

[38] Margaret Speight, 'Local government and politics in Devon and Cornwall, 1509–49, with some reference to the South-Western Rebellion of 1549', Ph.D. thesis, University of Sussex (1991), p. 190.

[39] Rose-Troup, *Western Rebellion*, p. 128, citing a contemporary account.

[40] Colin Kidd, *British Identities before Nationalism: Ethnicity and Nationhood in the Atlantic World, 1600–1800* (1999), p. 291.

[41] Rowse, *Tudor Cornwall*, p. 272.

[42] Ibid., p. 270.

[43] Nicholls, *Two Kingdoms*, p. 126.

[44] Rowse, *Tudor Cornwall*, p. 275.

[45] Ibid., p. 130.

[46] Payton, *Cornwall*, p. 105; And see also Keith Robbins, *Great Britain: Identities, Institutions and the Idea of Britishness* (1998), p. 41.

[47] Arthurson, *Perkin Warbeck*, pp. 213–14.

[48] Incidentally shattering confident kernowsceptic rejections of a cult of King Arthur on the grounds that 'there is little or nothing in the way of drama or literature to prove it' (Cooper, *Propaganda*, pp. 108–9).

[49] Chynoweth, *Tudor Cornwall*, p. 208.

[50] Cooper, *Propaganda*, pp. 64–5.

[51] Rowse, *Tudor Cornwall*, p. 138.

[52] Rhymer, 'Rebellions of 1497', p. 33; Rowse, *Tudor Cornwall*, p. 263.

[53] Mark Stoyle, 'The dissidence of despair: rebellion and identity in early modern Cornwall', *Journal of British Studies* 38 (1999), 423–44.

[54] Stoyle, '"Pagans or paragons?": images of the Cornish during the English Civil War', *English Historical Review* (1996), 299–323.

[55] G. R. Lewis, *The Stannaries: A Study of the Medieval Tin Miners of Cornwall* (1965), p. 254.

[56] John Norden, *Speculi Britanniae Pars: A Topographical and Historical Description of Cornwall* (1728), p. 28.

[57] Richard Carew, *Survey of Cornwall* (1811), p. 184.

[58] Stoyle, 'Pagans or paragons', p. 321.

[59] Ralph Griffiths, *The Fourteenth and Fifteenth Centuries* (2003), p. 20.

[60] Cooper, *Propaganda*, p. 257.

[61] Oliver Padel, 'Cornish Language Notes: 3', *Cornish Studies,* 3 (1975), 22.

[62] This evidence is collected together in Matthew Spriggs, 'Where Cornish was spoken and when: a provisional synthesis', in Philip Payton (ed.), *Cornish Studies Eleven* (2003), pp. 228–69.

[63] Bernard Deacon, *The Cornish Family* (2004), pp. 77–90.

[64] Stoyle, *West Britons*, pp. 48–9.

[65] John Angarrack, *Breaking the Chains: Propaganda, Censorship, Deception and the Manipulation of Public Opinion in Cornwall* (1999), p. 51.

[66] Estimate of 1549 casualties from Stoyle, 'Dissidence of despair', p. 443. French casualties from Keegan, *The First World War* (1998), p. 6.

[67] Lewis, *Stannaries*, pp. 253–4.

[68] Gillian Brennan, 'Language and nationality: the role of policy towards Celtic languages in the consolidation of Tudor power', *Nations and Nationalism*, 7 (2001), 317–38.

[69] Stoyle, *West Britons*, p. 46; Cooper, *Propaganda*, p. 64.

[70] Brennan, 'Language and nationality', pp. 327–9, 334.

[71] Stoyle, *West Britons*, pp. 41, 43 and 49.

[72] For the argument that 1548 was quite separate from 1549 see Speight, 'Local government and politics'.

[73] Rose-Troup, *Western Rebellion*, p. 80.

[74] Ibid., p. 70.

[75] A. L. Rowse, *Tudor Cornwall*, pp. 283–4.

[76] Philip Edwards, *The Making of the Modern English State, 1460–1660* (2001), p. 179.

[77] Joanna Mattingly, 'The Helston shoemakers' gild and a possible connection with the 1549 rebellion', in Philip Payton (ed.), *Cornish Studies Six* (1998), pp. 23–45.

[78] Chynoweth, *Tudor Cornwall*, p. 238.

[79] Payton, *Cornwall*, p. 127.

[80] Stoyle, 'Dissidence of despair', p. 438.

[81] Stoyle, 'Pagans or paragons', p. 322.

[82] Cf. Brigden, *New Worlds*, p. 146.

[83] Cooper, *Propaganda*, pp. 177–8 and 237.

[84] Philip Jenkins, 'The plight of pygmy nations; Wales in early modern Europe', *North American Journal of Welsh Studies*, 2 (2002), 1–11.

[85] Matthew Spriggs, 'William Scawen (1600–1689) – a neglected Cornish patriot and father of the Cornish language revival', in Philip Payton (ed.), *Cornish Studies Thirteen* (2005), pp. 98–125.

[86] Cooper, *Propaganda*, pp. 186–7.

[87] Michael Braddick, *State Formation in Early Modern England c1550–1700* (2000), p. 353.

[88] Payton, *Cornwall*, p. 128.

[89] Chynoweth, *Tudor Cornwall*, p. 272.

[90] Ibid., p. 256.

[91] Graham Haslam, 'The Elizabethan Duchy, an estate in stasis', in R. W. Hoyle (ed.), *The Estates of the English Crown 1558–1640* (1992), p. 88.

[92] Ibid., p. 111.

[93] Cooper, *Propaganda*, p. 175.

[94] Ibid., pp. 171–87.

[95] Graham Haslam 'Jacobean phoenix: the Duchy of Cornwall in the principates of Henry Frederick and Charles', in R. W. Hoyle (ed.), *The Estates of the English Crown 1558–1640* (1992), p. 269.

[96] Ibid., pp. 295–6.

[97] Anne Duffin, *Faction and Faith: Politics and Religion of the Cornish Gentry before the Civil War* (1996), p. 205.

[98] Cooper, *Propaganda*, p. 199.

[99] Ibid., p. 193.

[100] See Jonathan Barry, 'Population distribution and growth in the early modern period', in Roger Kain and William Ravenhill (eds), *The Historical Atlas of South West England* (1999), pp. 110–17.

[101] Carew, *Survey*, p. 185.

[102] A. L. Beier, *Masterless Men: The Vagrancy Problem in England, 1560–1640* (1985), p. 34.

[103] H. S. A. Fox and Oliver J. Padel (eds), *The Cornish Lands of the Arundells of Lanherne, Fourteenth to Sixteenth Centuries* (2000), p. lxxxi; James Whetter, *Cornwall in the 17th Century: An Economic Survey of Kernow* (1974), p. 22.

[104] Duffin, *Faction and Faith*, p. 24; Chynoweth, *Tudor Cornwall*, p. 147.

[105] Ibid., p. 23.

[106] Chynoweth, *Tudor Cornwall*, pp. 55–6.

[107] Duffin, *Faction and Faith*, p. 8.

[108] Stoyle, 'Pagans or paragons', p. 303; Duffin, *Faction and Faith*, p. 212.

[109] Stoyle, 'Pagans or paragons', p. 303.

[110] Stoyle, 'Dissidence of despair', p. 439, and 'Pagans or paragons', p. 303.

[111] Mary Coate, *Cornwall in the Great Civil War and Interregnum, 1642–60* (1933), p. 70.

[112] Ibid., p. 100.

[113] Simon Schama, *A History of Britain: The British Wars 1603–1776* (2001), p. 147.

[114] Mark Stoyle, '"Sir Richard Grenville's creatures": the New Cornish Tertia, 1644–46', in Philip Payton (ed.), *Cornish Studies Four* (1996), pp. 26–44.

[115] Ibid., p. 34.

[116] For the details of the Gear rising see Mark Stoyle, '"The Gear rout": the Cornish rising of 1648 and the Second Civil War', *Albion*, 32 (2000), 37–58.

[117] Mark Stoyle, 'The last refuge of a scoundrel: Sir Richard Grenville and Cornish particularism, 1644–6', *Historical Research*, 71 (1998), 31–51.

[118] Cooper, *Propaganda*, pp. 57 and 66–8.

4

Industrializing Cornwall: economic and cultural transformation, 1640s–1840s

The events of the 1640s signalled the virtual demise of a Cornish ethnic identity based on the Cornish language. The most unequivocal linguistic reminder of Cornwall's non-English roots withered away over the next century and a half and with it disappeared a large chunk of Cornish distinctiveness. Nonetheless, the 1640s also saw the first halting appearance of a sense of Cornishness more attached to territory than language. Richard Grenville's desperate plan of 1644 had attached political meaning to the idea of Cornwall and hinted at newer, more modern demands for autonomy and devolved powers. However, this devolutionary impulse was soon swamped in a tide of hyper-loyalism after the Restoration of King Charles II in 1660. The sketch of a separate Cornish political identity tantalizingly held out in 1645 soon dissolved in the face of a growing acceptance that Cornwall was a 'county' of England. But Cornwall was not, as may have seemed during this time, doomed to a future as a bog-standard English county. For, during the eighteenth century, its precocious industrialization produced a new economic distinctiveness and, furthermore, reopened connections away from the English core, to the north to south Wales and, with Cornwall's emerging role in the global mining economy, overseas. Industrialization also provided the basis for new cultural distinctions, guaranteeing the reproduction of a new sense of Cornish identity by the 1820s, albeit one that in some respects looked back to the past. This identity ultimately laid the foundations for renewed demands for political recognition of Cornwall's status to re-emerge in the second half of the twentieth century.

Cornwall's industrialization also radically changed the nature of its religious identity. In the early eighteenth century Cornish Toryism rested on an establishment Anglicanism. But the roots of this politico-religious identity were being sapped even as it dominated representations of post-Restoration Cornwall. Economic changes eroded this identity by the mid-eighteenth century, exposing the fragile social control of the clerical–gentry ruling class and replacing Anglicanism with a new religious allegiance more relevant to Cornish working people – Methodism. In this chapter I begin with an account of Tory Cornwall, before reviewing the factors that produced Cornwall's precociously early industrialization. The chapter ends with a discussion of the emergence of Methodist Cornwall.

Tory Cornwall

Mark Stoyle concludes that the 'perceptions of what it meant to be Cornish were transformed forever as a result of the Civil War'. The image of the Cornish as an inherently rebellious people now gave way to one of super-loyal subjects of the restored Stuart monarchy. In Cornwall itself, the gentry assiduously presented an identity of 'exaggerated loyalty'.[1] The Cornish royalist tradition, reforged in the wars of 1642–5, was embellished in order to celebrate a particular kind of regional distinctiveness that, existing safely in the past, served to underpin a conservatism in the present. In many ways this prefigured that loyalty to martial British imperialism of a later generation of Scottish gentry.

In the Cornish case it did not just entail loyalty to the crown, but also unswerving allegiance to the Church of England. It is often remarked how Cornwall was untouched by religious dissent as gentry support for the established church combined with popular loyalty to Anglican rites.[2] However, although this view neatly fits the myth of Cornish royalism, the very success of that myth exaggerates it. In fact, Cornwall was not immune from the religious turmoil of the mid-seventeenth century, years in which Presbyterians called for a church without bishops, Independents (often later known as Congregationalists) emphasized the rights of congregations to run their own churches, Baptists rejected infant baptism and Quakers went further in dispensing with outward ritual and ordained ministers. In the 1650s there was an attempt by some Cornish clergy to form a Presbyterian organization. In 1654 George Fox visited Cornwall and spent time in Launceston jail for his pains. And in 1662, when one in ten Anglican clergymen in England and Wales were expelled from their livings for refusing to commit themselves to the Act of Uniformity, which restored the bishops, a similar proportion of clergy in Cornwall were also ejected.[3] At least thirty-eight dissenting meeting places were recorded in Cornwall in 1672 or 1690.[4] Moreover, the proportion of dissenters in the Compton Census of 1676 in Cornwall looks little different from Devon. In around 27 per cent of parishes more than 2 per cent of the people were dissenters, while the equivalent proportion of parishes in Devon was 30 per cent.[5] Divergence occurred not in the middle quarters of the seventeenth century but after 1680. By 1715 only an estimated 2 per cent of the population of Cornwall were dissenters, far lower than Devon's 10 per cent. The number of dissenting meeting places had shrunk to just eleven, at the same time as dissent had flourished in Devon, especially in the east of that county.[6] Jonathan Barry offers one explanation for this; the urban structure of late seventeenth-century Cornwall was weaker and this meant a lack of that 'critical mass of potential middling supporters'.[7] Certainly, the dissenting congregations that survived in 1715 were restricted to the towns – the largest being in Launceston, Liskeard, Looe, Fowey, Falmouth, Penzance and St Ives. But it is also possible that in the fiercest phase of persecution of dissenters, in the early 1680s, there was less toleration of religious nonconformity in Cornwall. For the Tory view of society tied the divine rule of bishops over the church strongly to the sanctity of kingship. The royalism of Cornwall's ruling gentry therefore had little space for religious dissent, seen as dangerously seditious. Life for a Cornish dissenter was apt to be difficult. With no large towns, there was no countervailing urban power to set against the wrath of the royalist gentry.

By 1715 the lack of religious dissent in Cornwall mirrored its political culture. This was the high point of Cornish Toryism. Acquiescing silently in the 'Revolution' of 1688, when the legitimate King James II was deemed to have forfeited his throne because of his unrepentant Catholicism, Cornish Tories kept their heads down in the reign of William of Orange. But during Queen Anne's reign, especially from 1704, they increasingly found their voice as war with France began to affect local commerce and the tin trade. In 1710 George Granville (1667–1735), the leading mouthpiece of Cornish Toryism and a grandson of Bevill Grenville, was elected as one of the two county MPs, along with J. M. Trevanion, another high church supporter. They were joined by thirty-nine more Tories and only four Whigs from Cornish seats in the Parliament of 1710 and Granville took a leading position in the Tory government of 1710. Yet in 1714, on the accession of George I, the duchy influence on Cornwall's MPs was sufficiently reasserted to reduce the number of Tories to just eleven.[8]

However, Tories kept their hold on the county seats, indicating a degree of support from the landowners and their larger tenant farmers. In the two decades after 1715 boards displaying King Charles' letter of 1643 to the Cornish people were prominently displayed in churches across Cornwall.[9] But this was more of a ritualistic gesture than a robust expression of poplar Toryism. For the ultimate trial of Cornish Toryism had in the mean time arrived and been shirked – the Jacobite rising of 1715.

For the Cornish royalist tradition, as for all Tories, the 'Glorious Revolution' of 1688 presented a quandary. A legitimate monarch was overthrown, but partly because of the dangers James II's Catholicism posed for the established church. Tories were caught between support for the church and support for legitimate monarchy. In 1715 the dilemma was thrust from the realms of principle into the reality of practice when the earl of Mar raised the standard of rebellion in Scotland and proclaimed James the rightful king. But Mar fatally hesitated, building his strength in Scotland. In the meantime the government clearly thought Cornwall was a potential source of Jacobite rebellion, sending troops to Plymouth to stifle any rising.[10] They had good reason. George Granville, now Lord Lansdowne, had overtly adopted the Jacobite cause. But in the end the expected Cornish Jacobite rising was a damp squib. The Tory gentry failed to make their move. That there was some support for James is possible from the account by Henry Jenner of James Painter, of Trekenning at St Columb, who had planned to read James's declaration at St Columb market place on 6 October 1715. Painter was arrested but acquitted at the next assizes at Launceston. The claimed 'rejoicing' at this acquittal was enough for Jenner to assert the existence of a 'good deal of Jacobitism in Cornwall'.[11] However, Jenner, himself a romantic royalist, may have over-egged things. Boasts by Tory landowners such as Sir John St Aubyn (later County MP from 1722 to 1741) that he could 'place himself at the head of some 10,000 tinners for the Jacobite cause' had been exposed as empty bragging. Attempts by Jacobites to incite the tinners on the grounds that the church and kingly government were being threatened, even if they occurred, had plainly not struck much of a chord. By 1715, however much the Cornish gentry were wedded to the Cornish royalist tradition, the Cornish people had become more ambivalent.

And not just the people. While Tories such as Granville, Trevanion and St Aubyn went up to and beyond the brink of rebellion, others procrastinated. Perhaps more significant as a symbol of Cornwall's political role in these years was the career of Sidney Godolphin (1645–1712). Godolphin entered the court as a young man as a page to Charles II.[12] Milking connections made at court, not the least of whom was the future Lord Marlborough, Godolphin became MP for Helston and built a parliamentary career. His experience as a Treasury minister in 1688 was recognized by his eventual position as lord treasurer in Queen Anne's governments from 1702–1710. Godolphin had been counted with the Tories in the crisis years of the 1680s and made tentative contacts with Jacobites around 1700. But although at first a Tory minister, he gradually brought Whigs into the government. His pragmatic non-partisanship, his management of the financing of the long War of the Spanish Succession against France and his role in promoting the Act of Union with Scotland in 1707 have led some to suggest that he has better claim than Robert Walpole to have been England and Britain's first prime minister.[13] Godolphin's long years at the heart of government also reinforced the centrality of Cornwall in the governing process. The large phalanx of forty-four Cornish MPs, almost 10 per cent of the House of Commons, played an important part in bolstering Godolphin's support, and helped to undermine Walpole's Whig ministry in 1737, when many rallied to the cause of Prince Frederick, heir to the throne and duke of Cornwall. In the subsequent election of 1741 the government's majority fell to a mere nineteen and Walpole's days were ultimately numbered, largely due to electoral damage inflicted in Cornwall (and in Scotland).[14]

Being an MP was one way the Cornish gentry could exert influence on government. Another option remained the Stannary Convocation. It has been argued that the heyday of the Stannary Parliament came in the period from 1660 to 1688.[15] Meeting regularly to pronounce on mining matters and to debate the tin pre-emption rate, the price at which the duke agreed to buy a certain amount of Cornish tin, the Stannary Parliament was central to the Cornish royalist tradition. This was even more so as the lord warden of the stannaries was John Grenville, son of Bevill Grenville. However, after 1688 its precarious position became clear. The Convocation could only be summoned by the duke, or the monarch in the absence of a duke. William III did not renew the pre-emption contract and called no Convocation. In the eighteenth century the Convocation was to meet just four times, in 1703, 1710, 1750 and 1752. The Convocations of 1710 and 1750 were the most fractious. In 1710 it seems to have served as a surrogate for the fierce Tory–Whig political battles surrounding the Westminster parliamentary elections later in the same year. Convocation split on 'country' versus 'court', or anti and pro-government lines, and was accompanied by a near riot of up to 6,000 tinners.

While the Convocations of 1703 and 1710 were used by the dominant group of Cornish Tory gentry to press their wider political points, the Convocation of 1750 was an altogether more interesting affair. Though by this time utterly dominated by the same landed gentry who manipulated the parliamentary elections of Cornwall, this Convocation began to flex some long under-used muscles. It demanded the right to adjourn itself, just as the House of Commons did. This led to a breakdown in relations with the lord warden, Thomas Pitt of Boconnoc, and the Parliament was prorogued with no legislation agreed. After a stand-off, the lord warden eventually in 1752 assented to various legislation that tended to benefit landlord and large merchant interests. The demands of the 1750s Convocation are intriguing, foreshadowing some of the later demands of parliamentarians in America for greater independence from the 'mother of Parliaments'. They have been seen as a Cornish 'unilateral declaration of independence', demanding restoration of sovereignty to the Stannary Parliament and finally making good the powers implied by the 1508 Charter of Pardon.[16] On the other hand, the Stannators were very indirect representatives of the sovereign people. Chosen by the Corporations of Liskeard, Truro, Helston and Lostwithiel, those from the first three were in reality nominees of the Eliots, Boscawens and Godolphins. These families used the Convocation to embarrass the duchy, reflecting more the complex political squabbles of the Westminster Parliament than real demands for Cornish sovereignty.[17] In the final analysis, unlike the later American revolutionaries, the 1750 Convocation baulked at making a direct appeal to the people to assert their claim to sovereignty. Indeed, unlike 1710, there is little evidence of popular involvement in these events.

Economic and social change in the west

The palpable lack of support from the commons for Cornwall's Tory landowners in the eighteenth century may reflect the economic changes of the seventeenth. Recent work has concluded that, in terms of material wealth and domestic comfort, Cornish households became relatively poorer over the course of the 1600s.[18] In the first decades of the seventeenth century inventories in Cornwall were valued at around the same level as those in Hertfordshire and Worcestershire. By 1700 they were only half their value.[19] Relative decline had already set in before the Civil Wars of the mid-century, associated with a spread of cheaper goods from other regions, which led to a fall in household production activities such as textiles, found in half of Cornish households in 1600 but only 10 per cent by 1700.[20] Household economies in Cornwall were becoming as a result relatively more specialized in the 1600s with less evidence of by-employments. Specialization was not associated with growing wealth in seventeenth-century Cornwall but the reverse, as the options open to households for earning an income shrank. A growing tin-mining industry after 1660 at first only made this process worse, with the biggest falls in material wealth occurring in western mining parishes. Mired in poverty as a 'consequence of its integration into the English economy',[21] people in Cornwall at first suffered from the proletarianization that accompanied the growth of mining. As a result, they did not participate in the growing consumerism noticeable in the late seventeenth century in the south-east of England. In contrast, 'Cornwall experienced relative deprivation and exploitation more reminiscent of the Irish than the English experience of this period'.[22] The gulf between material culture in Cornwall and the south-east of England was further widened as households in Cornwall spurned new consumer goods even when they could afford them.

Nonetheless, tin production rose steadily after the Restoration to peak in the late 1680s. Over the next ten years there was some falling away but by 1703 the previous peak had again been surpassed.[23] The proportion of inventories with evidence of mining activity rose from 5 or 6 per cent before 1660 to 14 per cent by the 1720s.[24] In the mid-seventeenth century the tin industry had still resembled the late medieval period with predominately part-time tinners alternating between tin streaming and farming. However, a series of factors allowed miners to access deeper ores. Prominent amongst these was cheaper gunpowder to break ground, plus a more efficient use of water power to drain mines and to raise ore.[25] At first, technological change was not accompanied by any great change in the industry's organization. The bulk of the rise in tin production was achieved by a multiplication of small units. Moreover, the flexibility of an impoverished labour force was ideally suited to the uncertainties of the industry.[26] In contrast, the real revolution of the seventeenth century involved pulling in new finance for mining and this, ultimately, led to its transformation. As mines were worked deeper, the time required to break the 'dead' ground before reaching the productive ores lengthened. Consequently, credit was required to pay for development costs while waiting for ore sales to begin. Initially, this was supplied by London pewterers and tin dealers but gradually local merchants took over. By the 1700s a tightly knit all-Cornish group controlled the financing of the tin industry.[27] The involvement of merchant capital enabled some of the smaller operators to consolidate. By the 1720s, while many mines were still run by partnerships of working miners often linked by kinship, others were much grander. Poldice Mine in Gwennap was by this time 600 feet deep and employed a colossal 800 to 1,000 workers,[28] rivalling the collieries of north-east England 'in scale, complexity, the numbers of people they employed and the size of the capital investment they represented'.[29]

By the 1720s the benefits of Cornish mining growth at last began to trickle down into the middling groups as levels of material wealth rose faster than in some agricultural English counties.[30] But the two generations from the 1660s to the 1720s had been hard ones, especially for those in the west. There, very rapid population growth from 1660 to 1750, of 89 per cent in Penwith and 79 per cent in Kerrier Hundreds, had been stimulated by the growth of mining but the greater number of people increased pressure on resources and led to falling standards of living. In contrast, in Powder and Pydar in mid-Cornwall there was a much more modest 29 per cent and 6 per cent growth respectively, while population actually fell in eastern Cornwall.[31] The dramatic internal contrast within Cornwall again served to increase west–east differences after 1650, following a century and a half of economic convergence. In the west, population boomed as had relative deprivation; in the east population fell but household wealth held up. The years from the early 1600s to the 1730s were a transition phase in the Cornish economy. At first, buffeted by competition from England, it stagnated with the relatively diversified economy of the fifteenth century by now a dim memory. Yet, underneath this stagnation the seeds of growth were germinating, as tin production expanded after the 1660s. This combination of population growth and lower incomes accompanied an economic transformation of west Cornwall – with a slow penetration of consumer goods, the abandonment of domestic textile production and the concentration on cattle raising at the expense of corn. And it had other temporary effects on society.

David Cullum claims to have discovered the evidence for large extended households of seven to ten people in the far west. According to his research, half of married couples shared a house-hold with another couple.[32] This dramatically overturns the traditional view that everywhere in northern Europe the nuclear household of parents and children was the dominant domestic experience. In West Penwith, Cullum argues, 'a large household engaged in both mining and farming could more finely tune its efforts to prevailing economic harmonies', with younger men working in mining and older men in farming.[33] However, rather than a survival of an older extended household structure, it is more likely that this extended family structure was a temporary response to growing population and a shortage of housing, a situation similar to that of rapidly industrializing British regions such as the east Midlands later in the eighteenth century.

In the same districts where there were unmistakable signs of economic transformation, Cornwall's traditional language and the culture it had sustained for many centuries was entering its terminal phase. By 1700, when the Welsh Celticist Edward Lhuyd visited Cornwall, it was restricted to a strip of coastal parishes from St Keverne in the south to St Ives in the north. The efforts of a small band of enthusiasts who continued the work of the first Cornish revivalist, the east Cornish landowner William Scawen, and recorded various examples of written and oral Cornish, were to no avail.[34] These men, later known as the 'Newlyn School', included the Boson family of Paul (near Penzance) between 1660 and 1730. Nicholas Boson and his relatives Thomas and John wrote a series of short pieces in Cornish.[35] They were joined by William Rowe, baptized in 1666, a farmer of Sancreed, who even began to translate parts of the Bible into Cornish, unfortunately getting no further than Genesis 3 in the Old Testament and Matthew 4 in the New. Somewhat later William Gwavas (1676–1741), a Penzance barrister, collected together many scraps of the language, but this was its swansong, a final desperate flurry of activity by a small group of western intelligentsia, invaluable in capturing the spoken prose of the late seventeenth and early eighteenth centuries but unable to delay the end of Cornish as an everyday language. This fate finally befell it somewhere in the 1790s. Socially, once the small group of middling men who comprised the Newlyn School dispersed, the language was confined to the poorest and most marginalized strata of local society, labouring and fishing families.

More important things occupied the minds of eighteenth-century educated men than an apparently doomed language. Chief amongst these was the business of making money. Although the poor had struggled, landlords owning mineral rights benefited from the growth of tin mining. Hugh Boscawen spent £17,000 in the 1660s and 1670s on land purchases in Lincolnshire and Cornwall from mining proceeds.[36] Later, the exploitation of copper meant other established families gained. In the 1720s and 1730s the Bassets of Tehidy made £2.53 profit from mining investments for every £1 income from the rest of their estate.[37] Families who had moved into the gentry by other means found that growing income lifted their standard of living 'onto a new level'.[38] For example, Samuel Enys, whose family originally profited from the Fowey import and export trade, took £20,000 profits from mining in just twenty-five years, an annual income from mining equivalent to that of fifty-six labourers at the tin stamps. With rising income new houses could be built, or existing houses rebuilt. The Rashleighs entirely rebuilt Menabilly near Fowey in 1710–15, benefiting from the growth in commerce.

It has been claimed that merchants could not purchase estates and attain the status of country gentlemen until the late eighteenth century.[39] If this were the case elsewhere, it was certainly not true in Cornwall. While large landlords gained from mining profits, mining also held out opportunities for less exalted families. One of the most striking examples was that of William Lemon, born in Germoe in 1696 of a yeoman farming family. Entering service as a youth at Chyandour tin-smelting works near Penzance, Lemon took a keen interest in the growing mining industry. In 1720 he took on Wheal Fortune in partnership with others and made £10,000 profit in a few years. Adding to this by a good marriage to Isabel Vibert of Gulval, Lemon moved into the burgeoning copper mines of Gwennap, where he really made his fortune. By 1737 he was mayor of Truro and in the 1740s bought the Carclew estate at Mylor. His grandson William Lemon was to become county MP, baronet and a respected figure in late eighteenth-century Cornwall. Social mobility like this tended to subvert notions of a traditional social hierarchy in Cornwall. It contrasted with the idea of a conservative, unchanging and hierarchical society inherent in the Cornish royalist tradition, which was quite literally undermined by the dynamism of mining.

Cornwall's industrial revolution, 1740s–1810s

Demand for copper ore began to grow sharply in the early 1700s, mainly from the brass manufacturers of Bristol and Birmingham, responding to demand for brass combs from the woollen textile industry. And the relatively flexible, low-cost mining industry of Cornwall, coupled with a positive institutional structure and political tranquillity, allowed Cornish mines to meet this demand.[40] Later in the eighteenth century, the sheathing of the bottoms of ships with copper and the growth in the number of ships both for trade and war, added yet more demand. Writing in 1733, the Cornish historian Thomas Tonkin pointed how copper had been 'turned to very great account' in the previous couple of generations.[41] Twenty years later William Borlase noted that copper was 'a happy addition these 40 or 50 years to the employment and reserve of this county'.[42] Indeed, by the 1750s income from copper began to match that of the old staple tin. For the historian of Cornwall's industrial revolution, John Rowe, the 1740s marked the onset of a 'revolutionary transformation' of mining.[43] Copper mining was 'extremely volatile. It was exciting, stimulating and always changing and expanding.'[44] As a result of its growth Cornish communities began to move to the rhythm of those global capitalist markets that were beginning, in the eighteenth century, to transform the world. Copper mining lay at the heart of the transformation of west Cornwall into 'one of the most advanced engineering centres in the world' by the 1780s, one of Europe's early industrial regions.[45]

In order to develop the mines to meet the demand for copper a large amount of capital was required. The Cornish cost book system was ideally suited for this. Cost book companies were a form of extended partnership but with some limited liability. They combined the advantages of a close-knit partnership with the ability to draw in more investors and generate more capital and provided the flexibility required by the speculative industry of mining. Cost book financing has sometimes been condemned as a 'financial and managerial eccentricity' and 'fragile and ultimately ephemeral', leading to the 'long term underdevelopment of many Cornish mines'.[46] This is a view overinfluenced by hindsight and the ultimate collapse of mining. In the eighteenth century what is noteworthy is not the 'fragility' of the cost book system but its huge success in diverting capital into mining. This was a financing system dependent on trust, thriving on the close-knit, often extended family, relationships that criss-crossed the small Cornish mining region of the eighteenth century.[47]

In the 1770s competition from the low-cost mines of Anglesey brought a temporary halt to rising copper production. Where possible, Cornish mines turned their attention back to tin. Another response was an 'attempt to cartelize copper in the 1780s'.[48] The Cornish Copper Metal Company in 1785 set out to raise capital of £500,000, a remarkable sum for the time and 'one of the most heavily capitalised enterprises in the whole of the eighteenth century economy',[49] in order to buy up the copper produced in Cornwall and thereby push up the price. Ultimately unsuccessful, the Company was wound up when copper ore prices began to rise of their own accord in 1792, by which time the Anglesey mines were already becoming exhausted. After some difficulties from 1805 to 1815, when the inflated wartime price of copper began to ease back, the value of copper ore mined then steadily rose to the 1830s. In the earlier part of this long boom, in the middle of the eighteenth century, when mines were shallow, immense profits were made from copper. At a cost of a mere £100 the first two weeks working of the aptly named Wheal Virgin in Gwennap in 1757 produced copper ore worth £5,700. In the next three weeks another £9,600 worth of ore was raised for just £200 costs.[50] Such spectacular profits meant that adventurers (share-holders), the mineral lords, who received a proportion of sales whether or not profits had been made, and even working miners could make a lot of money very quickly. The chance of similar riches lured others into this dynamic business.

Nonetheless, occasional bonanzas notwithstanding, fortunes were lost as well as won in what remained a risky speculation. The real gainers were the smelters. Copper smelting, unlike tin, was by the 1780s based predominantly in south Wales. Only Copperhouse at Hayle continued to mount a challenge to the Welsh smelters.[51] Following the maxim that if you can't beat them you can always join them, the capital amassed through copper mining allowed 'the great Cornish families (to take) control of their own destinies during the early decades of the nineteenth century by moving their money into

Welsh smelting'.[52] The Vivians of Truro led this exodus, eventually
setting up the Hafod copper works in 1809/10.[53] They were soon
joined by the Fox family, who also invested in Welsh mines,[54] and the
Williamses, who began to invest on a large scale in Welsh copper
smelting in the 1830s.

By the early nineteenth century, west Cornwall was one of Britain's
industrial regions, its capitalists investing in other regions, and
providing 'best practice' examples for its leading export industry,
metal mining. Indeed, only cotton textile output grew faster than
Cornish copper before the 1830s. And even cotton had grown more
slowly before 1770.[55] This very early industrialization, combined with
the particular problems of managing large labour forces in underground mines, also produced a distinctive payment system. Groups
of miners were paid according to the value of ore raised (tributing) or
ground broken (tutwork). In these piece-work contracts the miners
retained considerable autonomy over their work practices. Such
payment methods harked seductively back to the memory of the
independent tinner-farmers who leased mining setts on their own
accord or in partnership with other working tinners. Yet this was not
quite a traditional survival. Although tributing was known in the
medieval period it was one wage payment system among many. In
the seventeenth century, as mines became more heavily capitalized,
the dominant form of payment was a wage paid by the day or week.
This, however, was not conducive to maximum effort in the unsuper-
vised dark recesses of a mine. Thus, tributing was the compromise, in
the interests of economy producing what later became seen as a
'traditional' system. In fact it was a product of the eighteenth century
and of deep copper mining, becoming the usual form of payment for
underground labour by the 1760s.[56]

Moreover, tributing, while giving to the working miner some independence as well as the ever-present possibility of making
considerable gains on any single bargain if the ground favoured him,
was accompanied after the middle of the eighteenth century by tightening labour discipline. Carew wrote in the late 1500s of tinners
working no more than four hours underground, while Tonkin in the
1730s felt that they had so many holidays and feast days that 'they do
not work one half of the month for their owners and employers'.[57]
But by the 1750s miners were working six- or eight-hour spells and by
1750 a three-shift system was in operation.[58] Holidays survived somewhat later but were under attack by the 1790s. By 1808 miners'

holidays were reported to be much reduced and by 1842 miners outside one or two mines in the St Just area in theory 'enjoyed' just Christmas Day and Good Friday as holidays, along with the majority of the rest of the British labouring population.[59]

Early industrialization therefore produced new traditions such as tributing while subjecting Cornish miners to common processes such as growing labour discipline. Also common to the process of industrialization was the use of new technology. Here, the Cornish industrial region played a central role, one that was by the 1820s to produce its own Cornish 'tradition'. By the 1730s three of Newcomen's 'fire' engines were at work in Cornwall, two near Redruth and one at Polgooth to the west of St Austell.[60] By 1776 there were forty steam engines in Cornwall,[61] each located within its own 'house', producing that distinctive icon of the modern Cornish landscape. From 1777 to 1800 fifty-two Boulton & Watt engines were erected in Cornwall together with perhaps as many as thirty piracies, engines built by local engineers such as the two Jonathan Hornblowers, father and son, Edward Bull and Richard Trevithick. One third of all the savings overall achieved by the Watt engine were accounted for by Cornwall, which played a crucial role in the development of the steam engine from the 1750s to the 1820s – 'the significance of the Cornish copper and tin mines in the spread of best practice technology in the eighteenth century cannot be exaggerated'.[62] And again, the relative earliness of this involvement should be stressed – in the years from 1734 to 1780 only the north-east English coalfield saw more steam engines erected.[63]

Once Boulton & Watt's patent ended in 1800 Cornish engineers were free to develop the steam engine further. Arthur Woolf eventually produced the first Cornish high pressure condensing engine in 1812.[64] By the 1810s the quest for higher efficiency and the interest of adventurers in the competition between engineers was institutionalized in *Lean's Engine Reporter*, a news sheet reporting the duties achieved by the larger steam engines. The tables of this publication appear to have been as avidly perused as are early twenty-first-century sports pages. Spurred on by such public interest, the Cornish engine reached the 'highest level of technological accomplishment in its field between, say, 1815 and 1840'.[65] But no one breakthrough invention had reproduced this; rather it was the result of a mass of critical ingenuity flourishing in the hot house of a dynamic industrial region. In this culture a series of 'on-the-job' improvements were rapidly diffused through a geographically small region. It was a culture of 'empirical tinkering', its hero the working engineer rather than the scientific genius.[66] Moreover, this open 'collective invention setting', where consistent increases in productivity were achieved between 1810 and the early 1840s, was the result of a financial context where adventurers bought shares across different mine ventures, encouraging collaboration across the industrial region. This ensured that technical innovations were released quickly into the public sphere, contrasting with industries and regions where patents and secrecy were the norm.[67]

Empirical tinkering encouraged the growth of an engineering industry, the first sign of diversification, although this never matched the high expectations raised in mid-eighteenth-century Cornwall about copper smelting, porcelain works and pewterware manufacture.[68] The nascent Cornish engineering industry soon centred itself on Hayle. In 1758 the Cornish Copper Company, which had begun smelting copper at Camborne in 1754, moved to Hayle Copperhouse.[69] They were joined by what was eventually to become the largest engineering works west of Bristol, when John Harvey moved his forge to Hayle in 1779.[70] Elsewhere in the eighteenth century the other main foundry was Perran Foundry on the Fal, owing its origins to the Fox family in 1791.[71] A larger quay at Hayle in 1790 was only part of the infrastructural improvements of the second half of the eighteenth century; other quays were built at Portreath, St Agnes and at places like Pill, Restronguet and Point in the Fal estuary.[72] By 1820 312 miles of turnpike road also helped to improve the roads although land transport remained slow and costly. Long mule trains carried coal from port to mine and ore back and were an increasingly common sight by the late 1700s. In this respect the breakthrough had to await the 1810s, when a tramway was constructed from Portreath to Poldice mine in Gwennap. At first pulled by horses, it was not long before engineers like Richard Trevithick were puzzling over the best means of applying steam power to this new method of transport.

As well as increasing the demand for mules and horses for transport, mining also boosted the coastal shipping industry. In 1720 around forty ships were engaged in the ore trade up and down the Bristol Channel, between west Cornwall and Bristol/south Wales. By 1824 109 ships were engaged in the trade with Swansea alone.[73] Moreover, these were increasingly likely to be Cornish-owned. In St Ives shipowning brought new wealth to middle-class families, widows, tradesmen and sea captains taking shares in the boats. In addition, the sea had for centuries supplied a livelihood to coastal communities through its harvest of fish. In terms of value, the part-time seine fishing of pilchards dominated. Seine fishing was an inshore fishery that exploited the large shoals of pilchards that appeared annually off Cornwall's coasts. It was also a highly capital-ized industry which since the fifteenth century had been dominated by merchants and shareholders who were not themselves fishermen, employing men to fish and women to salt the fish for a hectic month or two each year. In the middle of the eighteenth century the main seining port was still Mevagissey, although it was about to give way to St Ives, as the centre of gravity of the fishing industry migrated west-wards.[74] The 'poor-man's fishery' at this time was drift fishing. However, even here a first-class boat would in the early nineteenth century have cost around £180, or at least four years' average income. A complete net would be almost as much, around £120 in value. In consequence those fishermen who owned boats and/or nets would be far better off than their neighbours who only owned their labour. The latter were 'more emaciated and sickly looking, whilst they are a less spirited set of men than their more fortunate brethren, possessed of a little capital in the shape of boats or nets'. By the 1840s the long depressed eastern ports of Mevagissey and Looe boasted housing 'of the most straitened and filthy description', in which at Mevagissey cholera wrought deadly havoc in 1848. But in the west, although there was 'much domiciliary wretchedness' at St Ives, in Mounts Bay the 'bulk of the houses are comparatively good'.[75]

In the later eighteenth century drift fishermen turned increasingly to smuggling to supplement, and sometimes more than supplement, their income. John Rowe estimated that this trade, connived at by the local gentry, averaged three times the value of pilchards exported. In the 1770s 469,000 gallons of brandy were smuggled into Cornwall annually, along with 350,000 pounds of tea, employing the equivalent of 300 seamen.[76] When the long years of war after 1793 disrupted the fisheries, particularly seine fishing, whose traditional markets in the Mediterranean were closed, smuggling was boosted, peaking in the first two decades of the nineteenth century. Although the value of goods smuggled into the south-east of England, close to France and yet with a huge London market to supply, dwarfed the Cornish trade, in Cornwall violent clashes between smugglers and customs men were more common.[77] Eventually, after 1825, a combination of falling excise duties, in particular the end of the salt duties, a more efficient customs service and possibly a more conscientious Cornish magistracy all had their effects. Smuggling declined and the arrival of free trade in the 1840s effectively made it redundant. Meanwhile, after the Napoleonic Wars, full-time offshore drift fishing expanded. The estimated 900 drift fishermen of 1785 had almost doubled to 1,600 by 1827, with perhaps 200 to 300 boats.[78] Cornish fishermen were already by the 1810s participating in the herring fishery off Ireland. Over the next half century the balance of the fishing industry gradually swung towards deep sea drifting, which was to enjoy its halcyon years in the 1870s and 1880s, when easier railway communications opened up markets.[79]

But this is to jump ahead. In the eighteenth century Cornwall had secured a role for itself in the 'vanguard of . . . world industrialisation', with its financial structures, management systems and organisation of labour a 'model for latecomers in manufacturing industry' and its engineering industry 'a world leader in steam engineering'. In short, 'Cornwall helped to provide the raw materials, the strategic technology and the organisational experience for that new world to emerge'.[80] By 1800 possibly 20 per cent of employed adults in Cornwall were working directly for the mining industry, the dynamic sector of Cornwall's precocious industrialization. Yet it remained a very compact industrial region before 1810; 'Practically the entire copper mining region was within eight miles of the summit of Carn Brea'.[81] In the 1790s the ten largest copper mines produced over 75 per cent of all the value of ore mined.[82] Consolidation and concentration on this tight industrial region had stimulated a 'critical mass' of capital and an equally critical mass of inventive expertise. At one time in the 1790s, Richard Trevithick was tinkering with his steam engine in Camborne, while the Scottish engineer William Murdoch was inventing gas lighting four miles down the road in Redruth and Thomas Macadam pondering over new road surfaces another ten miles away at Falmouth. A culture of technical ingenuity was attracting some of the most inventive minds in Britain.

The Cornish industrial region, producing great wealth for its gentry and its merchant capitalists, was ringed by the towns of Truro, Falmouth and Penzance, each housing over 3,000 people by 1801. In Truro and Penzance especially, town houses for the gentry sprang up, along with 'fashionable amusements', including theatres, assembly rooms and cock-fighting pits, as well as grammar schools. However, the industrial region was still in the main a rural one. Only Redruth, at the heart of the region, was large enough in 1801 to be termed a town. Camborne at this time, though growing very rapidly, was still an overgrown village of around 700 souls. But in this rural industrial region a cultural revolution had occurred.

Cornwall's cultural revolution: Methodism

The decay of old dissent between 1680 and 1715 meant the Church of England virtually totally dominated Cornwall's religious culture, at least in theory. But underlying formal Anglicanism was a popular disengagement, a set of beliefs that revolved as much around magical charms, superstitions, witchcraft and the supernatural as the formal teachings of the church.[83] Not that these were entirely in opposition to the church. In many ways they flourished in the rites and fabric of churches and churchyards and the church remained at the centre of the calendar of parochial festivals and rituals. Nevertheless, there remained a gap between popular religion and the institution of the church, one deepened by a widening social gulf between the people and the clerical gentry who staffed the eighteenth-century church. While this had already qualified popular support for the Cornish royalist tradition, after the 1740s what support there was dissolved rapidly as the religious culture of the masses took a new direction.

During the 1730s renewed fears of Roman Catholic advances in central Europe had triggered a 'Great Awakening' among Protestants as some communities turned to evangelism. Evangelism involved a reaction against a rationalizing tendency in theology and a turn to open-air preaching, camp meetings and domestic piety. Mass 'revivals' in Wales and in North America in the 1730s were followed by a revival in Lanarkshire in 1742. At the same time, a vigorous transatlantic evangelical network made full use of print culture in spreading the news of these. In 1738 the clergyman John Wesley was converted to evangelism and in 1743 he arrived in Cornwall, preceded by his brother Charles, in response to an invitation from a Presbyterian Society at St Ives that was clearly already connected to the transatlantic network. John Reed, son of hard-working, church-going farming parents in Stithians, later remembered the first arrival of Wesley.

This soon occasioned a great rumour, and induced hundreds and thousands of people to assemble together, in various places, where notice was given for the new preachers to discourse to the people . . . And now there was no small stir among the people respecting this *new Religion*. The kingdom of darkness was attacked and the devil did all in his power to prevent the success of that gospel which directly tended to overthrow it.[84]

The devil in this respect worked through the magistrates of west Cornwall in 1745, when fears of Jacobite unrest and worries about large crowds assembling in a volatile political atmosphere spurred on some of the landed class to try to control John Wesley's preachings. Principal among Wesley's adversaries was the Reverend Walter Borlase. However, Borlase stopped short of imprisoning Wesley. Though hauled before the magistrates, he continued his tour of preaching and only met a large hostile crowd at Falmouth, a place where the presence of seamen added to excitability. At other places the crowds of Methodists often outnumbered their opponents.

Even in 1743, on his first visit, Wesley attracted large crowds, up to a thousand at St Ives, where, according to his diary, there was 'huge approbation'. His final sermon, at Gwennap in late September attracted, according to Wesley himself, 10,000 hearers. While this figure, almost one in ten of the whole Cornish population, was clearly inflated, it is equally clear that the largest crowds turning out to hear him were found in the mining districts. From the beginning Wesley struck a chord there which reverberated throughout the rest of the century. In 1767, when reliable membership statistics first appeared, Cornwall supplied 10 per cent of all British Wesleyans. In 1771, the proportion of the population who were members was over four times the rate in England. In the 1780s the number of new chapels, at least thirty, almost doubled the stock in Cornwall. But the growth of membership did not occur steadily and incrementally. Instead there were major membership surges in 1770–1 and 1781–4, when membership grew rapidly, only to fall off thereafter. This was the result of the emerging role of mass revivalism in Methodist growth. It has been stated that the 'characteristic image of English [Methodism] is *not* that of John Wesley preaching to great crowds in the sunken outdoor ampitheatre at Gwennap in Cornwall' but of him in 'a barn talking to a knot of people'.[85] But, if 'patient persistent Evangelism' was the story of eighteenth- and early nineteenth-century English Methodism, it was patently not the preferred narrative in Cornwall, where Methodist diffusion was more akin to North America than

England. In 1764 we can dimly detect the first mass revival in Wendron, where 'the work of God greatly revived this year in almost every place in the circuit'.[86]

Recurrent mass revivals were the main mechanism of Methodist growth in Cornwall, despite being increasingly frowned upon by Wesleyan leaders. Revivals were times of mass conversion, when people wrestled with their sins before becoming convinced of salvation. During periods of revival the chapels stayed open with around the clock prayer-meetings, business ground to a halt and sense of near hysteria gripped communities. 'The chapel was crowded to suffocation. The steam ran down the walls; the gallery stairs were flooded with it and had not all the windows been opened, every light would have gone out.'[87] Made more impressionable by lack of sleep and food, young people, and most converts during revivals were in their teens and twenties, staggered out of the hot and steaming chapels, their faces 'beaming with joy' and 'united . . . to religious society'.[88] Historians of Cornish Methodism credit these revivals with the function of binding communities together, providing a periodic ritual whereby a new generation of Methodists were publicly welcomed into the fold. John Rule has proposed that Cornish revivalism was the product of Methodism's status as a *Volkskirche* in Cornwall.[89] This repeats the argument of David Luker, who pointed out how Methodism in Cornwall was marked by a relatively high proportion of adherents to members. Around three times as many people attended Methodist chapels as were members.[90] Revivals occurred in this space, regularly drawing many of the younger adherents into active membership and serving as a rite of passage. Mass revivals could therefore only occur when Methodism had reached a certain level of penetration, reached in many places by the 1780s. With weak control from above, either from the Wesleyan Conference itself or local secular leaders, revivals could progress unimpeded, often triggered by some external threat or uncertainty.

By 1785 Methodist societies were present in 31 per cent of Cornish parishes. A generation later, in 1815, this figure was 83 per cent.[91] The years between, and particularly from 1798 to 1814, saw Methodism establish itself as Cornwall's dominant religious institution. These years were bracketed by the two greatest mass revivals of Cornish Methodism's history, those of 1799 and 1814. In each revival membership doubled, although there was much 'backsliding' after each one, particularly that of 1799. Moreover, these two revivals occurred in a more general climate of an outburst of itinerant preaching, as 'cottage evangelicalism' spread rapidly at a time of economic and social disruption and uncertainty caused by war, commercialization of agriculture and industrial change.[92]

What was this phenomenon that had swept across rural industrial Cornwall like a winter's storm, reordering communities in its wake? John Rowe viewed Methodism as a new religion for a new class, 'the individualist assertion of self-made men who gained fortunes by mining enterprise set the tempo of a new age'.[93] John Rule, on the other hand, draws attention to the way in which the simplicity and starkness of Methodist theology, the role it gave to divine will or satanic intervention, meant that 'Methodist superstition matched the indigenous superstition of the common people'.[94] Far from being a new religion finely tuned to thrusting industrialism, Methodism's strength flowed from its ability to penetrate the customary and traditional world view of the people. For David Luker, Methodism owed its pre-eminence in the early nineteenth century not to the fact that it was new or old, but both, a bridge from an older to a newer society.[95] It played a particular role in preserving communal culture by re-emphasizing the place of household and community in the great days of cottage religion before the 1820s. At the same time it 'offered philosophical and ethical support to a rising demand for greater personal autonomy'.[96] After the 1830s the latter role gradually replaced the former and in the process the early history of Methodism was rewritten.

Within this context of a convenient bridge linking an older to a newer society we can identify a number of reasons for the outstanding success of Methodism in Cornwall. First, Wesley's message of justification through faith and the possibility of universal redemption offered the hope of salvation for all, however humble. Even the poor cottager, rarely more than a payday away from destitution and hunger, could be 'saved' and find peace. Although there was no equality on earth, at least Methodism offered the prospects of an equality in heaven. Moreover, the role it gave to divine providence explained the twists and turns of fortune ever present in mining and fishing and provided a powerful draw. Methodism was also institutionally flexible, occupying an ambivalent space until John Wesley's death in 1791 on the margins of the Church of England. Methodism could be seen both as part of that church, its members partaking in its communion, and yet as something new, with its own vibrant organizational life. This ambiguity meant that Methodism could change appearance whenever circumstances demanded. Though proclaimed by Wesley as part of the church and therefore not a dissenting congregation, Methodism's organizational structures had obvious advantages over those of the Church of England. While the latter was anchored to a medieval parochial administration, Methodist preachers could pop up anywhere. The somewhat perplexed comment of the Anglican minister at Gwennap as early as 1744 hinted at the restless fluidity of early Methodism: 'there is a constant succession of teachers, that run up and down the country'.[97] Methodism could go where the people were. It could move 'into some of the yawning gaps of the Anglican parochial system'.[98] During the eighteenth and early nineteenth centuries expanding copper mining produced new villages, places such as Four Lanes, Chacewater, Pendeen, Leedstown, Carharrack, St Day and Lanner. Such villages, distant from their parish church, posed no problems for Methodists who held their class meetings and societies in them, and then soon built their first small chapels. Methodist itinerants were supplemented by scores of lay preachers, local men, and at first women, who could interpret the gospel in the dialect and idiom of the common people. These lay preachers were fundamental in the west of Cornwall to the creation of an indigenous Methodism, rough and ready but grounded in popular revivalism and in the spiritual world of local communities.[99]

While the internal organization of Methodism and its message were important features of its eighteenth-century growth, its pastoral machinery could only operate at full capacity when other external factors were present. These included the religious environment - the competition Methodists faced - and the secular environment, which provided both opposition and opportunities for eighteenth-century Methodism. The weakness of the Church of England has often been cited as a reason for the success of Methodism in Cornwall – 'large parishes, remote churches, pluralism and absentee clergy had produced a virtually heathen population in Cornwall'.[100] The first two of these did, it is true, make it difficult for the Church to respond to changing population patterns. Yet the indolence and corruption of the eighteenth-century Church of England, and the picture of heavy-drinking, worldly clergymen, more interested in hunting foxes than caring for souls, has been overinfluenced by the nonconformist histories of the nineteenth century. Work on eighteenth-century

Anglicanism in other parts of Britain has restored to it a degree of dynamism hitherto denied. It must be remembered, after all, that some of John Wesley's earliest supporters were evangelical clergymen, such as George Thompson of St Gennys, John Bennet of Tresmeer and John Torney of Week St Mary.[101] More important than the state of the Church of England was the lack of opposition from old dissent. Its weakness meant that Methodism could establish an effective monopoly of revivalist enthusiasm. The contrast with Wales is striking. There, though there was an earlier Methodist 'awakening', Methodism suffered personal and doctrinal disputes from the 1750s.[102] There was then a haemorrhage of members to the dissenting churches – Independents and Baptists – and it was not until after the 1780s that Welsh Calvinist Methodism, separated from Wesleyan Methodism and with its distinctively Welsh ethos, mounted an effective challenge to old dissent.

The opposition of the Cornish magistracy to Wesley in 1745 was relatively short-lived and feeble and suggests that secular opposition in Cornwall was limited. The relatively sparse presence of great gentry and their indirect hold over labouring communities gave them little influence over the religious culture of the latter, even had they been willing to exert it. Methodist dissemination was ineffectively constrained from above and prospered in an industrial society where deference was lacking.[103] In 1826 it was written from Hayle: 'There is not so much deference paid to the higher ranks. Aforetime no person left the church after the service was over until the parson had walked out and he received the obeisances of the congregation as he went down the aisle. Now the congregation leave at once without waiting for the parson'.[104] After the 1780s, as Methodism moved from a status of 'alternative religious community' to 'community religion', indigenous Methodism was strongest in such independent, industrial places. There, in this critical period from the 1780s to the 1820s, it buttressed traditional ways of life, providing inner discipline and a sense of spiritual immediacy that allowed families and communities to resist external pressures.[105] In its positioning as the undisputed Cornish version of cottage religion, Methodism also gave a new role to women, at least before the 1810s, in the work of Methodist dissemination. In 1771, Ann Gilbert was

> going one day to preaching in the adjoining village, the preacher happened not to come; I therefore gave out a hymn and went to prayer, according to my usual custom; I then told the people they need not be disappointed, for

the Lord was present to bless them . . . All the people were melted into tears, and many were convinced of sin . . . I endeavoured to the utmost of my power to be diligent in every duty, both public and private, especially meeting my classes, visiting the sick, and attending the prayer meetings.[106]

The active role given to women like Ann Gilbert, who was, moreover, partially sighted, and the emphasis on domestic piety and the cottage made Methodism particularly attractive to women in the eighteenth century. It is noticeable how women made up a majority of members in most of the Methodist societies of 1767. And this was almost invariably the case in mining parishes.[107]

By 1801 there was a larger proportion of Methodist members in relation to population in Cornwall than in any English county. In 1823 only the Isle of Man showed a larger proportionate Methodist membership.[108] In 1829, an Anglican clergyman, Richard Tyacke of Sithney, gloomily wrote in his diary that 'the Church was but thinly attended the rain pattered down so thick and fast, though at evening I observed the roads that led to the Methodists' chapel were thronged in every direction'.[109] Tyacke explained this popularity partly by the fact that lay preachers were 'generally selected from people from their own sphere in life' and partly because of the possibilities for the young to meet members of the opposite sex at the service. But this itself indicates how far Methodism had become the dominant community religion in Sithney by the late 1820s. In 1833 a vicar of a Cornish parish could lament that 'we have lost the people. The religion of the mass is become Wesleyan Methodism.'[110] Methodism was particularly strong in the west, where it had grown earliest and fastest and had more of a 'primitive' indigenous flavour, more independent and less constrained by top–down Connexional organization.[111] In the west the early emergence of popular Methodism established its revivalist and independent character at a time when the organization of Methodism, preceding John Wesley's death, was still fluid and evolving. The result was a Methodism in many ways at odds with formal Methodism, a 'tradition' that continued well into the nineteenth century and one that made local Methodism distinctively 'Cornish'. In contrast, in the agricultural east of Cornwall, Methodism was established later and in consequence direction from the top and circuit organization wielded more influence over societies and chapel congregations at the bottom.

Conclusion

The high point of the Cornish royalist tradition in the late seventeenth century had been a low point for Cornish standards of living,
falling rapidly behind places in southern England. Attached more
securely to English trading networks in the Tudor period, the Cornish
economy suffered growing competition from other regions in the
century after 1600. At first, mining expansion, by stimulating population growth, made things worse. Furthermore, economic changes
impacted in different ways across Cornwall. Impoverishment and
strains on resources were felt most in the west. There, a popular allegiance to the Cornish royalist tradition, kept alive by the stannaries,
was weakened by a growing social and economic gap between
commons and gentry.[112] By the 1730s and 1740s widespread indifference to the politico-religious gentry identity of Tory Cornwall
allowed John Wesley's message to implant itself in communities that
were just beginning to enjoy the benefits of the growth of copper
mining that heralded Cornwall's early industrial revolution.

By 1815 this had produced a society that was an amalgam of old
and new. It was, moreover, one that was sharply divided internally.
Divisions were social, between the landed gentry and merchants
enriched by the windfall profits of eighteenth-century copper mining
and the growing mass of labouring families dependent mainly,
though not totally, on wages. And they were geographical, between
the intense, dynamic industrial region between Truro and Penzance
and the agricultural districts of mid and east Cornwall. Methodism
added a religious dimension to these divides, possessing a different,
more 'indigenous' character in the west. Methodism was also a bridge
from the old to the new, providing a new social identity for labouring
communities at a time of exceptional economic and social volatility
from the 1760s to the 1810s. But this was a religious identity rather
than an ethnic one. The latter, with the apparent expiration of the
Cornish language, appeared to have suffered a fatal blow. From a
vantage point at the beginning of the new, nineteenth century, an
observer could be forgiven if they had assumed Cornwall's future was
to lose its former distinctiveness. Social changes were sweeping away
many older customs, industrialization was establishing new traditions
and deepening financial links with other parts of Britain and old
institutions such as the Stannaries were in decay. Cornwall, like many
other parts of the islands, was caught up in the British nationalism

that accompanied the long struggles against revolutionary and then Napoleonic France. And yet, just at the time when many might have concluded that Cornwall's future lay in looking eastwards, the seeds of a new identity were germinating. This was to blend the self-confidence generated by Cornwall's industrialization with rediscovered memories of Cornwall's past to construct a distinct regional identity in the early nineteenth century. Partly based on the economic and cultural distinctiveness of Cornwall's early industrialization, the restored Cornish popular identity outlived that society and provided the foundations for what in the twentieth century became viewed by some as the classic 'Cornish' identity. The next chapter looks at the emergence of these new representations of Cornwall.

Notes

[1] Mark Stoyle, *West Britons: Cornish Identities and the Early Modern British State* (2002), p. 157.

[2] Ibid., p. 166.

[3] Jonathan Barry, 'The seventeenth and eighteenth centuries', in Nicholas Orme (ed.), *Unity and Variety: A History of the Church in Devon and Cornwall* (1991), pp. 81–108.

[4] Calculated from 'Religion and the spread of nonconformity before 1800', in Roger Kain and William Ravenhill (eds), *The Historical Atlas of South West England* (1999), p. 224.

[5] Calculated from Anne Whiteman (ed.), *The Compton Census of 1676: A Critical Edition* (1986).

[6] William Gibson (ed.), *Religion and Society in England and Wales, 1689–1800* (1998), pp. 98–9.

[7] Barry, 'Seventeenth and eighteenth centuries', pp. 88 and 107.

[8] Stoyle, *West Britons*, p. 172.

[9] Ibid., p. 174.

[10] Frank O'Gorman, *The Long Eighteenth Century: British Political and Social History 1688–1832* (1997), p. 67.

[11] Henry Jenner, 'An incident in Cornwall in 1715', *Journal of the Royal Institution of Cornwall*, 20 (1921), 552–8.

[12] T. H. Murrin, 'Under the badge of a white eagle: the Godolphins', *Old Cornwall*, 8 (1977), 380–7 and 445–50.

[13] H. T. Dickinson, 'Goldophin, Sidney, 1st Earl Godolphin', in David Loades (ed.), *Reader's Guide to British History*, pp. 578–9.

[14] O'Gorman, *Long Eighteenth Century*, p. 84.

[15] Eveline Cruikshanks, 'The Convocation of the Stannaries of Cornwall: the Parliament of Tinners 1703–1752', *Parliaments, Estates and Representation*, 6 (1986), pp. 59–67.

[16] John Angarrack, *Our Future is History: Identity, Law and the Cornish Question* (2002), pp. 132–7.

[17] John Rowe, *Cornwall in the Age of the Industrial Revolution* (1953), pp. 45–6.

[18] Mark Overton, Jane Whittle, Darron Dean and Andrew Hann, *Production and Consumption in English Households, 1600–1750* (2004).

[19] Ibid., p. 140.

[20] Ibid., p. 47.

[21] Ibid., p. 176.

[22] Ibid., p. 177.

[23] G. R. Lewis, *The Stannaries* (1965), pp. 255–6.

[24] Overton et al., *Production and Consumption*, p. 39.

[25] Roger Burt, 'The international diffusion of technology in the early modern period: the case of the British non-ferrous mining industry', *Economic History Review*, 44 (1991), 249–71; Allen Buckley, *The Cornish Mining Industry: A Brief History* (1992).

[26] Burt, 'International diffusion'.

[27] James Whetter, *Cornwall in the 17th Century: An economic history of Kernow* (1974), p. 142: Gill Burke, 'The Cornish miner and Cornish mining industry 1870–1921', Ph.D. thesis, University of London (1981), p. 37.

[28] Roger Burt, 'The transformation of the non-ferrous metals industries in the seventeenth and eighteenth centuries', *Economic History Review*, 48 (1995), 23–45.

[29] G. A. Clay, *Economic Expansion and Social Change: England 1500–1700*, (1984), p. 59.

[30] Overton et al., *Production and Consumption*, p. 140.

[31] Jonathan Barry, 'Population distribution and growth in the early modern period', in Roger Kain and William Ravenhill (eds), *The Historical Atlas of South West England* (1999), pp. 110–17.

[32] David Cullum, 'Society and economy in west Cornwall, c1588–1750', Ph.D. thesis, University of Exeter (1993), p. 288.

[33] Ibid., p. 295.

[34] For William Scawen see Mark Stoyle, *West Britons*, pp. 134–56, and Matthew Spriggs, 'William Scawen (1600–1689) – a neglected Cornish patriot and father of the Cornish language revival', in Philip Payton (ed.), *Cornish Studies Thirteen* (2005), pp. 98–125.

[35] Oliver Padel, *The Cornish Writings of the Boson Family* (1975).

[36] James Rosenheim, *The Emergence of a Ruling Order: English Landed Society, 1650–1750* (1998), p. 76.

[37] Veronica Chesher, 'Some Cornish landowners 1690–1760: a social and economic study', B.Litt. thesis, Oxford University (1957), p. 214.

[38] Ibid., p. 212.

[39] O'Gorman, *Long Eighteenth Century*, p. 104.

[40] Burt, 'Transformation'.

[41] In Richard Carew, *Survey of Cornwall* (1811), p. 21.

[42] William Borlase, *Natural History of Cornwall* (1758), p. 206.

[43] Rowe, *Industrial Revolution*, p. 40.

[44] Buckley, *Cornish Mining Industry*, p. 16.

[45] Sidney Pollard, *Peaceful Conquest: The Industrialisation of Europe 1760–1970* (1981), p. 14.

[46] Philip Payton, *The Making of Modern Cornwall* (1992), pp. 79–80.

[47] Derek Giles, 'Did the cost book company contribute to the efficient organisation of mining in Cornwall in the eighteenth and nineteenth centuries, or was it a prime cause of its decline?', unpublished paper (no date).

[48] Pollard, *Peaceful Conquest*, p. 14.

[49] John Rule, *The Vital century: England's Developing Economy, 1714–1815* (1992), p. 178.

[50] Borlase, *Natural History*, p. 206.

[51] That this challenge was not a hopeless one is demonstrated by Newell's conclusion (Edmund Newell, 'The British copper ore market in the nineteenth century, with particular reference to Cornwall and Swansea' D.Phil., Oxford University (1988)) that ore could be smelted in Cornwall at a healthy profit, 'despite the costs of transporting coal'.

[52] Buckley, *Cornish Mining Industry*, p. 24.

[53] Rowe, *Industrial Revolution*, p. 121.

[54] Edmund Vale, *The Harveys of Hayle: Engine-Builders, Shipwrights and Merchants of Cornwall* (1966), p. 51.

[55] Calculated from Pat Hudson, *The Industrial Revolution* (1992), p. 43, and Robert Hunt, *British Mining: A Treatise on the History, Discovery, Practical Development and Future Prospects of Metalliferous Mines in the UK* (1887), p. 887.

[56] John Rule, 'The labouring miner in Cornwall c1740–1870', Ph.D. thesis, Warwick University (1971), pp. 64–5.

[57] Carew, *Survey*, p. 35.

[58] Rule, 'Labouring miner', p. 81.

[59] Ibid., p. 79.

[60] Rowe, *Industrial Revolution*, p. 7.

[61] Ibid., p. 51.

[62] Nick von Tunzelmann, *Steam Power and British Industrialisation to 1860* (1978), p. 22.

[63] John Kanefsky and John Robey, 'Steam engines in 18th century Britain', *Technology and Culture*, 21 (1980), 162–86.

[64] Nick von Tunzelmann, 'Technological diffusion during the Industrial Revolution: the case of the Cornish pumping engine', in R. M. Hartwell (ed.), *The Industrial Revolution* (1970), pp. 77–98.

[65] Ibid., p. 263.

[66] For the concept of empirical tinkerers, see Joel Mokyr, 'Technological change, 1700–1830', in Roderick Floud and Donald McCloskey (eds), *The Economic History of Britain since 1700*, vol. 1, *1700–1860* (1994), p. 35.

[67] Alessandro Nuvolari, 'Collective invention during the British industrial revolution: the case of the Cornish pumping engine', *Cambridge Journal of Economics*, 28 (2004), 347–63.

[68] Rowe, *Industrial Revolution*, p. 49.

[69] Vale, *Harveys of Hayle, pp.* 37 and 41.

[70] Ibid., p. 11.

[71] Ibid., p. 51.

[72] Peter Stanier, 'Lost mining ports of the south Cornish coast', *Industrial Archaeology Review*, 3 (1978), 1–16.

[73] Peter Stanier, 'The copper ore trade of south west England in the nineteenth century', *Journal of Transport History*, ns 5 (1979), 18–35.

[74] Rowe, *Industrial Revolution*, pp. 271–2.

[75] P. E. Razell and R. W. Wainwright (eds), *The Victorian Working Class: Selections of Letters to the* Morning Chronicle (1973), p. 19.

[76] Rowe, *Industrial Revolution*, pp. 275–6.

[77] Ibid., pp. 286–7.

[78] Ibid., pp. 291 and 299.

[79] John Rule, 'The south western deep-sea fisheries and their markets in the nineteenth century', *Southern History*, 22/23 (2000/1), 168–88.

[80] Roger Burt, 'History of metalliferous mining', in G. B. Selwood et al. (eds), *The Geology of Cornwall* (1998), p. 215.

[81] Rowe, *Industrial Revolution*, p. 66.

[82] 'Report from the select committee adopted to enquire into the state of the copper

mines and copper trade of the Kingdom', *British Parliamentary Papers* (1799), pp. 152–8.

[83] Owen Davies, 'Methodism, the clergy, and the popular belief in witchcraft and magic', *History*, 266 (1997), 252–65.

[84] Thomas Kelk, 'The life and death of Mr John Reed', *Methodist Magazine*, 27 (1804), 193–200.

[85] John Walsh, '"Methodism" and the origins of English-speaking evangelicalism', in Mark Noll et al. (eds), *Evangelicalism: Comparative Studies of Popular Protestantism in North America, the British Isles, and Beyond, 1700–1900* (1994), pp. 33–4.

[86] Kelk, 'Life and death'.

[87] Cited in John Rule, 'Explaining revivalism: the case of Cornish Methodism', *Southern History*, 20/21 (1998–9), 168–88.

[88] William Carvosso, *A Memoir* (1850), pp. 51–2.

[89] Rule, 'Explaining revivalism'.

[90] David Luker, 'Revivalism in theory and practice: the case of Cornish Methodism', *Journal of Ecclesiastical History*, 37 (1986), 603–19.

[91] David Luker, 'Cornish Methodism, revivalism and popular belief, c.1780–1870', D.Phil. thesis, Oxford University (1987), p. 82.

[92] Ibid.

[93] Rowe, *Industrial Revolution*, p. 31.

[94] John Rule, 'Methodism, popular beliefs and village culture in Cornwall, 1800–50', in Robert Storch (ed.), *Popular Culture in Nineteenth Century England* (1982), pp. 48–70.

[95] Luker, 'Cornish Methodism'.

[96] Ibid., p. 396.

[97] Cited in H. Miles Brown, *Episcopal Visitation Queries and Methodism* (1962), p. 7.

[98] Walsh, 'Methodism', p. 30.

[99] Luker, 'Cornish Methodism'.

[100] John Gay, *The Geography of Religion in England* (1971), p. 160.

[101] Rowe, *Industrial Revolution* (1993), p. 67. 12.

[102] Geraint Jenkins, *The Foundations of Modern Wales; Wales 1642–1780* (1987), p. 365.

[103] Luker, 'Cornish Methodism', p. 92.

[104] Cedric Appleby, 'Wesleyan Methodism in Hayle – 1826', *Journal of the Cornish Methodist Historical Association*, 7 (1985), 13–18.

[105] Luker, 'Cornish Methodism', p. 144.

[106] Joseph Taylor, 'The experience of Mrs Ann Gilbert, of Gwinear, Cornwall', *Methodist Magazine*, 18 (1795), 42–6.

[107] 'Book of Methodist Societies in Cornwall West circuit, June and July 1767', Cornwall Record Office AD 350.

[108] *Methodist Magazine*, 3 (1824), 378–9.

[109] Diary of Richard Tyacke of Antron, Cornwall Record Office AD 715.

[110] Cited in Rule, 'Labouring miner', pp. 262–3.

[111] Luker, 'Cornish Methodism', p. 281.

[112] E. P. Thompson, *Customs in Common* (1991), p. 5.

5

Reformed Cornwall: from material to mythical difference, 1810s–1860s

By the end of the Napoleonic Wars in 1815 two core elements of the quintessentially Cornish landscape were in place. Small Methodist chapels were scattered, apparently randomly, across Cornwall after the 1760s and had exploded in number as a result of the great revivals of 1799 and 1814. This grid of chapels was, by the 1800s, superimposed on an emerging landscape of smoking engine houses and encroaching mine burrows. Engine houses had begun to appear slightly earlier and multiplied as each upturn in the economic cycle triggered more mining ventures. But it was not just the physical landscape that was transformed by industrialization between the 1730s and the 1810s. Cornwall's moral landscape had also, according to contemporaries, undergone a revolution. By the 1840s the beneficial effect of Methodism in reforming the manners of the miners of Cornwall was being regularly remarked upon. They were described as 'leading habitually excellent and religious lives ... the brightest picture we have met with, of the condition of any considerable body of the labouring class'.[1] This matched local claims in the nineteenth century that Methodism had transformed behaviour.

But to ascribe the decline of old sports such as hurling, wrestling, bull-baiting and cock-fighting wholesale to Methodism was to exaggerate its moral effect. For example, hurling was condemned by Daniel Defoe as early as the 1720s as a game fit only for barbarians and at least one version of the game, pitching the men of one parish against their neighbours and ranging over several miles of open country, was virtually extinct by the 1790s. In 1744 Charles Wesley claimed that Gwennap miners had given up wrestling, but he was a little premature in this claim. A century afterwards the sport was still attracting large crowds, estimated in 1843 as up to 4,000 at a competition at Helston. Even Gwennap wrestlers were still around and winning prizes at the St Austell wrestling a year later.[2] Wrestling as a popular spectator sport in Cornwall had survived a hundred years of Methodist censure and recurrent attacks on it from the pulpit were a sign of its vitality and not its demise. Methodism therefore played a part in the reformation of popular culture but it was not the agent of change that was later claimed. Similar changes occurred in regions where Methodism was much weaker and a number of general factors were involved, not the least of which was the reduction of holidays and leisure time and a tightening of labour discipline.

Nonetheless, although Cornwall shared in some modernizing tendencies common to all the industrializing areas of Britain, a unique social compromise heightened differences between Cornwall and other regions. This chapter traces the outlines of a society that combined relatively independent labouring communities with weak social control from above. Although industrializing Cornwall looked on the surface more 'English', locked into wider economic processes, at a deeper level it was freer of metropolitan influence in the early nineteenth century than it had been at any time since the Reformation. A Cornwall-wide industrially oriented regional identity was flourishing by the 1840s, but then social changes started to unravel the material underpinnings of Cornish 'difference', leading to renewed convergence with the English core and more landward influence.

A proto-industrial society of dispersed paternalism

Cornwall's early industrialization reproduced a small-scale landscape, with the cottages of the miners distributed among the small fields, lanes and footpaths filling the space between mines and settlements. This domestic scale was reinforced by a continuing role for the family unit even into the deep copper mining era of the eighteenth century. Father inducted son into the skills of underground working (usually from around 10 to 12 years old) and other younger sons and daughters worked at the surface breaking up the ores. This, together with a less than total dependence on wages for meeting family needs, has led Roger Burt to characterize Cornish mining as proto-industrial, retaining certain older forms, and a stage before full industrialization.[3] His notion is a useful one, especially when widened to include the social terrain. Proto-industries were a product of merchant capitalism, where capitalists – merchants and gentry – had a looser, more indirect control over their labourers than classic factory- and workshop-based industrial capitalism, where owners were more directly involved in day-to-day oversight. Merchant capi-

talism provided a space in which 'independent' community life flourished, in the process creating new 'traditions'.[4] Thus, the 'tribute'
form of wage payment harked back to the days of the free tinner,
while miners' communities grew up outside the direct control of
either landlords, employers or the urban professional classes, aiding
the development of a Methodist religious culture.

By the 1790s the respectable classes were looking on such communities with some trepidation. In 1796 three Cornish JPs wrote to the
Home Secretary, concerned that 'no magistrate can attend [mining
villages] in person . . . for the Civil Power to venture amongst them,
unattended by the Military, would . . . be unsafe, dangerous and thoroughly ineffectual'.[5] Of course, this was a time when respectable
nerves were thoroughly jangled by events in France. What made
mining communities dangerous was their crowd culture. In 1842 the
miners' habit of meeting together on a Saturday, the 'crowds of idle
youths', the 'congregating in large numbers on market days' and the
tendency to 'congregate in large masses, without efficient discipline'
were all noted with concern.[6] Crowds carried the potential for
trouble. And Cornish miners had become notorious during the eighteenth century for their quickness to engage in food 'riots' when prices
of grain, particularly barley, the Cornish staple, rose too high. Rule
notes widespread food rioting in Cornwall on fifteen occasions
between 1729 and 1847.[7] Two earlier incidents push the origins of this
behaviour back into the seventeenth century. In 1690 tinners boarded
a ship at Falmouth to remove salt, a necessity for curing pilchards
and pork, and in 1700 a group of tinners attacked a corn store in
Truro.[8] The term 'riot' is however inappropriate, as these events
contained evidence of considerable discipline on the part of the
crowd. Grain was often paid for, rather than taken, but at a 'fair price'
imposed by the crowd. Thus the 'quarrymen at Port Isaac [in 1795]
seized barley warehoused for export, paying the reasonably high price
of 11s a bushel'. For E. P. Thompson this was evidence of a 'rebellious traditional culture', one that looked to custom and tradition – a
'moral economy' – rather than to the market economy.[9] Cornish
labouring communities at the end of the eighteenth century were
acting in ways reminiscent of those of the early sixteenth century,
even though the context of their conservative rebelliousness had radically altered.

Collateral aids

The strong sense of moral economy in Cornish labouring communities well into the nineteenth century, a generation later than in other
industrial regions, rested on labouring communities' access to various
forms of 'collateral aids'. These crystallized pre-capitalist, non-
market forms of commodity production and sheltered families in
industrial Cornwall from the full brunt of sudden price changes,
which could have an immediate effect on earnings and standards of
living. The classic collateral aid was a smallholding. During the eighteenth century the practice grew up on the Basset estate in Illogan of
granting miners a three-life lease on marginal land.[10] Such leases
could guarantee security of tenure for the lifetime of a miner, his wife
and one of his children. In the St Agnes district Stephen Davey, a
Redruth merchant and magistrate, and his brother William continued
this form of leasehold at least until the early 1840s. Smallholdings,
usually under five acres, contributed up to half the cash value of an
average family's food budget.[11] In 1841 it was estimated that just
under a quarter of miners in Redruth, St Just and St Blazey had
access to some land over and above any gardens attached to their
cottages, and in other parishes the proportion was much higher –
almost a half in St Agnes, over half in parts of Wendron.[12]

For those mining families with no smallholding, an alternative
collateral aid was the potato allotment, 'a common and growing'
practice in 1841.[13] Large-scale growth in potato cultivation has been
dated to the 1790s and potatoes, in Cornwall as well as Ireland, fed
the rapidly expanding population.[14] Farmers would allot some land
to the miner, who would plant and draw the crop, while the farmer
prepared the land and carted the manure provided by the miner. No
money changed hands, the farmer gaining improved land for the next
grain crop, while mining families could raise enough potatoes to feed
a pig or two.[15] Widespread access to common land for cutting turf or
furze for fuel was another element in this system. Although small-
holdings were fewer, collateral aids were both most concentrated and
most diverse in the far west by 1840. In St Just potato allotments were
supplemented by joint ownership of dairy cows and shares in fishing
boats, all of which diversified sources of income for a labouring
family. Collateral aids in the rural mining districts of Cornwall, and
as many as three-quarters of all miners still lived outside the towns as
late as 1851, was part of a wider 'economy of makeshifts'. This

involved income from paid labour as well as such things as charity, savings, customary rights, help from neighbours and kin, together with less than generous poor law provision and has been identified in the pastoral regions of northern England as well as in the south-west and Cornwall.[16] It contrasted with the far greater dependence on the poor law and the lack of options open to the poor in the more arable regions of southern and eastern England.

Work on the smallholding or potato allotment or excursions to collect furze involved women as well as men and produced a distinct set of gender relations. The expansion of copper mining had led to the employment of young unmarried women at the surface works. As early as 1736 William Borlase, the Cornish antiquary and naturalist, was complaining of the difficulties of obtaining servants as young women preferred to work at the copper mines.[17] The spell of economic independence between childhood and marriage gave women in the mining districts a taste for economic and social independence symbolized by conspicuous spending on clothes and, it is argued, a lack of deference towards men.[18] Relatively independent women lived within relatively independent communities where notions of a moral economy were embedded. Furthermore, 'independence' was not confined solely to mining villages. At Mousehole in 1766, Thomas Carlyon of Truro, owner of fish cellars, bemoaned the 'ungrateful behaviour of the masons in leaving the work [on Mousehole quay] . . . I could never discover any great sense of gratitude or honesty amongst the lower class of people'. Two years later Carlyon was at Newlyn trying to abolish a custom whereby the cellar women, engaged in curing pilchards, had a right to the dregs of the catch. But five months afterwards the women were still holding out and Carlyon was forced to consider bringing in women from elsewhere to 'break the back of all those wicked combinations'.[19]

Communities like these clearly cherished their customary rights. Yet ties of paternalism and dependence still operated. Thomas Kevill, steward of the Basset farm at Tehidy, was reported as acting 'as an imperious Nabob within the district' of Camborne–Redruth.[20] And the writer of these words, the local Lanhydrock steward, William Jenkin, was quick to dispense charity to poor miners on his estate's land, in 1799 'to drop a small matter into the hands of poor distressed families which lie within the neighbourhood of Tincroft Mine as their distress happens to come to my knowledge'.[21] Whatever was happening in other parts of Britain the Cornish gentry still recognized that paternalism and patronage also involved obligations and responsibilities. The webs of deference and paternalism were there; but they were fitful and fragile, mediated indirectly through land stewards and mine captains. In consequence they stopped short of controlling the 'character of independence – something American – [of] this population'.[22]

The Cornish identity

Such a society, turbulent but conservative, with its own customs and religious culture, was diverging from other places by the 1790s. Industrialization occurred in regions specializing in different products; copper in Cornwall, cotton in Lancashire, metalware in the west Midlands, coal in Northumberland and Durham. It had produced a series of dynamic growth poles, which acted as lightning rods for the emergence of a number of culturally distinct, occupationally specific regions in the early throes of industrialization.[23] Cornwall had, apparently, lost the distinction of a spoken Celtic language by 1800, but it had gained a unique culture. David Luker has gone so far as to argue that this was 'a buttress to Cornish "nationalism" in the face of encroaching forces and influences from "up-country" England'.[24] However, we need to qualify this description.

First, it was a private identity, revolving around a desire for close fellowship, the family and the home and based on loyalty to small-scale moral codes which looked to local dynasties for leadership.[25] Second, such dispersed local identities were, for the most part, inarticulate, with a rich, dense community culture but few public narratives. The narrative that had emerged by 1815 was religious rather than 'nationalist'. The great revivals of 1799 and 1814 transformed Methodism into the religion of the people and ensured that it took on a public role as the identity of whole communities. From the 1810s a repeated narrative of early persecution, a time when these communities went though a baptism of fire, suffering 'the most fierce and determined opposition', became the norm. But this greatly exaggerated the actual opposition of 1745.[26] Furthermore, this religious identity was located within a 'county' narrative. It did not look back to some historical golden age, as did some Scottish evangelists who made explicit allusion to the Covenanters of the seventeenth century. There was nothing similar in Cornwall. Instead, when Cornwall's 'British' past was invoked, it was part of the Cornish royalist (and

Tory) tradition, which was by no means entirely dead and buried. At a meeting in 1819 the inhabitants of Truro resolved that 'as true Britons and, especially as the "faithful Cornish", we are determined "One and All", to support the just prerogative of the Crown, and the authority of the Government, standing firm in defence of the throne and of the altar'.[27]

Finally and critically, dispersed paternalism was not Cornwall-wide. Before the 1810s it was centred on the mining districts of Cornwall west of Truro. Similar places could be found east of Truro, for example in the fishing villages of Mevagissey and Gorran Haven or around the tin mine of Polgooth, west of St Austell, or the slate quarries of Delabole and St Teath. But its heartland was geographically restricted to the industrial region that had emerged out of the ashes of the Cornish-speaking culture that had held sway in the west. Ethnic distinctions had given way to more subtle occupational and religious differences that marked off Cornwall, especially the west, from other regions. But it was not long before the particularities of past and present were soldered together and, moreover, extended to the whole territory of Cornwall.

Merchants, landed gentry and 'county' institutions

With a new industrial society came a new social class – the merchant bourgeoisie. Such families had risen by financing the growth of copper mining in the eighteenth century and tended to be found in or near the towns of Truro, Falmouth and Penzance, as well as at Redruth and Gwennap. Amongst the three most prominent were the Williamses, Bolithos and Foxes. They followed different paths to riches. The Williamses were tinners in Stithians in the seventeenth century, but had moved to Gwennap by the early 1700s, where they became heavily involved in the excavation of the Great County Adit, an ambitious series of drainage tunnels linking mining setts across Gwennap, Redruth and Illogan. By 1800 the family 'controlled or managed over a quarter of the copper mines in Cornwall.[28] John Williams's grandson, also John (1753–1841), established the real family fortune, entering in 1822 into a partnership which invested in copper smelting in Swansea and opened places of business in London, Liverpool, Manchester and Birmingham. By 1840 the company's capital was £400,000 and John Michael Williams, who left

£1.6 million in his will in 1880, was described as 'probably the most wealthy man in Cornwall'.[29]

As the Williamses diversified from mining into smelting, banking and other trading, their counterparts in the west, the Bolithos, moved in the opposite direction. Some time before 1740 this family, tanners and merchants of Penryn, moved to Madron, near Penzance. Thomas Bolitho (1765–1858) leased lime pits and in 1805 joined in a partnership which owned the tin-smelting works at Chyandour. Their next significant move was into banking, establishing the Mounts Bay Commercial Bank in 1807 and going into partnership in the East Cornwall Bank at Liskeard. From this base they invested heavily in tin mines and by the 1840s dominated tin mining. By 1885 the family was wealthy enough to be described as the 'merchant princes of Cornwall'.[30] The third success story of the Cornish industrial revolution was the Fox family. Moving west from Fowey to Falmouth somewhere in the early eighteenth century the Foxes, a tight-knit Quaker family, made money from the pilchard and timber trades and become major investors in mining by the 1790s as well as leading a consortium that built the Perran Foundry. They were the principal backers of the restarting of Dolcoath mine at Camborne in 1799 and provided the financial muscle behind Cornwall's first railway, from Portreath to Gwennap, in the 1800s.[31]

Such families were only the most prominent of a growing group, which included the Daveys of Redruth, Daniells of Truro, Harveys of Gwennap and Fosters of Lostwithiel. They made up a dynamic merchant class, tightly knit through trading links and, in the early 1800s, increasingly by marriage. It was this class that was important in stabilizing the mining economy after 1815, their interlocking portfolios helping to dampen the volatility of the war years.[32] Yet, ultimately, they did not challenge the gentry; instead they joined them as soon as was decently possible. Within three generations at the most, merchant families had purchased their landed estate. In 1866 Thomas Simon Bolitho bought Trengwainton, just outside Penzance, built by Sir Rose Price in 1814 from the profits of slavery and Jamaican sugar plantations. The Foxes spread across the pleasant south-facing countryside north of the Helford, buying or building Trebah, Penjerrick and Glendorgan and sowing the seeds, literally, of Cornwall's early twenty-first-century garden tourism. Michael Williams (1785–1858) also made the symbolic move away from the Gwennap district in 1854 when he bought Caerhays, the building of which had almost bankrupted its former owners, the Trevanions.

The power of the new merchant bourgeoisie was exercised mainly in the economic sphere. It was the landed gentry's representation of Cornwall that still held sway, of a county still tinged with the Cornish royalist tradition. The end of the eighteenth century, years when a distinct working-class customary culture had been created, also saw the emergence of gentry-led institutions through which this 'county' identity was reproduced. These came in three waves. In 1792 the Cornwall Library and a Cornwall Agricultural Society were formed.[33] In the 1810s a second wave of institutions appeared, by this time including the new merchant bourgeoisie. The Cornwall Geological Society was formed at Penzance in 1814 and the Cornish Philosophical Institution, later to become the Royal Institution of Cornwall (RIC) at Truro in 1818. These were two of the three 'county' literary institutions that dominated nineteenth-century Cornwall's intellectual life. In 1833 the third, the Royal Cornwall Polytechnic Society, was born at Falmouth, closely following the Cornwall Horticultural Society of 1832,[34] both of these being of a more practical bent than the earlier literary societies. In the midst of this burst of institution-building a Cornish press appeared. In 1800 the *Cornwall Gazette* began to publish. This paper, espousing Tory politics, was followed in 1810 by the *West Briton*, which adopted a reforming agenda explicitly in opposition to the *Gazette*. The location of the two 'county' newspapers at Truro staked an early claim for that town to be considered Cornwall's 'capital', although such pretensions would be vigorously challenged throughout the century. Moreover, the ubiquitous epithet 'Royal' sought and attained by the majority of these institutions, indicate both the persistence of the royalist tradition and a search for status that led to an active courting of the landed classes. This contrasted with the literary societies of the northern English industrial cities, where the professional and business middle classes more clearly dominated.[35]

Cornwall as industrial civilization

If the eighteenth-century merchant bourgeoisie ultimately preferred to join the landed class rather than challenge it, industrialization threw up another group which looked potentially more capable of shaking the old order. In 1791 fifty-one leading Cornish lay Methodists converged on Redruth, in the heart of the mining district, to discuss the administration of affairs after the death of John Wesley. There, they produced a remarkable document that demanded a series of democratic reforms. In language resonant of the Constitution of the United States of 1787, the meeting called for members to choose their leaders who were to possess a right of veto over the travelling ministers appointed by Conference. As John Probert observes, the document, had it been adopted, 'would have revolutionised Methodism'.[36] This group of leading Methodists was dominated by mine captains and tradesmen.[37] In the society of dispersed paternalism of the mining districts pastoral responsibility had been to some extent appropriated by the 1790s by such self-made and newly financially secure men. It was they who acted as the mouthpiece of the egalitarian and socially homogeneous communities in which they lived and worked, channelling the independent temper of places where John Wesley had alleged people were 'apt to despise and [be] very willing to govern their preachers'.[38]

Underneath the gentlemanly strata, a view of Cornwall was crystallizing by the 1820s that gloried in its role as an industrial region. Cornwall, it was agreed, was an example rarely matched and unlikely to be exceeded. This view, articulated by the small-town middle classes, partly grew out of the culture of Cornish rural industrialization and partly borrowed from broader nineteenth-century notions of 'progress' and the ideology it spawned. It revolved around three axes – independence, combination and enterprise. It was these that made Cornwall special. The independence of Cornish labouring communities was generalized to become part of the Cornish 'natural' character: 'Among the prevailing propensities of the Cornish . . . their spirit of independence not only pervades their general actions but it enters into their various views'.[39] Independence could easily, of course, dissolve into individualism. Methodist secessions after 1815, disagreements over competing railway plans in the 1840s, the rivalry between Cornish towns and the absence of trade unionism could be and were interpreted as a natural consequence of Cornish individualism. 'Never was a small people more curiously and readily divisible into factions.'[40] However, individualism became a more widespread self-image later in the nineteenth and in the twentieth century when it served as a convenient scapegoat for the failure to surmount deindustrialization.[41]

Before the 1860s, independence was tempered by the second component in the ideology of Cornwall as industrial civilization –

combination. The motto 'one and all', generally used in the eighteenth century in any British crowd action, had, with the decline of food rioting and the moral economy elsewhere, become confined to Cornwall and viewed as peculiarly Cornish by the 1830s. Twenty years later, it was described as the 'watch word of and battle cry of the Cornish . . . of great antiquity'.[42] For, 'accustomed to associate in bodies they [the Cornish] mutually encourage each other to persevere, even on occasions when all rational hopes of success have taken their leave'.[43] Enthusiastic combination also underpinned the 'camp meetings, temperance parties and monster tea drinkings' observed in the 1850s.[44] The third component of Cornish self-representation was 'enterprise'. 'Few', argued Cornish historian and Methodist theologian Samuel Drew, 'are more active, more enterprising or more persevering' than the Cornish.[45] When Cornish people began, in the 1840s, to emigrate in large numbers, it was attributed to their enterprise.[46] Outsiders echoed this. As early as the 1790s, Fraser reported that 'the people of Cornwall also possess a great degree of perspicacity and acumen; they attend to new improvements; if they find them successful, they are not slow in imitation'.[47]

The local myth became one of progress from darkness to light, from 'West Barbary' to 'industrial civilization'. In Cornwall the science-based discourse of technological progress and industrial civilization was contrasted with a former state of 'barbarism'. In the retelling industrial civilization became more glitteringly civilized, while 'West Barbary' became more barbaric. And this was further encouraged by Methodism, which claimed for itself the credit for the moral revolution. Without the idea of a pre-industrial West Barbary 'industrial civilization' would not thrive. So insiders in particular in the nineteenth century adopted the idea of 'West Barbary' in retrospect and constantly reaffirmed it as the alternative to the newly dominant discourse of the Cornish working class as paragons of industrialization, ingenious, inventive, civil, well-mannered and alert.[48]

History and antiquarianism

The clerical antiquarianism of William Borlase and the Toryism of his fellow cleric Richard Polwhele drove attitudes to Cornwall and its past, although from the 1820s they were joined by the writings of smallholder's son and Methodist Samuel Drew.[49] Borlase and Polwhele built on Richard Carew's *Survey* to construct their own view of Cornish history. Both agreed that the Cornish had a common origin as Britons, fleeing before the Saxons, before retiring into Wales and Cornwall and then Brittany.[50] Borlase recognized a 'national enmity betwixt the Britons and the Saxons'; from the tenth century Cornwall was to be considered 'under the Saxon yoke'.[51] Drew went even further, constructing this settlement in recognizably nationalist and modern terms; the events of the tenth century were 'both fatal and final to the independence of the Cornish. This, amidst all the struggles that Cornwall made to preserve her liberty untainted . . . this was the era of the first subjugation of the Cornish by the English'.[52] These 'fathers of Cornish history'[53] drew clear boundaries between Saxons and Cornish in the first millennium. But, although the raw materials were in place by the 1830s for a Cornish history distinct from that of the English, it was confined to the distant past. Ideas of Cornwall as 'another and different nation from the English'[54] coexisted with pride in Cornwall's contribution to English politics and industry and with Cornwall's modern status as a county.

In the nineteenth century, regional identities tended to be conservative, 'in the sense that they accepted the status quo, accommodated themselves to the Union Jack, and sometimes explicitly to the monarchy, as in the case of pearly kings and queens'.[55] Popular memories of Cornish history show how a master narrative of English nationalism could structure regional patriotism. Francis Harvey was a lay preacher in the engineering centre of Hayle. Emigrating to South Africa in the 1850s, he wrote a rambling eulogy to his homeland. The Cornish, he wrote, were the men

> who, of all England battled and nobly withstood the ancient oppressive forces of the north, leaving the defeated marauders, when leaving our shores discomfited and hopeless in their grief, to exclaim 'they are only waille' (foreigners), hence 'kornu-waille', the horn in the sea possessed by foreigners.[56]

In this narrative the real marauders, the English of the ninth century, were replaced by the actual allies of the Cornish, the Danes. In a similar way, the distinct myth of origin that Geoffrey of Monmouth's *History* had bequeathed the Cornish – as descendants of Corineus – had by the nineteenth century changed in the popular imagination. By the 1830s it was commonly believed that the Cornish were descended from the Phoenicians, despite Borlase's explicit rejection of this myth in the 1750s,[57] or were one of the lost tribes of Israel or the descendants of Spanish settlers. But significantly the popular descent myth remained exotic and gave the Cornish an origin that was separate from that of the English.

While the popular myth looked to Phoenicians, the middle classes were becoming increasingly nostalgic. In 1806 Polwhele claimed that, because of its 'intercourse with other provinces, if [the manners] of the Cornish were in any way peculiar, it could only have been in former ages'.[58] Industrialization had swept away former customs. And yet, thirty years later, the same Polwhele was asserting that the superstitions of Cornwall 'assimilate in a surprising manner' to those of Scotland, Ireland and Wales. Here we see the early appearance of the antiquarian-romantic impulse to recover the fragments that were being irrevocably lost. Despite the comments of a number of visitors around 1810 that the Cornish were a 'rational' people, free from 'the shackles of these terrors of the imagination', by the 1860s Cornwall was home to an 'air of antiquity which pervades [it] and seems, like the morning mist, half to conceal and half to light up every one of its hills and valleys'.[59] It was not only outsiders, intoxicated with the first heady attractions of the 'Celtic twilight', who began to represent Cornwall in this way. Even as Cornish mining boomed and Cornwall seemed set fair for an industrial future, the Cornish landed and middle classes also turned to nostalgic romanticism in the face of rapid change. A search for old ways seeped into every nook and cranny as the local middle class, desperate to assert Cornwall's distinctiveness, heaped superstitions and old customs indiscriminately onto the bandwagon marked 'local peculiarities', along with icons of industrialization like the steam engine and popular enthusiasms such as religious revivals. Although superstitions and industrial imagery may seem strange companions they coexisted quite amicably as representations of mid-nineteenth-century Cornwall, as in Robert Hunt's later activities, combining as he did a scientific interest in Cornish mining with a pursuit of customs and folk tales.[60]

Amongst these 'peculiarities' was the Cornish dialect. Dialect tales, performed orally or written in pamphlets, became incredibly popular in the 1840s, mirroring the rise of dialect literature in the industrial regions of the north of England.[61] Although, unlike in northern England, no working-class literature emerged, Cornish dialect literature was different from that of the south of England where the principal themes concerned the small farmer and agricultural labourer. In contrast, dialect tales in Cornwall almost invariably concerned mining. The literature, dense with mining references, acted to reinforce the connections of industry and region. It was, moreover, claimed that 'only in the mining districts' in the 1840s was the 'Cornish provincial dialect . . . to be heard in its full richness'.[62] The stories reached a wide audience. *The humorous adventures of a Cornish miner at the Great Exhibition* by Jimmy Trebilcock, printed at Camborne in 1862, sold at least 5,000 copies within just two years.[63]

Reform

A regional pride fed by industrialization and a consistent group history that included 'British' origins and 'golden ages' set in the tenth and seventeenth centuries underpinned what was probably the most successful campaign of modern Cornish history. In 1846, agitation began for a separate diocese of the Church of England, restoring the bishop granted to Cornwall in 994 but then, just as abruptly, removed in 1050. This reassertion of Anglicanism appealed to Cornish distinctiveness, a combination that retained more than a hint of the Cornish royalist tradition. The agitation was at its most sustained and intensive in the 1850s and 1860s when Cornwall's Celtic origins supplemented other evidence for occupational, religious and indeed, racial difference between Cornwall and Devon. Cornwall was mining, Methodist and Celtic; Devon was agricultural, Anglican and Saxon.[64] In 1876 victory was achieved and the neo-Gothic cathedral at Truro began to rise over the town centre, somewhat paradoxically in the long run adding to the Englishness of the town.

Meanwhile, after the 1810s, Methodism too had begun to change. The years from 1815 to the 1850s saw a series of vigorous secessions from the parent Wesleyan Methodist body,[65] either protests against the growing respectability of Wesleyan Methodism or results of demands for more lay control. The most successful, the Bible Christians, founded by William O'Bryan in 1815, were wedded to a popular revivalism, although their work tended to be concentrated in rural agricultural districts like north Cornwall, areas where Wesleyanism was relatively lightly implanted. In practice, despite the secessions, amounting to more than 40 per cent of all Methodists in Cornwall by 1856,[66] the real distinction within Cornish Methodism remained one between town and village rather than between denomination and denomination. Village Methodism, of whatever hue, tended to be more revivalist and by the 1840s more 'traditional', harking back to the great days of cottage religion in the 1790s and 1800s. In the towns the increased choice provided by new chapels tended to produce a social discrimination between congregations. The more 'respectable' classes attended the Wesleyan chapels; the poor were more likely to worship at the Bryanite (Bible Christian) or the Primitive Methodist chapel.

Urban Methodism's growing respectability accompanied and over-lapped an emerging political reform movement after 1800. During the eighteenth century the jostling between new and old wealth was reflected in political disputes. In 1774 the role of new money was spectacularly recognized when Sir William Lemon, grandson of a tinner, was elected as one of Cornwall's two county MPs.[67] This both broke the hold of the older families – the Carews, St Aubyns, Molesworths and Bullers – over county politics and symbolized a shift in power from east to west and from farming to mining. Lemon was sympathetic to the calls for reform of the electoral system for the House of Commons and in 1782 the first meeting occurred of those supporting calls for parliamentary reform. These reformers were mainly younger men of lesser gentry families, excluded from the borough-mongering of the Bassets, Boscawens, Eliots, Edgcumbes and Hawkins, who fought to control Cornwall's borough seats in the 1780s and 1790s. Partly in reaction against this, the call for parlia-mentary reform was coupled with opposition to corruption and electoral abuses.

The reformers were joined after 1800 by professionals and traders in places like Bodmin, Truro and Liskeard, resentful of continuing landlord control over their boroughs. In 1814, during debates over Roman Catholic emancipation, the reformers, ably led by John Colman Rashleigh (1772–1845), succeeded in opening up county meetings to all (male) inhabitants and not just freeholders. Allying themselves with tenant farmers led by John Penhallow Peters from the Roseland, they seized the initiative from the older Tory-inclined gentry. In 1826 Edward Pendarves's election as a county MP marked the victory of this reforming alliance, who then turned their attention to the towns, where anti-slavery societies after 1825 spearheaded a dynamic reform movement. Parliamentary reform in 1832, reducing the number of Cornwall's MPs from forty-four to fourteen, appeared to mark the victory of reform. However, Cornwall's reputation as a centre of Liberalism and Radicalism had to wait another forty years. It was certainly the case that after 1832 aristocratic control over some boroughs was lost, notably at Truro and Liskeard. But, in the 1840s, disagreements over protection of agriculture and unhappiness with the Tithe Commutation Act of 1836 effectively shattered the farmer–reformer alliance. By 1841 the East Cornwall seat was back in the hands of the Conservatives. Indeed, before 1857 the Conservatives could also hold their own in the boroughs. This was partly due to the continuing power of patrons but partly also because urban, Methodist middle-class householders were as likely to vote Tory as Liberal at this time.

The mature mining region

These small-town middle classes benefited in the first half of the nineteenth century from growing trade and mining activity. In the 1810s, large-scale copper mining began in the Crinnis and Fowey Consols district of St Blazey and Tywardreath and was followed, in the 1830s, by the Caradon copper boom north of Liskeard. This, coupled with new silver-lead mines at Menheniot and the reopening of older mines east of Callington, produced an eastwards shift of mining as miners and capital moved from the older mining districts west of Truro. The migrants brought elements of their culture with them and expanded the industrial region until its boundaries became almost coterminous with the territory of Cornwall. From the 1840s to the 1870s, there was a brief period when the influence of mining was felt across the majority of Cornwall. Cornwall could be viewed as a coherent and relatively homogeneous region more easily in the mid-nineteenth century than at any time since the early medieval period. Long-standing linguistic divisions were now a matter of history as east Cornwall moved to a greater degree, though never totally, into the sphere of mining, with its epicentre in the west.

While expanding production of copper depended on the opening of new mines in new eastern mining districts, older mines dependent on tin experienced a resurgence from the 1830s, led by the mechanization of Wheal Vor. By the 1850s the deeper copper mines of the Camborne–Redruth district, such as Dolcoath, had discovered that copper gave way to tin ore bodies at depth and the balance in the Central Mining District began to swing back to tin. During the mid-century decades signs of diversification also began to appear. New foundries were established in the 1840s, for example at St Austell and Charlestown.[68] These met the needs of the small clay works that were beginning to mushroom on Hensbarrow Downs. Meanwhile, the granite quarrying industry was growing fast in the Penryn and Caradon districts and Cornish firms began to dominate the market for safety fuse.[69] To service these new developments ports were constructed at Charlestown, Pentewan and Par and railways were built. In the 1830s Hayle was linked to Redruth; in the 1840s a railway helped to join the new Caradon mining district to the port of Looe; and from 1852 people could travel from Penzance to Truro on the new West Cornwall Railway.

The expansion of the industrial region did not stop at the Tamar. In 1844 very rich copper reserves were discovered at Devon Great Consols just across the border near Tavistock. This was recognized in the title of the first permanent institution established by the mining industry in 1859 – the Mining Association of Cornwall and Devonshire. The title of this body, dominated by mine captains, was significant. By encompassing Devon, even though in practice the Association was 'almost entirely a Cornish venture',[70] the mine captains were doing two things. They were laying claim to a mining region that was larger than Cornwall alone and they were distancing themselves from the elite who thought only in 'county' terms. Of course, in the long term the risk with this strategy was that when the economic pendulum swung back, the dominant partner in this relationship would no longer be Cornwall but its bigger neighbour Devon.

The turning point of the 1840s

In the 1840s, the unique social relations of industrial Cornwall based on a balance of industrialization and tradition, modernity and custom, began to be fatally undermined, ironically at the very time the administrative territory became wedded to the industrial identity. This happened even as a more public sense of civic Cornishness emerged, fuelled by the new local press, by literary institutions and by such things as dialect literature. The potato blight that hit Ireland and the western parts of Great Britain in the mid-1840s was felt particularly severely in Cornwall, where potatoes had become an important part of the diet by 1800 and potato allotments a key mechanism in collateral aids.[71] In 1846 the potato harvest in Cornwall was described as 'not one hundredth part of a crop, and so wretchedly poor that many will say they are unfit to use'.[72] Three years later it was being reported that 'the loss of the potato has been a great blow to the miner'.[73] In the short term the blight threw labouring families back onto a reliance on bread and salted fish (access to the latter saving Cornwall from an Irish scenario). Cornish industrial communities also adopted their traditional resort to the moral economy, and food riots exploded across the length and breadth of Cornwall in 1847. But this episode of food rioting was the final spasm of a fading customary way of life. Henceforward, riots were confined to single places and issues: elections in St Austell, the Irish in Camborne, fishing in Newlyn and tourism in Newquay.[74] In the longer run, reliance on potato allotments was not to return. For a variety of reasons, perhaps the most important being the attractions of commercial farming, farmers were unwilling to reinstate this tradition once the worst of the blight was over. This was exacerbated by pressure on customary rights to fuel and grazing and growing competition for smallholdings posed by the continuous population growth since the early eighteenth century, which was beginning to put a strain on finite resources of land.

However, an alternative strategy had appeared – emigration. Emigration was not a new phenomenon; Cornish men and women were numbered among the American colonists of the sixteenth century. The emergence of a global market for mine labour had led to the emigration of miners to Mexico and Latin America in the 1820s and the Wisconsin lead mines in the 1830s. What was new by the end of the 1830s was the activity of emigration agents, such as Isaac Latimer of Truro. Latimer was agent for the South Australian Colonization Commissioners and energetically publicized the attractions of life in South Australia through lectures and newspaper adverts.[75] Latimer and his colleagues made up an 'emigration trade' linking Cornwall into a global communications network and providing an obvious outlet in bad times. In the later 1840s Cornish families, both in agricultural areas in the north-east and in the mining districts of the west, responded in their thousands. Mass emigration had become acceptable, even desirable, and when better times returned after the difficult years of 1845–8, emigration remained an ever-present option, presenting families with a new strategy. As the system of collateral aids came under pressure from the 1840s Cornwall's position as a leading mining region made emigration the inevitable alternative.

Politically, we can also detect a shift in the 1840s. Despite the reputation of Cornish miners and others as irascible consumers, quick to 'riot' in the eighteenth century, they had been slow to join the new working-class political institutions of the early nineteenth century – trade unions and Chartism. For John Rule this was part of a 'configuration of quietism' pervading the Cornish labouring classes.[76] However, 'quietism' hardly seems the appropriate term to describe a ready resort to direct action in defence of customary rights. And Cornish communities were not averse to organization *per se*, as the relatively high proportion of friendly society members in the early 1800s suggests.[77] However, 'quietism' becomes even less appropriate a descriptor for the 1840s. For example, strikes, very unusual before 1840, became more frequent thereafter. In 1842 there was a strike at Consolidated Mines, Gwennap; in the 1850s industrial action in the St Just mining district. While a generalized attempt to form a miners' union had to wait until 1866, other groups of workers were organizing by the 1840s.[78] The quarrymen at St Blazey, Luxulyan and Bodmin had already joined the Operative Stonemasons and they were then joined by quarrymen in Truro, Penryn, Constantine and Penzance. Shoemakers, engineers, building workers and clay workers were all willing to take strike action in the 1850s. Similarly, when the first major surge of co-operative societies appeared outside Lancashire in the 1860s, Cornish examples were plentiful. By 1872 there were more co-ops in Cornwall than in larger Devon.[79] Though the Chartist missionaries who visited Cornwall in 1839 found the going tough, Chartist branches were maintained throughout the next decade in Penzance, Truro, Camborne and St Ives.[80]

What this flickering of working-class collective activity in the mid-nineteenth century suggests is that Cornwall was converging with other industrial regions politically. And it was not just the working class who were converging. In the towns a respectable Methodist middle class increasingly turned its face against the emotional popular revivalism that made Cornish Methodism most obviously 'Cornish'. By the mid-1840s the connexional authorities of Wesleyan Methodism felt strong enough to challenge local traditions and stationed two itinerant ministers at Truro in 1845 with the specific task of redirecting indigenous Methodism into more orthodox channels.[81]

Mid-century identities

By the 1840s a unique regional identity had emerged in Cornwall, confident, dynamic and increasingly articulate. Underpinning it was the buoyancy of the mining industry. Socially, Cornwall's rural indus-trialization had created a society that still possessed many proto-industrial forms, growing out of the social relations of dispersed paternalism. Central to this were the multiplying varieties of Methodism, producing a religious culture that clung to revivalism long after other parts of the Methodist family rejected it. Cornish industrial communities, with their worldview stitched onto older discourses of popular moral economy and custom, were clearly distinctive. Their recreated cultural distinctiveness fuelled the growing confidence of the local lesser gentry and middle classes and gave birth to a vigorous and assertive sense of regional pride and 'difference'.

At the same time, middle-class respectability looked to the cultural centres of middle class Victorian England for its inspiration. The Foxes of Falmouth, for example, were closely linked into English society and culture. Working-class respectability was similarly boosted by the arrival of teetotalism which, at least temporarily, wreaked havoc on traditional drink- and gambling-related sports and feasts in Cornwall, as thousands deserted these to sign the pledge. Teetotal missionaries from the north of England made an immediate impact in 1837. At St Austell in January 1838 'about a thousand' attended a public meeting addressed by James Teare. A reputed 240 signed the pledge, encouraged by a teetotal society already formed 'principally through the exertions of an individual, an operative mechanic'. [82] The teetotal movement in mid-nineteenth-century Cornwall awaits its historian but it played a major role in dissolving the older customs and leisure pursuits that had survived almost a century of Methodism. Simultaneously, it diverted energies and enthusiasm into teetotal activity, one element in the difficulties faced by Chartist agitators in 1839. Teetotalism subtly changed local iden-tities after the 1840s, pushing them closer to that of respectable, independent working-class regional identities elsewhere in Britain. That said, at mid-century the discourse of a moral economy, a 'customary' kin and family life based on access to collateral aids and independent communities clung on, though increasingly restricted to the longer established rural mining parishes of the west. But it was precisely these places, communities where access to housing and patches of land enabled the costs of emigration to be met more easily, where mass emigration began to be felt most keenly. Thus communities where 'tradition' was strongest were also those which were subject to the most pressure after the 1840s.

By the 1850s and 1860s we can detect two processes. On the one hand there was cultural convergence with English regions, as a cultural 'blending' began to produce a British culture.[83] On the other Cornishness had emerged as a public identity. At a time when mass emigration and growing respectability was undermining the practices of Methodist folk religion, its symbols were being appropriated as icons of Cornishness and being attached in new ways to other symbols. The same people who were avidly consuming the burgeoning dialect literature of the 1840s and 1850s and attending literary society meetings were beginning to cherish aspects of local history. Thus Edward Boaden, a solicitor's clerk who entered the Wesleyan Methodist Association ministry in 1849, spent time copying out the Apostles Creed in Cornish as well as in English.[84] Two of Cornwall's leading mid-century Methodists, George Smith and Charles Thomas, also professed an interest in antiquities and the Cornish language.[85] These people were evidence for a remade, more public and more articulate regional identity. As part of that identity, Methodism took on symbolic overtones, along with mining and the Celtic heritage, as the birthright of the Cornish people, at the very time when revivalist fervour was beginning to wane, energies sapped by the need to pay for the administrative fabric and the new chapels of the Methodist denominations.

In the 1860s, as later, this confident articulated regional pride overlapped other identities. First, there was an unmistakable mid-century drift by Methodists to fuse into a wider nonconformist Protestant identity. Well into the 1830s, Methodists, especially Wesleyans, remained ambivalent about their relationship with the Church of England. But in the 1840s the appearance of Tractarianism, the counter-offensive of a renewed high church Anglicanism, eased the transition of Methodists from the borders of established religion to nonconformity. As an example, anti-Catholicism played a large part, along with local patriotism, in the biography of early nineteenth-century Methodist reformer and merchant Thomas Pope Roseveare of Boscastle (1781–1853).[86] Men like Roseveare later provided the voting strength for Gladstonian Liberalism in Cornwall. In 1881 a letter from the Liberal solicitor, William Grylls, pointed out that Wesleyan Methodist 'preachers and people may be depended on, much more than 25 years ago, as Liberals'.[87] Although local Methodists had joined with reformers in the 1820s and 1830s over specific issues such as anti-slavery and church rates the links between Methodism and Liberalism were still not fully forged in the 1840s. By the 1880s Methodism and Liberalism had become virtually synonymous.

A Cornish regional identity, for all its strength, nested within increasingly explicit English and British identities, fuelled by mass literacy and a patriotic local press. And, from within this English identity, Cornwall's status as an English county appeared secure. At the same time the flow of emigrants made the Cornish open to late nineteenth-century imperialist identities. The embers of the residual Cornish royalist tradition lay ready to be co-opted into an empire loyalism after the 1870s. However, the most common destination for Cornish emigrants, the United States, also took them beyond the parameters of the British Empire. Cornish and yet also English, influenced from England but looking overseas to other continents, British imperialists and American Republicans, Cornish people in the 1860s were still being moulded by a variety of sometimes conflicting pressures. But then the foundation of their nineteenth-century confidence, the mining industry, began to falter, and their world again began to turn.

Notes

[1] J. D. Tuckett, *A History of the Past and Present State of the Labouring Population*, vol. 2 (1846), pp. 536–7.

[2] *West Briton* (7 July 1843; 14 June 1844).

[3] Roger Burt, 'Proto-industrialisation and "stages of growth" in the metal mining industries', *Journal of European Economic History*, 27 (1998), 85–104.

[4] See Bernard Deacon, 'The reformulation of territorial identity: Cornwall in the late eighteenth and nineteenth centuries', Ph.D. thesis, Open University (2001), pp. 241–5.

[5] Cited in Roger Wells, *Insurrection: The British Experience 1795–1803* (1983), p. 258.

[6] 'Report of Commissioners for inquiring into the Employment and Condition of Children in Mines and Manufactories', *British Parliamentary Papers* (1842), p. 761.

[7] John Rule, *The Labouring Classes in Early Industrial England 1750–1850* (1986), p. 348.

[8] Andrew Charlesworth, *An Atlas of Rural Protest in Britain 1548–1900* (1983), p. 82.

[9] E. P. Thompson, *Customs in Common* (1991), pp. 231 and 9.

[10] John Rowe, *Cornwall in the Age of the Industrial Revolution* (1953), pp. 225–6.

[11] *BPP* (1842), p. 830; Damaris Rose, 'Home ownership, subsistence and historical change: the mining district of West Cornwall in the late nineteenth century', in Nigel Thrift and Peter Williams (eds), *Class and Space: The Making of an Urban Society* (1987), p. 119.

[12] Deacon. 'Reformulation', p. 252.

[13] *BPP* (1842), p. 754.

[14] Mark Overton, *Agricultural Revolution in England: The Transformation of the Agrarian Economy 1500–1850* (1996), p. 102.

[15] *BPP* (1842), p. 88.

[16] Alan Kidd, *State, Society and the Poor in Nineteenth-Century England* (1999), p. 2.

[17] Cited in Rowe, *Industrial Revolution*, p. 8.

[18] Gill Burke, 'The decline of the independent bal maiden: the impact of change in the Cornish mining industry', in Angela John (ed.), *Unequal Opportunities: Women's Employment in England 1800–1918* (1986), p. 194.

[19] Letters from Thomas Carlyon to William Veale, 10 July 1766 and 26 May 1768, Cornwall Record Office ML 781, 793.

[20] William Jenkin, cited in A. K. Hamilton Jenkin, *News from Cornwall* (1951), p. 20.

[21] Jenkin, *News from Cornwall*, p. 65.

[22] *BPP* (1842), p. 759.

[23] John Langton, The industrial revolution and the regional geography of England', *Transactions of the Institute of British Geographers*, ns 9 (1984), 145–67.

[24] David Luker, 'Cornish Methodism, revivalism and popular belief, c.1780–1870', D.Phil. thesis, Oxford University (1987), p. xi.

[25] Cf. Alan Everitt, *The Pattern of Rural Dissent: The Nineteenth Century* (1972), pp. 64–6.

[26] Francis Truscott, 'A letter to the Rev. Jabez Bunting', *Methodist Magazine*, 43 (1820), 538–42.

[27] Richard Polwhele, *Traditions and Recollections, Domestic, Clerical and Literary* (1826), p. 584.

[28] Allen Buckley, *The Cornish Mining Industry: A Brief History* (1992), p. 16.

[29] George Boase, *Collectanea Cornubiensis* (1890), col. 1252.

[30] Cited ibid., cols 1332–40.

[31] Crispin Gill, *The Great Cornish Families: A History of the People and their Houses* (1995), p. 37; D. Bradford Barton, *A History of Copper Mining in Cornwall and Devon* (1961), p. 112.

[32] Jim Lewis, 'Cornish copper mining 1795–1830: Economy, structure and change' in Philip Payton (ed.), *Cornish Studies Fourteen* (2007), pp. 164–86.

[33] Denise Crook, 'The early history of the Royal Geological Society of Cornwall, 1815–1850', Ph.D. thesis, Open University (1990), pp. 13–14; Christopher Riddle, '*So Useful an Understanding': A History of the Royal Cornwall Show, 1793–1993* (1994).

[34] Alan Pearson, 'A study of the Royal Cornwall Polytechnic Society', MA thesis, University of Exeter (1973).

[35] Mark Billinge, 'Hegemony, class and power in late Georgian and early Victorian England: towards a cultural geography', in Alan Baker and Derek Gregory (eds), *Explorations in Historical Geography: Interpretative Essays* (1984), pp. 28–67.

[36] John Probert, *Dr Boase of Redruth* (n.d.), p. 2.

[37] John Rowe, *Industrial Revolution*, p. 261. 3.

[38] John Wesley, *The Works of the Rev. John Wesley* (1841), p. 102.

[39] Fortescue Hitchins and Samuel Drew, *The History of Cornwall*, p. 710.

[40] Herman Merivale, 'Cornwall', *Quarterly Review*, 102 (1857), 289–329.

[41] For example, see A. K. Hamilton Jenkin, *The Cornish Miner: An Account of his Life Above and Underground from Early Times* (1927).

[42] George Henwood in Roger Burt (ed.), *Cornwall's Mines and Miners: Nineteenth Studies by George Henwood* (1972), p. 231.

[43] Hitchins and Drew, *History*, p. 711.

[44] Merivale, 'Cornwall', p. 311.

[45] Hitchins and Drew, *History*, p. 708.

[46] Merivale, 'Cornwall', p. 317.

[47] Robert Fraser, *General View of the County of Cornwall* (1794), p. 13.

[48] Hitchins and Drew, *History*, p. 727.

[49] Hitchins and Drew, *History*.

[50] William Borlase, *Antiquities, Historical and Monumental of ghe County of Cornwall* (1769, first published 1754), p. 40; Richard Polwhele, *The History of Cornwall* (1806), p. 25.

[51] Borlase, *Antiquities*, p. 42.

[52] Hitchins and Drew, *History*, p. 725.

[53] P. S. Morrish, 'History, Celticism and propaganda in the formation of the Diocese of Truro', *Southern History*, 5 (1983), 238–66.

[54] William Borlase, *Natural History of Cornwall* (1758), p. 304.

[55] Paul Ward, *Britishness since 1870* (2004), p. 70. See also Patrick Joyce, *Visions of the People: Industrial England and Question of Class 1840–1914* (1991).

[56] Francis Harvey, *Autobiography of Zethar: St Phillockias, Cornu-waille, England* (1867), p. 29.

[57] Edward Spender, *Fjord, Isle and Tor* (1870), p. 126; Borlase, *Antiquities*, p. 13. For the Corineus myth see Oliver Padel, 'Geoffrey of Monmouth and Cornwall', *Cambridge Medieval Celtic Studies*, 8 (1984), 20–7.

[58] Polwhele, *History*, vol. 7, p. 133.

[59] Richard Warner, *A Tour through Cornwall in the Autumn of 1808* (1809), p. 303; Max Muller, 'Cornish Antiquities', *Quarterly Review*, 123 (1867), 35–66.

[60] Robert Hunt, *Popular Romances of the West of England: The Drolls, Traditions and Superstitions of Old Cornwall* (1871) and *British Mining: A Treatise on the History, Discovery, Practical Development and Future Prospects of Metalliferous Mines in the UK* (1887).

[61] Patrick Joyce, *Visions of the People: Industrial England and the Question of Class 1840–1914* (1991), pp. 279–301.

[62] Jan Trenoodle (alias William Sandys), *Specimens of Cornish Provincial Dialects* (1846), p. 1.

[63] George Boase and William Courtney, *Bibliotheca Cornubiensis* (1874), col. 1012.

[64] Morrish, 'History, Celticism and propaganda'.

[65] Rule, 'The labouring miner in Cornwall c1740–1870, Ph.D. thesis (1971), pp. 264–82.

[66] Calculated from Peter Hayden, 'Culture, creed and conflict: Methodism and politics in Cornwall, c.1832–1979', Ph.D. thesis, Liverpool University (1982), pp. 428–9.

[67] Edwin Jaggard, *Cornwall Politics in the Age of Reform* (1999), p. 25.

[68] T. W. McGuiness, 'Population changes in the St Austell-Bodmin-Padstow district', *Journal of the Royal Cornwall Polytechnic Society* (1942), p. 91.

[69] Peter Stanier, 'The granite quarrying industry in Devon and Cornwall, Part 1 1800–1910', *Industrial Archaeology Review*, 7 (1985), 171–89; Edmund Newell, 'The British copper ore market in the nineteenth century, with particular reference to Cornwall and Swansea', D.Phil., Oxford University (1988), p. 60; Bryan Earl, *Cornish Explosives* (1978).

[70] Patrick Keane, 'Adult education and the Cornish miner: a study in Victorian initiative', *British Journal of Educational Studies*, 22 (1974), 261–91.

[71] Rule, *Labouring Classes*, p. 53. For an expanded version of this argument of this section see Bernard Deacon, 'Proto-industrialisation and potatoes: a revised narrative for nineteenth-century Cornwall', in Philip Payton (ed.), *Cornish Studies Five* (1997), pp. 60–84.

[72] *Royal Cornwall Gazette* (1 Jan. 1847).

[73] P. E. Razell and R. W. Wainwright (eds), *The Victorian Working Class: Selections of Letters to the* Morning Chronicle (1973), p. 28.

[74] Though 'Cornish traditions' have still been cited as present in the anti-Irish riots in Camborne in 1882. See Louise Miskell, 'Irish immigrants in Cornwall: the Camborne experience, 1861–82', in Roger Swift and Sheridan Gilley (eds), *The Irish in Victorian Britain: The Local Dimension* (1999), pp. 31–51.

[75] Philip Payton, '"Reforming thirties" and "hungry forties": the genesis of Cornwall's emigration trade', in Philip Payton (ed.), *Cornish Studies Four* (1996), pp. 107–27.

[76] John Rule, 'A "configuration of quietism"? Attitudes towards trade unionism and Chartism among the Cornish miners', *Tijdschrift voor Sociale Geschiedenis*, 2/3 (1992), 248–62. See also John Rule, *Cornish Cases: Essays in Eighteenth and Nineteenth Century Social History* (2006).

[77] Martin Gorsky, 'The growth and distribution of English friendly societies in the early nineteenth century', *Economic History Review*, 51 (1998), 489–511.

[78] Bernard Deacon, 'Attempts at unionism by Cornish metal miners in 1866', *Cornish Studies*, 10 (1982), 27–36.

[79] Martin Purvis, 'Popular institutions', in John Langton and R. J. Morris (eds), *Atlas of Industrialising Britain 1780–1914* (1986), p. 195.

[80] Alf Jenkin, 'The Cornish Chartists', *Journal of the Royal Institution of Cornwall* ns 9 (1982), 53–80.

[81] Luker, 'Cornish Methodism', pp. 362–3.

[82] *West Briton* (26 Jan. 1838).

[83] Keith Robbins, *Nineteenth Century Britain: England, Scotland, and Wales – The Making of a Nation* (1989).

[84] Anon., 'Edward Boaden and the Apostles Creed in Cornish', *Journal of the Cornish Methodist Historical Association*, 4 (1973), 92–3.

[85] Charles Thomas, *Methodism and Self-Improvement in Nineteenth-Century Cornwall* (1965), p. 17.

[86] Luker, 'Cornish Methodism', p. 232.

[87] Cited in Jaggard, *Cornwall Politics*, p. 203.

6

Post-industrial Cornwall: blending into Britain, 1870s–1914

Cornwall's industrialization engendered a robust, confident, even arrogant, public identity. The lawyer and writer Herman Merivale, who had lived at Helston in the 1840s, summed up the Cornish as 'considerably self-opinionated ... the thorough Cornishman's respect for his own shrewdness and that of his clan is unbounded, or only equalled by his profound contempt for "foreigners" from the east ... this feeling increases ludicrously in intensity as we advance further west'.[1] This geography of Cornishness reflected the geography of industrialization. In west Cornwall, the district of the oldest and most advanced industrialization, feelings of Cornishness were at their height. Moreover, the accident of mineral geology was reinforced both by distance from London and the lingering reminders, in place names, surnames, folk tales and dialect, of Cornwall's Cornish-speaking past. But the regional identity contained ambiguities and tensions. This chapter unearths some of them before noting a shift in self-presentation apparent by the 1860s. It then unravels the contradictions exposed in the failed campaign for a Sunday Closing Bill in the early 1880s. Having established the limits of Cornwall's industrial identity, deindustrialization provides the backdrop for a period described as Cornwall's 'great paralysis'. However, recent work suggests that Cornwall in this period was less 'paralysed' than we might have thought.

The Cornish identity in the 1860s

When John Harris, the Camborne poet, won the Shakespeare Tercentenary Prize in 1864 he jumped with glee, shouting 'We have beaten them all! Hurrah! Hurrah! The barbarians of Cornwall are at the very top of the tree!'[2] Joy at winning the award was intensified by a feeling that the Cornish were somehow viewed as inferior 'barbarians'. As a Methodist, Harris was influenced by the myth of progress that had enthusiastically recreated the pre-Methodist common people of Cornwall as 'barbarians'. But an uneasy inkling remained that barbarity lay not only in the past but was a potential label in the present. Sensitivity to alleged or real stereotyping was echoed in a splendid polemic written in South Africa in the 1860s by Francis Harvey. He was sure that the West Barbary myth was alive and well and ascribed its origin to London.

> 'These West Barbary Barbarians' and 'not of England', as many scapegrace, evil-minded Cockneys have derisively in their stupidity, falsely named us, were, thank God! too sternly honest and noble, to learn the vile strategy, or imitate the viler doings of their slimed accusers . . . those mere distortions of humanity, creeping and limping in debased Cockneydom![3]

Harvey was proud to be English at the same time as outspoken in his Cornish patriotism. Cornwall, he claimed, was 'England's first, best county'.[4]

Another striking example of interpreting Cornish patriotism within a Protestant English identity was Robert Stephen Hawker's *Song of the Western Men*, published anonymously in 1825 and built around an older fragment possibly referring to the imprisonment of the royalist Sir John Trelawny in the Tower in 1628.[5] Hawker transferred this to the imprisonment of Bishop Jonathan Trelawny by James II in 1688. In doing so Cornish anti-Protestant rebelliousness became pro-Protestant rebelliousness, a more suitable history for nineteenth-century nonconformist Cornwall. The rapid popularization of the Trelawny myth – within a generation it was being described as a 'soul stirring patriotic and favourite song' while the Cornish regarded Trelawny as 'a demigod' on a par with King Arthur[6] – both indicated the intensity of the Cornish identity and its accommodation within a broader English identity. Such accommodation was echoed in the appeals of miners in the bitter labour disputes in east Cornwall in 1866 to their rights as 'free-born Englishmen'.[7]

Confronted by statements that Cornwall was 'not of England', Harvey responded that they were a slander put about by Cockneys.

> Cornwall may justly be proud, as being in all her history, in her internal, priceless worth, and in the glorious elements with which she has served and aided, and honoured every valuable interest of the nation; of being in truth, if 'not of' yet superior by far to England, if really 'not of it'.[8]

Underlying this confusing reaction was a desperate need to be accepted. The Cornish role at the forefront of technological and industrial advance amply justified their recognition as central to 'English' industrialization. Yet whispers of 'West Barbary' and 'non-Englishness' were conspiring to deny them the accolades they so richly deserved. There is more than a hint here of the hyper-loyalism of the Cornish royalist tradition, one capable of being transformed into a 'conservative rebelliousness' if slighted or rebuffed. While Harvey swung between ultra-loyalism and aggressive and hostile independence, other emigrants appear to have found a better way of reconciling their Cornishness with 'grander' projects of British identity. Philip Payton has noted the existence of self-representation as 'ancient Britons' in South Australia in the 1850s.[9] This linked the older non-English Cornish heritage to British greatness, in which Cornwall was centrally placed as a result of its industrial achievements. Like the Welsh, the Cornish employed their British inheritance as a badge of loyalty to the post-1707 British state. But, unlike the Welsh, they were also capable of merging Cornwall into England

However, Cornwall's British roots were always capable of being read differently. During the 1860s such a reading emerged, one that began to make Cornish 'difference' potentially more oppositional. The intensity of the Cornish sense of belonging already approached that of a national identity, the novelist Wilkie Collins in 1850 noting; 'a man speaks of himself as Cornish in much the same way as a Welshman speaks of himself as Welsh'.[10] In the 1860s this began to be overlain by more consistent references to the Cornish as a Celtic people. As early as the mid-eighteenth century Borlase was using the term 'Celt' but he included within it a broad group of Scythians, Celto-Iberians, Teutons and Germans, in line with contemporary usage.[11] At that time, 'ancient Britons' was the preferred description for Cornish, Welsh, Bretons and Cumbrians. But by the 1850s the term 'Celtic' was creeping back into use, Merivale writing of the 'Cornu-Britons, that small but strongly characterised Celtic people'.[12]

It was in 1860 that the Cornish middle class rediscovered their Celtic roots. In that year a paper on Carn Brea by Sir Gardner Wilkinson was published in the *Journal of the Royal Institution of Cornwall* and led to a communication from the Cambrian Society in Wales. Enthused by this, members of the Royal Institution of Cornwall fell over themselves in their rush to sign up as Celts; 'we are here at the utmost verge of the Celtic system; we want to connect our local antiquities with the antiquities of other Celtic tribes' stated their president Charles Barham.[13] Although there was still some ambiguity. After second thoughts about being lumped in with Welsh and Bretons, Barham in 1863 affirmed that 'it was from contact and communication with Phoenician civilisation, then the most advanced in the world, that the ancient inhabitants of Cornwall were raised above the level of other Celtic tribes'.[14] Nonetheless, the description Celtic had been quickly linked to the campaign for a separate Cornish diocese by the Reverend Wladislaw Lach-Szyrma, himself born in Plymouth and the son of a Polish exile: 'No contiguous counties in England contain populations so entirely different in race from one another as Devon and Cornwall . . . The Cornish . . . are mostly Celts, akin to the other Gaelic populations of these islands and Brittany . . . A distinct race requires a distinct mode of treatment.'[15] A modern sense of nationalism had made its appearance.

The Cornish Sunday Closing Bill campaign of 1881–1882

But the notion that the Cornish were a distinct Celtic nation had a long way to go. The unsuccessful campaign for a Sunday Closing Bill tellingly reveals, twenty years later, the political limits of Cornish patriotism. The Welsh Sunday Closing Act of 1881 has been described as a legislative recognition of the diversity of Wales.[16] Not too many months passed before people in Cornwall were demanding similar recognition of their own diversity. By July 1881 petitions in favour of a bill for the Sunday closing of public houses were circulating in mid-Cornwall and at some other places such as St Ives and Camborne.[17] In November the agitation was put on a more organized footing and by the spring of 1882 a phenomenal 119,000 signatures had been garnered from across Cornwall, east and west, testament to the organizing ability of the nonconformist denominational network of late Victorian Cornwall and the strength of its teetotal movement. As well as being geographically comprehensive, support for the Bill was widespread from the top to bottom of society. It had the more or less active support of eleven of Cornwall's thirteen MPs, while 477 of the 549 workmen at the Hayle Foundry were claimed to have signed the petition.[18]

The bill's supporters were not slow to link the campaign to Cornish patriotism. According to one, 'promoters of the Bill were possibly animated by the same spirit as those hardy miners of two hundred years ago, who joined so lustily in the song "And shall Trelawny die; full twenty thousand Cornishmen shall know the reason why"'.[19] Even the opposition that belatedly emerged during 1882 couched its arguments in the terms of the dominant patriotic discourse. A meeting of victuallers at St Austell concluded that the Bill 'had been to a very great extent promoted by travelling preachers who were only in the county two or three years, and were not Cornishmen at all'.[20] At times all-pervasive appeals to local patriotism were tinged with the newer discourse of Celticity. This was most strikingly seen in the speeches of William Copeland Borlase, great-great-grandson of William Borlase and MP for East Cornwall. Borlase, speaking at Penzance Wesleyan Methodist chapel in 1882, said 'it is a very remarkable thing that we in Cornwall should have taken up this movement next to Wales . . . it seems to me as if it is the light of other days coming back to us. It seems to me as if we are part and parcel of that ancient people, that we have part of the Celtic blood in us, which makes us regard what is evil as a veritable reality.'[21]

Nevertheless, appeals to shared Celtic blood were bound by the shackles of the English county discourse that had by now fully established itself in the popular imagination. This was neatly illustrated by the speech of Canon Arthur James Mason of Truro at the first major meeting of the campaign in November 1881. Mason, himself born in Wales in 1851 and resident in Cornwall since 1877, put forward his reasons 'why Cornwall should be treated in the same way as Wales'.[22] Echoing Lach-Szyrma's earlier formulation, Mason asserted that the 'Cornish people were different in birth. (Laughter and applause) They were the relics of a grand old race which were in possession of the whole of England before the Saxons came over, and the Cornish people preserved characteristics which were recognized as distinct (Hear Hear)' However, the laughter indicates a lack of seriousness, perhaps a nervous embarrassment, about such claims. For, although this was a recognisably proto-nationalist argument, Mason felt it necessary to remind his audience that 'Cornish people were very happy to be united to England, and they did not wish for home rule (laughter)'. Though willing to add the Celtic kinship card to appeals to 'one and all', no supporter of the Sunday Closing campaign took the logical step and demanded special treatment on the grounds that, like Wales, Cornwall was 'not England'.

Here lay the fatal flaw in the campaign. Opponents and sceptics were quick to ask why Cornwall, as an English county, deserved 'exceptional legislation'.[23] According to them this 'would be piecemeal legislation brought to an absurdity. However remote Cornwall may be from London, and whatever may be said in joke about it being out of England, it is still one of England's counties.'[24] Despite the depth of their support, the campaigners had no convincing answer. For 'one and all' coexisted with Englishness. The Liberal/Radical noncon-formist identity that flourished in the mid and later nineteenth century was, fundamentally, an English identity. It was locked into the taken-for-granted assumption that Cornwall was an English county. Even more than the conservative Cornish royalist tradition, it resisted the urge to look backwards and dream of lost golden ages and was unable to transcend a dominant discourse of (Cornish) county, (English) nation and (British) Empire. The Sunday Closing campaign illustrated the limits of the Cornish regional patriotism that had emerged in the great days of industrialization; it hinted at newer discourses that, para-doxically, looked more to a reinvented past; it reminds us of the continuing inter-weaving of seaward (Celtic) and landward (English) influence in late nineteenth-century Cornwall; and it may even carry some lessons still relevant for campaigns for special treatment for Cornwall in the twenty-first century.

Political developments 1873–1914

Cornish politics more broadly in this period were in many ways well ahead of the game.[25] Most historians date the coming of democratic politics to the election of 1885, the first to be fought on a franchise that gave votes to the majority of men (but not women). This election is regarded as heralding the beginning of the end for landed gentry control over party politics. Yet, as Ed Jaggard reveals, the Conservative gentry of east Cornwall had already ceded control as early as 1852 when the farmers' candidate Nicholas Kendall defeated the aristocratic nominee and sitting MP, William Pole Carew. Conversely, however, in west Cornwall, where no county election was contested between 1832 and 1884, the great Liberal families held sway to the 1860s. The drift of the Falmouth and Williams families towards Conservatism thereafter was matched by growing demands for more public involvement in candidate selection by the 1870s.

At the same time as emigration and economic crisis were combining to disrupt the previous customary working-class culture of west Cornwall, working people began to be influenced by the emerging trade unionism and Chamberlainite Radicalism of up-country industrial districts. This is best seen in the alacrity with which Cornish miners took the opportunity of the 1872 economic boom to demand the end of the 'five-week month', the system of payment by calendar month that meant an occasional five-week gap between pay days.[26] They took their lead from successful strikes from Penzance to Callington by foundry workers, coal porters, clay workers, building workers, tailors and even agricultural labourers. Among the first mine-workers to strike were bal maidens at Wheal Basset, near Redruth. From this epicentre at Illogan the strike wave spread across the mining districts from Botallack in St Just to Okel Tor in Calstock. Although some of the gains were lost during the fall in tin prices after 1873, strikes were by now no means unknown in Cornwall, despite a later over-emphasis on the innate individualism of the Cornish miner. Clay workers engaged in a 'grim winter of industrial trench warfare' in 1876/7 in a doomed attempt to impose a closed shop on the clay pits, an initiative met by a lock-out from their employers.[27] Bitter strike action was to be repeated in the well-known dispute, again over union recognition, in the clay country in 1913, one dramatized in the late twentieth century in the film *Stocker's Coppers*. Class conflict was present in other arenas too. Negotiations between the Basset family and Dolcoath adventurers over the renewal of the mine lease in the early 1880s were acrimonious and on the terms being made public in 1883 miners stopped work and marched through Camborne to the estate office. Disputes like this between the landed interests and the 'productive classes' blurred the capital–worker division but did help inject an enduring people versus aristocracy aspect into politics in Cornwall, one that reached its peak in the fevered elections of 1910, fought around the central issue of 'the peers versus the people'.

The emerging class politics of the 1870s and 1880s triggered their most spectacular outcome in the 1885 election in the new mining division of Camborne–Redruth, where Arthur Pendarves Vivian, Liberal MP for West Cornwall since 1868, was challenged by Charles Conybeare, a 32-year-old radical Liberal. Conybeare, with few family links with Cornwall, won a closely fought election on a platform that was one of the most progressive in the UK. He tacked on to an anti-landlord stance calls for the abolition of the House of Lords, disestablishment of the Church of England, a graduated income tax, Sunday closing of pubs, votes for women, triennial elections and

Home Rule all around. For a moment the mining constituency shone out as a beacon of the new democratic politics, occupying a place at the leading edge of British politics. The miners' democratic impulses were seen as 'as Cornish as the Cornish pilchard and Cornish humour'.[28]

However, it was a fleeting moment, and this democratic radicalism soon fragmented. Low-cost tin reserves in Bolivia and then Malaya cut short the recovery of mining in the 1880s. The miners who made up the backbone of Conybeare's voters began to disperse again to seek work overseas. At the same time the question of Irish Home Rule that had rumbled in the background of British politics since the 1860s finally ignited when Gladstone proposed his Home Rule Bill. The Liberal Party promptly split, Gladstonians staying with their leader in support of Home Rule but Liberal Unionists defecting, unable to accept it. In Cornwall the Liberal clean sweep of the 1885 election was transformed into a representation of three Liberal Unionist, three Gladstonians and one Conservative at the 1886 election. Although the tide of Liberal Unionism quickly ebbed elsewhere, it continued to run strongly in Cornwall through to the 1910s when the remaining Liberal Unionists finally threw in their lot with the Tories. Meanwhile, popular Conservatism remained very weak, the Primrose League, the mass movement formed by the Conservatives in 1885, having one of the lowest memberships anywhere outside Scotland and London.[29] So why did Liberals turn to Unionism? Garry Tregidga puts forward three factors that led Cornish voters to support Liberal Unionism.[30] First, anti-Catholicism made Cornish nonconformists more sympathetic to the arguments of Ulster Protestants. Second, fishermen in the west feared they might be excluded from the Irish herring fishery. Finally, the mass emigration of Cornish people to parts of the empire, in particular South Africa in the 1890s, reinforced an empire loyalty. This was vulnerable to arguments that moves towards Irish independence would herald the break-up of the wider empire, to which the fortunes of so many Cornish families were tied up by the century's end. Glossing these points, Philip Payton claims that Cornish support for Liberal Unionism highlighted 'the significance of Cornish issues and Cornish perceptions'.[31] He argues that it reflected a distinct Cornish politics, radical in social matters but unionist in its attitude to empire, implicitly hinting at continuity with the conservative rebelliousness of the sixteenth century.

But, even in the period when Liberal Unionism was supposedly at its height, it was not paramount. Voters were evenly split between

Unionism and Gladstonian Liberalism. In the longer run, far from reinforcing it, Liberal Unionism corroded the long-term vitality of Cornish political radicalism. It reflected a distinct, but increasingly conservative politics, where a radical shell was becoming hollowed out, transfixed by its Gladstonian past but unable to challenge the problems of a deindustrializing present. For the Liberal split resulted in two unmistakable processes. First, despite the continuing adherence of Liberal Unionist politicians such as Leonard Courtney, MP for East Cornwall to 1900, and Thomas Bedford Bolitho, MP for St Ives to 1900, to radical social policies such as women's suffrage, their alignment with a conservative British imperialism undermined Cornish radicalism by yoking a portion of it to Conservatism. Indeed, Liberal Unionism was the bridge to the working-class Toryism that became important in twentieth-century Cornwall. The Liberal split of 1886 also resulted in a loss of native leadership. Tommy Agar Robartes of Lanhydrock was the only Liberal MP between 1886 and 1915 who was born and bred in Cornwall.[32] The Irish Home Rule crisis precipitated most of Liberalism's remaining landed supporters into the Conservative camp, via Liberal Unionism. Combined with the process of out-migration and depopulation, which by the late 1880s was sapping the potential middle-class leadership cadres of local Liberalism, Cornish Liberalism found it increasingly difficult to find leaders with the resources, charisma or time to regenerate former enthusiasm.

The 'independent tradition' and new political stirrings

This was most clearly seen in the aftermath of the first elections to the new County Council in 1889. The Local Government Act of 1888 on the one hand confirmed Cornwall's traditional boundaries and provided democratically accountable local government and a potential sounding-board for trans-Cornish grievances. But, on the other hand, it shackled Cornwall to an English county discourse, acting as a constant institutional reminder of that status through the twentieth century. The County Council was also the midwife of the Cornish 'independent' local government 'tradition'.

In the second half of the twentieth century and even, to some extent, into the twenty-first, 'independent' non-party councillors seemed to encapsulate an older tradition of 'independence'. But in the mid-nineteenth century, Cornish borough politics were not noticeably less riven by party politics than boroughs east of the Tamar. Open Tory–Liberal contests were commonplace in Helston and Truro well into the 1860s. And in 1889 the first elections to Cornwall County Council were fought in most places on straight party lines, producing a council where Gladstonian Liberals were, just about, in the majority. However, it soon became clear that, when appointing aldermen, there were insufficient Liberals with either the right social cachet or sufficient leisure time to devote to daytime meetings. For councillors and aldermen in east Cornwall, these involved time consuming journeys of up to sixty miles to the new 'county' capital of Truro, which had quickly seen off Bodmin. So, although Methodist and nonconformist Liberals, small farmers and tradesmen in the main, controlled the voting power that would select the aldermen, a tacit deal was reached whereby the bulk of the latter came from Anglican, upper-class, landowning and merchant families. The resulting political compromise led to the rapid disappearance of party politics in ensuing County Council elections and the installa- tion of an 'independent' political tradition. Thus was born the twentieth-century 'Cornish consensus', where the potential voting strength of Liberalism was negated in pursuit of a social alliance at local government level between the small-town and rural middle classes and the landed class. This 'Cornish consensus', born out of the problems faced by Liberalism in the later 1880s, was to cast its shadow over Cornish local government for a century or more.

Achieving the 'Cornish consensus' was made easier by the growing social conservatism of Cornish society. Methodist respectability and the temperance tradition formed the small-town mentality of a popu- lation concentrating on the everyday struggle of making a living at a time of stagnating or declining markets. This was perhaps what lay behind D. H. Lawrence's acidic observation in 1917 that the Cornish were 'inertly selfish, like insects gone cold, living only for money, mean and afraid'.[33] And yet we must be careful not to let the preju- dices of a sojourning romantic wordsmith sway us too far. Progressive politics lived on, as Katherine Bradley's account of the suffragette movement in Cornwall reminds us.[34] Cornwall's social conservatism did not lead to widespread attacks on the suffragettes. On the contrary, in 1896 the proportion of Cornish signatures on a petition in favour of votes for women (at 1.1 per cent of the total) was higher than the Cornish proportion of the total British population (at this time around 0.9 per cent).[35] This suggests that Cornish people were more rather than less likely to support votes for women. In the immediate pre-First World War period nine branches of the National Union of Women's Suffrage Societies were formed, from Launceston and Saltash in the east to Penzance in the west, together with three branches of the more militant Women's Political and Social Union at Penzance, Falmouth/Penryn and Newquay.

Even in these years there were other hints of a newer politics. In Truro in 1904 W. A. Phillips 'came out boldly as a representative of the workers and a social democrat', yet still managed to win a municipal by-election in a straight fight with a Conservative.[36] Phillips was the nominee of a branch of the Social Democratic Federation, a Marxist-inspired socialist party. This small group played a role out of all proportion to its size in helping to restart trade unionism in the clay district.[37] That in turn led to the clay strike of 1913 and some violent scenes as the Liberal government introduced strike-hardened Welsh police to protect the clay-owners' property. Yet, significantly, the attraction of socialist ideas remained limited to Truro, and to railway workers and craftsmen, rather than the mining population of Camborne–Redruth. This was driven home to the SDF when they put up a candidate in the Mining Division in the 1906 general election. Jack Jones, a London docker, was soundly trounced, coming a very poor third with just 1.5 per cent of the votes. Although there was a minor surge of industrial activity in later Edwardian Cornwall, echoing the confrontations of these years in the industrial centres of Britain, the main divide in Edwardian Cornwall remained religion rather than class. It is no coincidence that the first Truro socialist councillor was also a Primitive Methodist, while his opponent in 1904 was an Anglican. The centrality of religious identity and its link to political Liberalism was demonstrated in the passive resistance campaign of 1903/4, when ratepayers refused to pay their rates in protest at the 1902 Education Act, which supported Anglican schools. The resistance was strongest in areas of the highest nonconformist church attendance and Liberal voting, such as St Austell, where a virtually community-wide resistance based on a religious, nonconformist identity could be found.

This is what underlay the striking Liberal success in the 1906 general election, when they won all seven seats and outpolled the Unionists 60–40. Even in 1910 Liberals held on to five seats and still managed to outpoll their rivals overall by a comfortable margin of

57–43. The period of Liberal Unionism, dominant in 1886, then sharing the electoral terrain from 1892 to 1900, was over and Cornwall had reverted to being the Liberal stronghold it was in 1885.

Cultural and social change

Cornish Liberalism had gone through a metamorphosis in the decades from the 1880s to the 1910s, retaining its difference but undergoing change, and so had Cornish culture more generally. By the 1880s, the culture that had flourished from the 1790s to the 1840s in Cornish customary communities was fast evaporating. Methodism ceased to be spontaneously revivalist in the 1860s and even country congregations were adopting newer and more respectable habits. Older folk customs were dissipating in the face of growing literacy, commercial change and influences from urban Britain. For example, the 'shallal' band, a serenade to a married couple using old tin kettles, buckets and anything similar that came to hand, or its darker version, the 'mock hunt' of moral transgressors, were fading by the late nineteenth century. [38] When in 1880 two people impersonating a pair who had infringed community morals were driven through the streets and jeered in Stoke Climsland this was unusual enough to receive considerable publicity. [39] Other customs were also going. Midsummer eve bonfires were 'fast dying out', while hilltop fires were generally discontinued in the 1880s. [40] As this residual culture ebbed it was captured by the collectors of folk tales. The antiquarian impulse of the mid-nineteenth century triggered the scientific scrutiny and categorization of Cornwall's culture as well as its geology and zoology. [41] This work of recording '"primitive" cultures vanishing in the face of the forward march of civilisation and reason'[42] was ably performed by Robert Hunt and William Bottrell, whose collections were published in the years from 1865 to 1880. Their 'mythic representations of Cornish difference',[43] an oral culture frozen in its final phase, coexisted with a dynamic and changing actual popular culture, which by the 1880s was beginning to diverge widely from the folk narratives of the collectors.

This new culture paralleled working-class cultural forms in other industrial regions of Britain, part of that 'blending' of national cultures in a late nineteenth-century Britishness. [44] The brass bands of mid-century were by the Edwardian period entering formal competitions such as the annual band festival at the appropriate venue of Bugle in the clay country. The popularity of bands and male voice choirs was also symbolized by the Cornwall Music Festival, first held in 1910. Leisure became more organized by the century's end, the prime example being the rise of codified rugby and association football from the 1870s, leading to greater interest in spectator sports. Furthermore, there was a wider choice of sports. Billiard halls appeared in Cornish towns from the early 1870s, and by the 1890s even swimming baths at Launceston and Penzance. In 1912 the formation of the Cornwall Bowling Association reflected the spread of bowling greens across the late Victorian urban landscape. Meanwhile, library provision was greatly boosted in the 1890s by the public library movement, the buildings of which were often financed by the Cornish philanthropist, the newspaper man Passmore Edwards. Technological novelties such as bicycles and the more short-lived craze of roller skates combined with shorter working hours and half-day holidays to produce a quality of life more obviously shared with communities across Britain. This changed popular culture, more organized, more eclectic and, for some, more hedonistic – in 1888 the Kilkhampton Bible Christians railed against the 'the practice of such games as dancing, skittles, cards, bagatelle etc.'[45] – has often been linked to the coming of the railway. The opening of Brunel's bridge in 1859 and the joining of the British network to the earlier West Cornwall Railway, signalled a major change. The chairman of the West Cornwall Railway welcomed the connection by explaining that before this Cornwall was 'neither within nor without the borders . . . but now we are part of England'.[46] Cornwall's ambiguous location as 'of England' but 'not of England' that had exercised (and irritated) many was apparently resolved. After 1859 the railway brought in its wake several changes, notably the adoption of Greenwich Mean Time, quicker mail and the telegraph, all of which 'proclaimed the full union of Cornwall with the rest of England'.[47]

It is true that in areas such as literature there had been a vast change from the writings of the early-century perambulating balladeers such as Henry Quick of Zennor (1792–1857), who, in the days before widespread newspaper reading, entertained and informed the dispersed communities of Cornwall. As Alan Kent points out however, Quick was not just the last relic of a dying culture, expressing in his words the end of an era:

> The Cornish drolls are dead, each one;
> The fairies from their haunts have gone:
> There's scarce a witch in all the land,
> The world has grown so learn'd and grand.[48]

He was also invigorated by modernity and industrial prowess and expressed the economic and social change going on around him.[49] Two generations later, Cornwall gave rise to its own version of the regional novel, in writers such as H. D. Lowry of Camborne and Edward Bosanketh of St Just. Lowry's *Wheal Darkness*, set in the Camborne–Redruth of the 1890s and combining various historical cameos from earlier decades, was resolutely realist and materialist in its depiction of a local culture dominated by mining.[50] In one sense the culture depicted in *Wheal Darkness* and Bosanketh's *Tin* was typical of small-town industrial communities across Britain. But in another it was different in that it depicted an industry – metal mining – with its own texture of life. And others were able to breathe more 'difference' into the Cornish regional novel. Charles Lee, not himself Cornish, wrote *Paul Carah, Cornishman*, published in 1898. This explicitly linked the Cornish identity to nationalism and Celticity and defined Cornishness as other than Englishness. Lee's novel hinted that the view of Cornwall as 'not of England' had not in fact been suppressed by the railway but still had considerable life in it.

> There edn' no kingdom on earth to come up to Cornwall; nor no nation fit to stand up in the sight o' the Cornish nation. 'Wan an' all' agin the world. That's we, brothers all! Hoorah for home an' a lovin' welcome, an' pilchers an' saffern an' true friends an' pasties![51]

If we look beyond the cultural changes linked to late Victorian modernity we detect other, more everyday, differences subtly marking Cornish society off from English norms. Cornish family structure changed in the final decades of the century, when family formation was disrupted. The traditional pattern of customary Cornwall was that couples pledging themselves to each other would more than often wait until the woman was pregnant before getting married. The proportion of brides who were already pregnant was thus high, especially in mining communities, into the 1850s and 1860s. Even Cornwall's Methodism had been unable to do much to dent this courtship practice before the mid-nineteenth century.[52] But the engagement was generally honoured and, in fact, illegitimacy rates in Cornwall were consistently lower than the English and Welsh averages in the first half of the century. After the 1840s the gap narrowed and, in a startling turnaround, illegitimacy in Cornwall kept rising into the 1870s and 1880s, while it fell elsewhere.[53] By the early 1880s illegitimate births were running about two percentage points higher in Cornwall than in England and Wales. This reversal was caused by economic problems, which postponed or prevented the planned wedding. The customary courtship pattern was disrupted and only began to readjust again in the 1880s.

High illegitimacy rates were one reason for an increase in the proportion of households in mining areas headed by women. Yet the biggest rise was in the number of households headed by a married woman but with no husband present. While fewer than one in ten households in England contained a single woman with children in 1881, in Cornwall this proportion was in many places one in five.[54] The proportion of extended families was also significantly higher in west Cornwall, reaching 27 per cent in Penzance. Higher numbers of children born out of wedlock, a greater likelihood of grandchildren or grandparents sharing the home and an absent male head all point to major changes in the family after the 1860s. Late nineteenth-century Cornwall was also, at least numerically, dominated by women. In 1861 there were 96 men to every 100 women in Cornwall; by 1901 there were only 85.[55]

The Great Migration

The explanation for these changes in Cornish family structure in the later nineteenth century lies in the mass out-migration that began in the 1840s. For Philip Payton this was 'the greatest saga in our history' and Cornish historians continue to display a fascination, verging on obsession, with the process of overseas emigration.[56] Indeed, in relative terms, Cornwall was 'probably an emigration region comparable with any in Europe', with emigration rates far higher than any part of England or Wales.[57] The basic story of Cornish emigration can be easily summarized.[58] Before 1841 the population of Cornwall had grown virtually in line with growth in England, suggesting that net out-migration was relatively limited. However, in the 1840s and 1850s, emigration began to affect Cornwall's population growth, which fell back to just 4 per cent a decade, compared with around 12 per cent in England and Wales. Over half of the out-migrants left, not for other parts of the British Isles, but for destinations overseas, primarily in the 1840s for North America and in the 1850s South Australia. Despite lingering myths of emigrants fleeing economic crisis, this emigration was not in those decades a result of economic necessity, save perhaps for the difficult years of 1846–8. For example, in 1855, at a time when Cornwall's mining industry was doing relatively well, there was a dramatic drop in the number of marriages right across Cornwall. This was a result of the short-term postponement of marriage as young men (and less often women) rushed to join the emigrant ships, most probably to the goldfields of Victoria in Australia. By the 1850s Cornish communities were wired up to a global communications network whereby news of developments in far-flung mining fields sent tremors of anticipation through the towns and villages of Cornwall. Cornwall's role as an early mining region meant the skills of its miners were a saleable commodity in a global mining labour market. The activities of emigration agents and the spread of newspapers oiled the links in the chain of information flows from the New World to the Old. Cornwall was ideally placed to provide desperately needed labour on world-wide mining frontiers and this drove the migration process, producing by mid-century a culture of emigration and drawing into the process the non-mining population.

In the later 1860s, however, there was a qualitative shift. In 1866 the price of copper crashed, ironically partly because of the new reserves pouring onto the world market from regions opened up with the aid of Cornish miners. This heralded a long-drawn-out mining decline. Copper extraction fell rapidly, although tin mining continued through a regular cycle of crisis and (unsustained) recovery. In consequence migration became less of a choice and more a necessity. Net overseas migration peaked in the 1860s and remained very high in the 1870s. But in the 1870s migration to other parts of the UK exceeded migration overseas. This, indeed, was crisis migration. In relatively good years such as the tin boom of 1871/2 miners built up savings needed for the journey to North America or Australia. In more straitened periods, such as the long years of depression between 1873 and 1878, conditions in Cornwall made it impossible to do this. Instead, greater numbers fled to industrial regions in England and Wales, in particular to parts of Lancashire, Furness, Northumberland, Durham and south Wales, often later moving overseas from these places.

The crisis migration of the 1870s, a decade when Cornwall's population fell by nearly 9 per cent in absolute terms, ebbed in the 1880s and 1890s as the economy recovered (though population still fell). The emigration of whole family groups common in the 1850s, particularly to Australia, was replaced by the migration of single, young men, usually to North America, though by the 1890s the goldfields of South Africa were the preferred destination. Such migration was less permanent, with many men returning to Cornwall. Of the 342 miners who died in the Central Mining District in 1900–2, 216, or 64 per cent, had worked abroad and all of these had been in more than one country.[59] These 'birds of passage' have been characterized by Gill Burke as the 'light infantry of capital', drawn hither and thither by the demand from capitalism for a labour supply.[60] Yet at the time Cornish emigration (though not, interestingly enough, the large movement to England and Wales) was viewed in a much more positive light. It was Cornwall's contribution to both empire and America, taking the spirit of progress and development overseas through individual effort and heroism, more the missionaries of capital than its light infantry. However, this positive interpretation began to give way by the end of the century to growing doubts. In 1900, J. H. Collins, an indefatigable proponent of Cornish mining, write that 'a Cornish correspondent in Colorado suggests that the Cornish character is itself deteriorating in this respect, owing to the fact that her more enterprising sons have been emigrating for many years past'.[61] This more pessimistic view echoed wider end-of-century angst in Britain about the 'deterioration' of its people, especially the urban poor, concerns triggered by the difficulties the British had in defeating the Boers and compounded by growing fears of German and American technical superiority and industrial competitiveness. By the 1900s voices were questioning the long-term value of the empire, a questioning that threatened to undermine the Cornish infatuation with empire, reproduced through the everyday involvement of its sons and daughters in the imperialist project.

Later twentieth-century historians of Cornwall, writing from a post-colonial vantage point, shared early twentieth-century doubts. By the 1990s the dominant view was that the consequences of the emigration saga, while on an individual and family level still heroic, were for Cornwall as a whole 'almost wholly bad'.[62] They pointed to the catastrophic poverty of the 1870s, the soup kitchens and contemporary remarks that concluded emigration was 'a serious calamity to the house owners and shop keeping class as well as to the ratepayers. There are 200 empty houses in [Redruth] parish and the cry is still

"They are going!"'[63] Emigration was seen as fostering a culture of loss, fatalism and poverty, with a passive, inert and undynamic population pitifully dependent on the remittances sent back from overseas.[64] This interpretation was linked to a model that stressed the role of deindustrialization in producing a wider social, cultural and political paralysis from the 1870s onwards.

Deindustrialization – a 'great paralysis'?

The underlying problem of Cornwall's industrialization was that it depended on the extraction of a finite natural resource. Of course there is nothing unusual in this, in that the same point could be made more broadly about the carbon-based industrialization of modern capitalism. But the ultimate unsustainability of mining was more obvious. An anonymous writer in the *Quarterly Mining Review* in 1832 predicted with uncanny accuracy that the Central Mining District's place in the history of steam technology would 'attract the attention of future generations, when, perhaps after a lapse of centuries, the mines of Cornwall shall have become exhausted, the population dispersed, the surface more barren and desolate than ever'.[65] All this indeed came about, but after just two generations in the case of copper rather than 'centuries'. The crises of 1866, the 1870s and the 1890s reduced miners from around 30 per cent of Cornwall's workforce at the census peak in 1861 to just 10 per cent by 1901.[66] Copper and lead production fell to insignificant amounts while tin mining struggled on in a much smaller number of larger mines. This central fact – the collapse of Cornwall's staple industry – is the staple ingredient of the view of late nineteenth-century Cornwall as a deindustrialized region. One of the first industrial regions of Europe was also one of its first deindustrialized regions. Although the rapidity of this transition has been greatly exaggerated by some historians, who seem to feel it transformed Cornwall instantaneously into a holiday resort,[67] it nonetheless involved a traumatic restructuring. It also underpins Philip Payton's influential interpretation of the closing decades of the nineteenth century as the onset of an 'economic paralysis', one that caused a parallel socio-cultural paralysis. 'Cornish society sank into a fatalism and resignation, a certain paralysis, mirroring the economic inertia'.[68] Economically, a lack of innovation and diversification fostered conditions of 'decline and stagnation'. Moreover, these 'fundamental characteristics [of paralysis] remained virtually unchanged from the late nineteenth century until the Second World War'.[69]

It is not difficult to find evidence for deindustrialization. The rundown of mining had rapid knock-on effects. Eight tin smelters closed in the three decades from 1861.[70] Engineering foundries dependent on the mining industry for their market soon went under. Copperhouse Foundry at Hayle closed as early as 1869.[71] It was followed by Perran Foundry, Charlestown Foundry, St Blazey Foundry and Hayle Foundry, once the showpiece of Cornwall's engineering industry, which staggered on until 1903.[72] Indeed, Hayle, losing its two foundries, became something of an industrial ghost town, badly hit by the decline in the complementary copper/coal trade with south Wales. The smaller sailing coasters began to be laid up from the 1860s.[73] In 1879 the Cornish Bank, Cornwall's oldest, failed. This followed the collapse of smaller banks at Helston, where two banks failed in the late 1870s, and at St Columb in 1866.[74] The shrinkage of Cornwall's financial infrastructure mirrored that of its transport infrastructure. The Portreath tramroad, the oldest railway in Cornwall, closed around 1870. Meanwhile, both the Chacewater Railway, taking ore to Devoran, and the Liskeard and Caradon Railway, built in the heady days of east Cornwall's mining boom in 1844, struggled on with declining revenue and increasingly antiquated rolling stock until inevitable closure in 1917.[75]

Outside mining and related industries another mainstay of the Cornish economy, fishing, hit hard times in the 1890s. A railway generated boom in the 1870s and 1880s had guaranteed a decent level of income for the Cornish deep sea drift fisheries, especially at Newlyn, where a new pier was built. But by the 1890s, while Cornish fishermen were reluctant to give up their small-scale way of life, steam drifters began to appear in Mounts Bay. East coast and even Brixham steam trawlers could outfish the Cornish luggers. 'Up-country boats come here, clear our seas, sweep our bays clean' lamented the chairman of the Cornwall Executive Committee for Fisheries in 1896.[76] Tensions in the same year led to serious riots at Newlyn, ostensibly over Sunday fishing, but at bottom a reaction against growing competition from more 'efficient' fishing practices. It was downhill from there on.

Social paralysis

The social effects of such changes are easily imagined. In 1903 it was reported that Cornish fishermen were leaving 'their homes in Cornwall for other ports, Southampton in particular, in the hope of obtaining berths on some of the numerous yachts fitting out'.[77] The sufferings of the fishing communities in the 1900s were repeating those experienced on an even worse scale in the mining districts a generation earlier. William Copeland Borlase, president of the Royal Institution of Cornwall, put this graphically in 1879 – 'an industry has for the present at least, if not for ever, departed from amongst us, carrying with it the loss of surplus wealth to one class, but well nigh life itself to another'.[78] Harrowing stories were aired in the local press, such as the couple and their five or six children at Marazion who lived for a week on fried turnips.[79] A County Distress Committee was belatedly established in December 1877, followed two years later by a Wesleyan Methodist Relief Fund, these bodies providing soup kitchens, giving grants to local work schemes and promoting emigration. Yet, during this crisis decade, expenditure on poor relief in the Penzance Poor Law Union hardly changed, a lack of response echoed in the other Cornish Poor Law Unions.[80] Instead, Cornish working-class families had to resort to their long-standing 'economy of makeshifts', including family, charity, savings and credit, with migration as an ever-present potential escape route.

The Cornish customary family of the early nineteenth century did not survive the combined pressures of more commercial farming and the decades of migration after the 1840s. Young couples found it ever more difficult to obtain access to three-life leases and to the small-holdings that provided a safety net for wage labour. Instead, emigration of the husband overseas with the intention of supporting wife and children left behind became commonplace. Thus was born a new Cornish family form – the dispersed Cornish family. In this family, husband and wife were more likely to be physically separated, sometimes by thousands of miles, for greater or lesser periods of their married lives. Women had considerably more decision-making and domestic independence in the context of the absent husband, although the control of the latter over the main source of family income became more total. When money was not sent home for any reason destitution could result. On the other hand, steady remittances from well-paid jobs on mining frontiers overseas could raise

living standards well above those of neighbours who were struggling
to live on locally generated income alone. The Cornish dispersed
family was, like the Cornish customary family, somewhat different
from the dominant patriarchal 'traditional' Victorian family that had
first appeared amongst the urban middle classes and then spread
widely into the respectable working classes of Britain by the 1890s.

At the heart of these social changes lay the once dominant mining
industry. Roger Burt has noted how a tightly knit group of busi-
nessmen and gentry, including the Robartes, Bolithos, Williamses,
Holmans and Harveys, still dominated the remaining profitable
mines of the 1880s and 1890s. Therefore a 'long term decline in
mining profits could produce an almost inevitable spiral of decline
affecting all aspects of the regional economy'.[81] And it did. In 1894
the most dramatic slump yet to hit tin mining halved tin prices within
a few months. This was the result of currency changes making
Malayan tin cheaper, together with the opening of large new mines in
Bolivia, now linked by rail to the Pacific.[82] A long overdue restructuring of Cornish mining was triggered. Those mines that had
survived earlier crises were either financially reorganized as limited
liability companies, amalgamated, as in the Camborne–Illogan
district, or closed down. According to Gill Burke, the 1890s marked
the demise of an entire social system. It was the final nail in the coffin
of the social relations that had accompanied Cornwall's phase of
merchant capitalism and semi-independent labouring communities.
For Burke, the 'handicraft' relations of Cornish mining were finally
transformed into 'full capitalist relations'.[83] The dominant influence
of mineral landlords and smelters over the mining industry was
removed, a turn graphically illustrated by the declaration of Michael
Williams in 1896 that he would withdraw all his holdings in Cornish
mining.[84] From this point, local banking families like the Bolithos
were drawn more into UK-wide and international finance. By the
early 1900s, Cornish banks were being swallowed up by Barclays and
Lloyds, while its railways were all owned by the Great Western and
the London and South Western Railway Companies. The formerly
all-encompassing mercantile/smelting/banking network, its wealth
based on mining, dissolved. From the mid-1890s onwards both
Cornish mercantile and landed elites and its working-class communities were inexorably affected more by the rhythm of British economic
and political change than they were by events on far-off mining
frontiers.

Greater dependency on the metropolitan core was accompanied by desperation in parts of Cornwall. Cornwall's prominent man of letters, Arthur Quiller-Couch (Q), in 1898 saw 'Cornwall impoverished by the evil days in which mining and . . . agriculture have fallen.'[85] But was Q mistaken? Were things really as bad as both he in the 1890s and Cornish historians in the 1990s stated? This is exactly what has been questioned by Ronald Perry.

The great paralysis rejected

Perry's reinterpretation of the period from the 1870s to the 1910s rests on both structural factors and the response of local agents to these factors. Structurally, the decline of mining was not as traumatic as it has been painted. In fact, it removed 'supply-side constraints' that had inhibited the development of a more diversified economic base and coincided with changing external demand benefiting goods and services where Cornwall had comparative advantages. Moreover, in stark contrast to the 'great paralysis' thesis, Cornish entrepreneurs were hardly lethargic and inert in their response to these changes. Quite the opposite; they were dynamic and entrepreneurial, introducing new managerial and technical skills to regenerate the Cornish economy but meeting resistance from an 'artisanal pragmatism' that did not wish to give up older ways. This 'modernising bourgeoisie', Perry claims, can be seen in action across many sectors of the Cornish economy, especially when we lift our eyes from an over-obsessive concern with mining.[86]

Even in the middle of the catastrophic 1870s Jonathan Rashleigh, president of the RIC, was remarking upon 'a new stimulus to production [which] has been given to Cornish agriculturists by the great demand for dead meat and butter for the London market'.[87] From the 1870s onwards European agriculture was hard hit by imports of cheap grain from North America and Russia. While most European countries adopted high tariffs to protect their farmers, the British government remained firmly wedded to free trade. But, while bad news for arable farmers and the grain-specializing regions of eastern England, tumbling grain prices were good news for pastoral farmers. Indeed, it played to Cornwall's strengths. Cornish farmers switched from growing wheat and barley to raising cattle and dairying, areas where they possessed obvious climatic advantages.[88] As a result, while rents of farmland in England fell by 17 per cent from 1872 to 1892, Cornish rents actually rose by almost 5 per cent.[89] To some extent farm rents may have been held up by greater competition for land from return migrants, armed with the savings accrued from spells overseas. However, like Cheshire and Cumbria, Cornwall also benefited by the movement in the terms of trade to pastoral farming. Natural advantages in stock-raising were taken advantage of by better railway links. In the 1880s flower growing first became remunerative and horticulture became of considerable importance in the Mounts Bay area, the Scillies and the Tamar Valley by the 1900s.[90] There were also attempts to develop a food-processing industry, as in a bacon factory at Redruth. True, farm rents fell by 7 per cent from 1892 to 1911, implying increasing difficulties from the 1890s, but this was still far less than the 12 per cent fall in England in the same years.[91]

As mining output declined, so clay output grew. Production more than trebled in the three decades from 1864[92] and productivity quadrupled from the 1850s to 1910. The clay industry became the major engine of change in the St Austell district where it dominated the economy by the end of the century in the same way that metal mining had done more generally fifty years previously. While clay was maintaining St Austell, shipbuilding and ship repairs at the dry docks constructed in Falmouth in the early 1860s became the mainstay of that town by the 1880s, making up for the loss of the Packet services in 1850. The other obviously new industry of the last decade of the century was tourism. Rail bookings began to rise in the 1890s and there was renewed interest in Cornwall as a winter resort, a role it had played to a small degree during the Napoleonic Wars.[93] However, it was not as a winter resort but as a summer destination that Cornwall began to attract visitors. The GWR's publicity campaign based on the concept of the 'Cornish Riviera' from 1904 sealed Cornwall's twentieth-century role as a tourist region. New resorts such as Newquay and Bude had emerged by 1910 while ports such as St Ives, Looe and Fowey began to see growing numbers of visitors, offsetting to an extent the problems of the fishing industry.

Such developments are taken by Perry as evidence of a growing diversification and continuing dynamism, which sometimes occurred even in more traditional industrial areas. While engineering foundries dependent on the domestic mining market followed their customers into oblivion, others were able to tap new overseas markets, as did

Holman's Foundry at Camborne.[94] New industrial enterprises also appeared during this period of supposed 'paralysis'. For example the National Explosives Company, based at Perranporth and at Upton Towans near Hayle, gave a new lease of life to devastated industrial centres and by 1906 was employing 700 people.[95] And not all the older industries declined as early as mining. Granite quarrying boomed into the 1890s, employing almost a thousand men, meeting a growing demand from government contracts for naval harbours. However, Cornish quarries could not produce granite fast enough and Scandinavian competitors were able to undercut their price by up to 20 per cent. In 1905 a major crisis ensued. Many quarries were closed and afterwards only 150 granite quarriers were still left in the major quarrying district near Penryn, compared with 800 at the height of the late nineteenth-century boom.[96]

Nonetheless, as the experience of the granite quarries was lending weight to the paralysis thesis, so mining gained a new lease of life. Even here it was not all doom and gloom. Productivity doubled, mainly as a result of the 1890s restructuring, and the mines of Edwardian Cornwall were better placed to take advantage of the upturn in tin prices that occurred in the 1900s. Several new mines were developed while old mines were reopened. The depression of the late 1890s seemed to be lifting. Even population numbers, after three decades of decline and stagnation, began to rise a little. Q, reluctantly concluding in 1898 that tourism was the only answer to Cornwall's economic problems, had changed his mind by 1906, feeling that he had 'despaired too soon . . . our industries seem in a fair way to revive'.[97] The prosperous clay industry, thriving agriculture, new fruit growing and flower farming enterprises, dynamite factories, ship repair yards and export-orientated engineering works all belie the picture of a 'great paralysis'.

Socially too, we can interpret this period as more than paralysis. Even in their response to deindustrialization, Cornish working-class families in the west had exercised considerable flexibility and agency in attempting, albeit unsuccessfully, to retain their traditional small-holding economy.[98] More crucially, emigration is read from within the revisionist view of the 'great paralysis' not as a sign of failure but success. Return migrants and financial remittances revitalized public life in late century Cornwall and injected capital and entrepreneurial energy, underwriting many of the ventures of this period, from food processing to hotel building. The growth of a 'transnational' Cornish community had, by the 1880s, created outward-looking global links between Cornwall and the New World, links that maintained a sense of pride in being Cornish and enabled Cornish communities to survive the restructuring of these decades.

Ironically, for those men left behind real wages rose faster than elsewhere after the 1870s. In 1867–70 only three English counties – Somerset, Dorset and Shropshire – had lower wages for agricultural labourers than Cornwall. By 1898, however, there were sixteen such counties.[99] Moreover, as the revisionists rightly point out, one reason for the historical over-fascination with mining is that newer economic sectors like tourism were dominated by women rather than men. And as Perry notes, the proportion of women employed in the Cornish economy rose slightly from 1861 to 1901.[100] However, this should be seen in the context of a fall in the overall numbers employed. Women's activity rates in Cornwall actually fell, from 33 per cent in 1851 to 29 per cent in 1911, slightly faster than in England and Wales during this same period.[101] Moreover, in 1851 32 per cent of Cornish children aged 10 to 15 were earning money. By 1911 this proportion was just 9 per cent. This time the fall was a lot faster than in England and Wales.[102] The restructuring may indeed have favoured women's activity, but not as much as the revisionists claim. Indeed, the decline in women's and children's paid employment suggests family income as opposed to male earnings fell when compared with other places.

Nevertheless, growing income in some sectors plus remittances did help support the shopkeeping and middle classes of Cornish towns in the last quarter of the nineteenth century. Social mobility is indicated by the rows of substantial late Victorian and Edwardian terraces in towns like Camborne, Redruth, Truro, Falmouth and Penzance, whilst examples of new consumer goods appeared in Cornwall not long after other places. For instance, the first car was owned in Camborne in 1896 and by 1899 people were already complaining that 'motor cars in Camborne are a perfect nuisance to horse traffic'.[103] Such signs of modernity coexisted with a cultural identity that reflected an earlier time of mining greatness. This was not mere nostalgia, as the existence of the Cornish transnational community into the Edwardian years acted as a reservoir for the classic industrial self-confidence. On the mining frontiers mining still fulfilled its role of being the 'primary differentiating symbol of "Cornishness"'.[104] As Dorothy Mindenhall has shown, non-mining emigrants were quick to lose their Cornish characteristics, choosing to merge into a 'British' identity rather than stress their Cornishness. But a transnational identity determined by mining fed back into Cornwall itself via return migration and kept this identity alive at home long after its actual material underpinnings were dismantled.

The most important consequence of the economic restructuring of the 1890s was also cultural. Perry reiterates that in this period 'the region was fragmenting from a monolithic community into a patchwork of local economic specialisms'. Economic diversification produced a 'mosaic of economic specialisms'; St Austell based on clay, Truro on local government and 'county' services, Camborne–Redruth on mining and engineering, Falmouth on ship repair, Newquay on tourism, Newlyn on fishing and so on.[105] Before the 1870s an occupational culture dominated by one staple industry – mining – helped to create a Cornwall-wide sense of identity and was a critical part of the regional pride that emerged in the early nineteenth century. By the 1900s that identity still existed, bolstered by transnationalism. Yet it was no longer being materially reproduced in everyday life. Instead, a tendency towards fragmentation, one that had always existed in the absence of a single dominant town, was given free rein. For example, attempts to amalgamate Cornwall's learned societies in 1842 and again in 1893 fell on stony ground.[106] The economic diversification and local specialisms of the 1880s and 1890s unwittingly reinforced local identities which worked to neutralize and undermine the Cornish level. This Cornish pattern of a squabbling group of small-town 'city-states',[107] rarely able to agree on a common direction, was intensified by the 'independent tradition' of the new County Council. Parochialism, therefore, became a major characteristic of twentieth-century Cornish life, constraining imaginations and looking to protect local interests before anything else.

The dynamism of the modernizing bourgeoisie and the growing diversification of late-century Cornwall all clearly undermine the thesis of a 'great paralysis' in the period 1870–1914.[108] But to view the whole of Cornwall as dynamic and diversified in this period is clearly not sustainable. A preferable narrative might view the period from 1873 to 1880 as crisis years, when relatively sudden adjustments, including major out-migration, had to be made in the face of the severe difficulties experienced by mining. Dislocation was followed by a period of constrained diversification, as recovery, depression and then recovery again succeeded each other from the early 1880s to the early 1900s. In the Edwardian years, there was a distinct mini-economic revival. This was based on the earlier diversification but it crystallized a society of economic fragmentation and laid down an ambiguous foundation for the coming century.

Rugby and identity

The period of mini-economic revival coincided with a mini-cultural revival that showed a sense of Cornishness was still alive and well, but coexisting with renewed parochial loyalties. Its catalyst was the new spectator sport of rugby. Rugby first appeared in Cornwall in the 1870s, as elsewhere organized through the influence of ex-public schoolboys.[109] But it quickly shed its elitist origins and became the spectator sport of choice west of St Austell. In 1883/4 the Cornwall Rugby Football Union was formed and, after a number of relatively unsuccessful years, in 1908 the Cornish team won the English county championship and ended up representing Great Britain in the 1908 Olympics. The progress of the team through to the final in 1908 attracted growing crowds of enthusiastic supporters. Not for the first time, observers noted the apparent paradox of a 'county' team supported in a manner reminiscent of 'national' sides. But this was not a paradox at all. For supporting Cornwall was both support for a 'county', by then viewed as a place located in England, and the expression of something else, an identification that had more ethnic overtones. Cornwall was still 'of England', but the Cornish were also 'not of England'. Rugby in Edwardian Cornwall acted as the catalyst for a public articulation of Cornishness and continued to do so periodically through the twentieth century. This was despite the fact that at first Cornwall's senior rugby clubs came from an astonishingly confined area, no more than twenty-four miles by eight, from Penzance in the west to Truro in the east. But this was also the area that had established itself in the eighteenth and nineteenth centuries as Cornwall's cultural heartland. Support for the Cornish team spilled outside this heartland to affect, to an extent, all of Cornwall. Q, for example, a Fowey man, wrote proudly in 1913 of 'young men between Redruth and Penzance . . . winning the English rugby football championship'.[110]

Rugby had further contradictory effects. For local clubs helped to institutionalize community loyalties and hostilities; for example, matches between Camborne and Redruth were often the occasion for near-riotous behaviour as groups of opposing supporters traded insults and sometimes stones.[111] As well as providing an outlet for local identity, rugby also reflected another level of identity, as teams from England, Scotland, Wales and Ireland began to play each other. The absence of Cornwall from this level meant that Cornish players began to appear in the English shirt and inevitably Cornish rugby followers also identified with the English team. In the same way as rugby confirmed the Britishness of Wales rather than contested it,[112] in Cornwall it confirmed the Englishness of Cornwall. Yet it simultaneously strengthened Cornwall's distinctiveness although not resulting, at least in this period, in nationalism. Cornish rugby therefore did not just reflect Cornishness, but rather refracted the complex multi-level identities of early twentieth-century Cornwall.

Notes

[1] Herman Merivale, 'Cornwall', *Quarterly Review*, 102 (1857), 289–329.

[2] John Harris, *My Autobiography* (1882), p. 92.

[3] Francis Harvey, *Autobiography of Zethar: St Phillockias, Cornu-waille, England* (1867), pp. 35–6.

[4] Ibid., p. 33.

[5] Piers Brendon, *Hawker of Morwenstow: A Portrait of a Victorian Eccentric* (1975), p. 56.

[6] George Henwood, *Cornwall's Mines and Miners: Nineteenth Studies by George Henwood*, ed. Roger Burt (1972), p. 220.

[7] Cited in Gill Burke, 'The Cornish diaspora of the nineteenth century', in Shula Marks and Peter Richardson (eds), *Internal Labour Migration: Historical Perspectives* (1984), p. 68.

[8] Harvey, *Autobiography*, p. 29.

[9] Philip Payton, 'Paralysis and revival: the reconstruction of Celtic-Catholic Cornwall 1890–1945', in Ella Westland (ed.), *Cornwall: The Cultural Construction of Place* (1997), p. 30.

[10] Wilkie Collins, *Rambles beyond Railways* (1852), p. 70.

[11] Colin Kidd, *British Identities before Nationalism: Ethnicity and Nationhood in the Atlantic World, 1600–1800* (1999), pp. 51–2.

[12] Merivale, 'Cornwall', p. 302.

[13] *Journal of the Royal Institution of Cornwall*, 43 (1861), 15–16. See also Simon Naylor, 'Collecting quoits: field cultures in the history of Cornish antiquarianism', *Cultural Geographies*, 10 (2003), 324.

[14] *Journal of the Royal Institution of Cornwall*, 45 (1863), 21.

[15] Cited in P. S. Morrish, 'History, Celticism and propaganda in the formation of the Diocese of Truro', *Southern History*, 5 (1983), 238–66.

[16] Keith Robbins, *Great Britain: Identities, Institutions and the Idea of Britishness* (1998), p. 110.

[17] *West Briton* (7 July 1881).

[18] *West Briton* (17 Aug. 1882).

[19] *West Briton* (22 Feb. 1883).

[20] *West Briton* (5 Oct. 1882).

[21] *West Briton* (28 Sept. 1882).

[22] George Boase, *Collectanea Cornubiensis* (1890), cols 540–1; *West Briton* (10 Nov. 1881).

[23] *West Briton* (3 Nov. 1881).

[24] *West Briton*, editorial (19 Jan. 1882).

[25] Edwin Jaggard, 'Political continuity and change in late nineteenth-century Cornwall', *Parliamentary History*, 11 (1992), 218–34.

[26] See Bernard Deacon, 'Heroic individualists? The Cornish miners and the five-week month 1872–74', *Cornish Studies*, 14 (1986), 39–52.

[27] Jack Ravensdale, 'The china clay labourers' union', *History Studies*, 1 (1968), 51–62.

[28] *West Briton* (24 Sept. 1885) and see Bernard Deacon, '"Conybeare for ever!"', in Terry Knight (ed.), *Old Redruth: Original Studies of the Town's History* (1992), pp. 37–43.

[29] Martin Pugh, *The Tories and the People 1880–1935* (1985), pp. 95–6.

[30] Garry Tregidga, 'The politics of the Celto-Cornish revival, 1886–1939', in Philip Payton (ed.), *Cornish Studies Five* (1997), p. 129.

[31] Philip Payton, 'Labour failure and Liberal tenacity: radical politics and Cornish political culture, 1880–1939', in Philip Payton (ed.), *Cornish Studies Two* (1994), p. 88.

[32] Tregidga, 'Celto-Cornish revival', p. 130.

[33] Cited in Denys Val Baker, *The Spirit of Cornwall* (1980), p. 16.

[34] Katherine Bradley, '"If the vote is good enough for Jack, why not for Jill?": the women's suffrage movement in Cornwall 1870–1914', in Philip Payton (ed.), *Cornish Studies Eight* (2000), pp. 127–46.

[35] Calculated from Bradley, 'Women's suffrage movement', p. 132.

[36] *West Briton* (12 May 1904).

[37] See Treve Crago, '"Play the game as men play it": women in politics during the era of the "Cornish proto-alignment" 1918–1922', in Philip Payton (ed.), *Cornish Studies Eight* (2000), p. 151.

[38] Michael Tangye, 'Shal-alling', *Old Cornwall*, 9 (1981), 184–6.

[39] Tony Deane and Tony Shaw, *Folklore of Cornwall* (2003), p. 25.

[40] Michael Tangye, 'Customs remembered', *Old Cornwall*, 9 (1982), 308–12; Cyril Noall, 'The Cornish midsummer eve bonfire celebrations', *Old Cornwall*, 6 (1963), 164–9.

[41] Naylor, 'Collecting quoits'.

[42] James Vernon, 'Border crossings: Cornwall and the English imagi(nation)', in Geoffrey Cubitt (ed.), *Imagining Nations* (1998), p. 96.

[43] Alan Kent, *The Literature of Cornwall: Continuity, Identity, Difference* (2000), p. 125.

[44] Robbins, *Great Britain*.

[45] John Probert, *The Worship and Devotion of Cornish Methodism* (1978), p. 109.

[46] Cited in John Corin, *Fishermen's Conflict: The Story of Newlyn* (1988), p. 20.

[47] Jack Simmons, 'The railway in Cornwall', *Journal of the Royal Institution of Cornwall*, ns 9 (1982), 11–29.

[48] Kent, *Literature of Cornwall*, p. 97.

[49] Ibid., pp. 97–9.

[50] H. D. Lowry and Catherine Dawson Scott, *Wheal Darkness* (1906); Edward Bosanketh, *Tin* (1888).

[51] Charles Lee, *Paul Carah Cornishman* (1898), p. 13.

[52] Henwood, *Cornwall's Mines and Miners*.

[53] Sub-Registrar General's Annual Statistics, *British Parliamentary Papers.*

[54] Bernard Deacon, *The Cornish Family* (2004), pp. 43–4.

[55] Sheila Johansson, 'The demographic transition in England: mortality and fertility change in Cornwall 1800–1900', PhD thesis, University of Indiana (1974), p. 276.

[56] Philip Payton, *The Cornish Overseas*, (1999), p. 42. Discrete Cornish migration streams are described in A. L. Rowse, *The Cornish in America* (1969); A. C. Todd, *The Cornish Miner in America* (1969); John Rowe, *The Hard Rock Men: Cornish Immigrants and the North American Mining Frontier* (1974); A. C. Todd, *The Search for Silver: Cornish Miners in Mexico, 1824–1947* (1977); Philip Payton, *The Cornish Miner in Australia: Cousin Jack down under* (1984) and *The Cornish Farmer in Australia* (1987); Richard Dawe, *Cornish Pioneers in South Africa: Gold, Diamonds, Copper and Blood* (1998); Sharron Schwartz, 'Cornish migration to Latin America: a transnational perspective', Ph.D. thesis, University of Exeter (2002).

[57] Dudley Baines, *Migration in a Mature Economy: Emigration and Internal Migration in England and Wales, 1861–1900* (1985), pp. 152 and 159.

[58] For an overview see Payton, *Cornish Overseas.*

[59] Gill Burke, 'The Cornish miner and Cornish mining industry 1870–1921', Ph.D. thesis, University of London (1981), p. 427.

[60] Ibid., p. 432.

[61] J. H. Collins, 'Capital for West Country Mines', *Royal Cornwall Polytechnic Society Report*, 68 (1900), 87–99.

[62] Burke, 'Cornish miner', p. 451.

[63] Cited in Frank Michell, *Annals of an Ancient Cornish Town, Being Notes on the History of Redruth* (1978), p. 171.

[64] Bernard Deacon and Philip Payton, 'Re-inventing Cornwall: culture change on the European periphery', in Philip Payton (ed.), *Cornish Studies One* (1993), pp. 62–79.

[65] Anon., 'On the mining district of Redruth', *Quarterly Mining Review*, 2 (1832), 201–25.

[66] C. H. Lee, *British Regional Employment Statistics, 1841–1971* (1979).

[67] Sidney Pollard, *Peaceful Conquest: The Industrialisation of Europe 1760–1970* (1981), p. 14; Maxine Berg, *The Age of Manufactures, 1700–1820: Industry, Innovation and Work in Britain* (1994), p. 112.

[68] Philip Payton, *The Making of Modern Cornwall* (1992), pp. 127–9.

[69] Ibid., pp. 125 and 139.

[70] D. Bradford Barton, *A History of Tin Mining and Smelting in Cornwall* (1967), p. 289.

[71] W. H. Pascoe, *CCC: A History of the Cornish Copper Company* (1981), p. 119.

[72] T. W. McGuiness, 'Population changes in the St Austell-Bodmin-Padstow district', *Journal of the Royal Cornwall Polytechnic Society*, 10 (1942), 83–116; Edmund Vale, *The Harveys of Hayle: Engine-Builders, Shipwrights and Merchants of Cornwall* (1966), p. 310.

[73] Peter Stanier, 'The copper ore trade of south west England in the nineteenth century', *Journal of Transport History*, ns 5 (1979), 18–35.

[74] C. E. Hicks, 'Cornish banks and bank notes', *Devon and Cornwall Notes and Quarterly* (1950–1), 183–6.

[75] Stanier, 'Copper ore trade', p. 20.

[76] Cited in John Rule, 'The home market and the sea fisheries of devon and cornwall in the nineteenth century', in Walter Minchinton (ed.), *Population and Marketing: Two Studies in the History of the South West* (1976), pp. 123–39.

[77] *West Briton* (23 July 1903).

[78] William Copeland Borlase, 'President's address', *Journal of the Royal Institution of Cornwall* (1879).

[79] Michael Tangye, 'The Wesleyan Methodist Relief Fund for the Cornwall District 1879', *Old Cornwall*, 7 (1969), 185–90.

[80] Gill Burke, 'The poor law and the relief of distress', *Journal of the Royal Institution of Cornwall*, ns 8 (1979), pp. 148–59.

[81] Roger Burt, 'Proto-industrialisation and "stages of growth" in the metal mining industries', *Journal of European Economic History*, 27 (1998), 85–104.

[82] Roger Burt and Martin Timbrell, 'Diversification in response to decline in the mining industry: arsenic and south-western metal production', *Journal of Interdisciplinary Economics*, 2 (1987), 31–54.

[83] Burke, 'Cornish miner', p. 30.

[84] Barton, *Tin Mining*, p. 222.

[85] Arthur Quiller-Couch, 'How to develop Cornwall as a holiday resort', *Cornish Magazine*, 1 (1898), 237–8.

[86] Ronald Perry, 'The making of modern Cornwall, 1800–2000: a geo-economic perspective', in Philip Payton (ed.), *Cornish Studies Ten* (2002), pp. 166–89.

[87] Jonathan Rashleigh, 'President's address', *Journal of the Royal Institution of Cornwall*, 5 (1876), 245–64.

[88] John Rowe, 'Cornish agriculture in the age of the Great Depression, 1875–1895', *Journal of the Royal Institution of Cornwall*, ns 3 (1959), 147–62.

[89] F. M. L. Thompson, 'An anatomy of English agriculture, 1870–1914', in B. A. Holderness and Michael Turner (eds), *Land, Labour and Agriculture 1700–1920* (1991), pp. 211–40.

[90] *Victoria County History* (1906), p. 579.

[91] Thompson, 'Anatomy of English agriculture', p. 226.

[92] *VCH*, p. 577.

[93] W. J. Bennett, 'Origins and development of the tourist industry in Cornwall', *Report of the Royal Cornwall Polytechnic Society*, 116 (1949), 33–53.

[94] Clive Carter, *Cornish Engineering 1801–2001: Holman, Two Centuries of Industrial Excellence in Camborne* (2001).

[95] W. H. Pascoe, 'Loggans – a history of transport', *Old Cornwall*, 8 (1974), 120–8.

[96] Peter Stanier, 'The granite quarrying industry in Devon and Cornwall, Part 1 1800–1910', *Industrial Archaeology Review*, 7 (1985), 171–89.

[97] Arthur Quiller-Couch, *From a Cornish Window* (1906), p. 194.

[98] Damaris Rose, 'Home ownership, subsistence and historical change: the mining district of West Cornwall in the late nineteenth century', in Nigel Thrift and Peter Williams (eds), *Class and Space: The Making of an Urban Society* (1987), p. 133.

[99] E. H. Hunt, 'Industrialisation and regional inequality: wages in Britain, 1760–1914', *Journal of Economic History*, 66 (1986), 935–96.

[100] Ronald Perry, '"The breadwinners": gender, locality and diversity in late Victorian and Edwardian Cornwall', in Philip Payton (ed.), *Cornish Studies Eight* (2000), p. 119.

[101] E. H. Hunt, *Regional Wage Variations in Britain, 1850–1914* (1973), p. 128.

[102] Ibid.

[103] M. E. Philbrick, 'The Redruth to Penzance turnpike roads', *Journal of the Trevithick Society* (1973), 79.

[104] Dorothy Mindenhall, 'Choosing the group: nineteenth century non-mining Cornish in British Columbia', in Philip Payton (ed.), *Cornish Studies Eight* (2000), p. 50.

[105] Ronald Perry, 'Cornwall circa 1950', in Philip Payton (ed.), *Cornwall since the War: The Contemporary History of a European Region* (1993), pp. 28–9; Perry, 'Breadwinners', p. 124; Perry, 'Making of modern Cornwall', p. 184.

[106] Denise Crook, 'The early history of the Royal Geological Society of Cornwall, 1814–1850', Ph.D. thesis, Open University (1990); Michael Stephens and Gordon

Roderick, 'The Royal Institution of Cornwall: initiatives in nineteenth century English adult education', *Pedagogica Historica*, 13 (1973), 85–106.

[107] Perry, 'Cornwall circa 1950', p. 28.

[108] Ronald Perry, 'Cornwall's mining collapse revisited: an empirical survey of economic re-adjustment in late Victorian and Edwardian Cornwall', *Cornish Historian* (2001).

[109] H. Grylls, *The Centenary of Redruth Rugby Football Club, 1875–1975* (1975), p. 10.

[110] Cited in Perry, 'Cornwall's mining collapse revisited'

[111] Ken Pelmear, *Rugby in the Duchy* (1960), p. 14.

[112] D. Andrews and J. Howell, 'Transforming into a tradition: rugby and the making of imperial Wales, 1890–1914', in A. Ingham and J. Loy (eds), *Sport in Social Development: Traditions, Transitions, and Transformations* (1993), p. 79.

7

Romanticized Cornwall: visionaries and escapists, 1880–1960

Cornwall's past has its blind spots, periods which are less intensively researched. The two centuries after Athelstan's 'settlement' is one, the fifteenth century another, as is the period from 1660 to the late-eighteenth century. And so, more surprisingly, is the twentieth century, a period when seawards influences ebbed and landwards influences were in the ascendant. There is a sense that little progress was made and that Cornish society stagnated, sunk in endemic economic difficulties, inward-looking, inert and undynamic. Paralysis can, indeed, finally be found in the inter-war decades. However, the doldrums of this period may be exaggerated by a paucity of work on the years after 1914. A lack of interest in Cornwall's twentieth-century economic and social history accompanies a growth of work on its romanticization, at its height in the inter-war years. That romanticisation had its roots in the years before 1914 and this chapter therefore overlaps with Chapter 6. I begin by deconstructing what I term the 'discovery school' of historians, before looking at the home-grown romanticism of the Cornish cultural revival. The chapter then provides an account of the economic background of the early twentieth century before concluding with a review of Cornwall in the 1950s.

The rise of romanticism

Most non-Cornish scholars have shown little interest in Cornwall since its industrial period – with one striking exception. There has been a growing fascination with the changing representations of Cornwall after the 1870s. Ella Westland has identified the way in which

> Cornwall, as a natural periphery, perfectly fits the notion of a remote Celtic land. During the century of High Romantic sensibility, say 1750 to 1850, it was in fact known nationally as a leading mining and maritime region . . .

[but] . . . Cornwall's modernity was always liable to suppression by the overwhelming urban need for an uncomplicated distant past.[1]

Therefore, in the late nineteenth and early twentieth centuries, Cornwall was reconstructed as a remote, more primitive, yet somehow purer ancestor and antidote to metropolitan civilization.

Several observers have argued that writers, artists and the publicity department of the Great Western Railway created the Cornish Celt in the period before the First World War. Jane Korey has claimed that a 'semantic vacuum' opened up in late nineteenth-century Cornwall as a result of the decline of mining. This left 'the region dispossessed of its past and its future, vulnerable to characterization by powerful outsiders . . . insofar as Cornwall had a separate culture, it was largely one created for it by Victorian gentlemen'.[2] This interpretation was echoed by Philip Dodd, who asserted that the Newlyn painters of the 1880s and 1890s had bestowed an identity on the periphery, constructing Cornwall as Celtic.[3] He later returned to this theme, arguing that painting 'has helped to give Cornwall a visibility and representational identity . . . Cornwall was particularly indebted to visiting painters for creating its iconography.'[4] This interpretation, reserving the major role in changing representations of Cornwall after the 1870s to the English intelligentsia, is a version of the wider argument put forward by Malcolm Chapman. His thesis is that the category of 'Celt' and 'Celtic' is largely a construction of an urban elite and one imposed on the inhabitants of the peripheries of Britain (and France) over the past two centuries.[5]

James Vernon has adopted a somewhat more sophisticated version of the 'semantic vacuum' argument.[6] For him, nineteenth-century English folklorists and antiquarians reconstructed the Cornish peasantry as a 'pastoral and deeply moral' people. This 'imperial imaginary' was picked up by both Newlyn artists and the Great Western Railway to 'evoke Cornwall as a foreign land still rooted in the natural essence of its uncorrupted, aboriginal peasantry – through which English tourists could view themselves with a mixture of self-satisfaction and anxious regret'. Vernon does admit that Cornish intellectuals then attempted to appropriate this imagery to critique English modernity. However, 'the only way . . . the Cornish subaltern could speak itself as a nation was by appropriating this English romance with the Cornish labouring poor'. Cornish intellectuals have been unable to escape the dominant narrative imposed by the English, even though Vernon admits that a constant flow of ideas between

'English imperial and Cornish nationalist imagineries' undercuts notions of both Cornwall and England as stable and secure nations. Furthermore, the 'four nations' approach to British identity 'tellingly ignores Cornwall or conflates its alterity with Englishnness'.

Vernon's analysis offers some intriguing insights but the broader notion of Cornwall as a semantic vacuum waiting to be filled by the representations of English intellectuals is flawed. The idea of an 'English romance with the culture of its labouring men' sits uneasily alongside statements by English observers about the Cornish people. The quasi-scientific ethnographic surveys of the 1890s drew on frankly racist categorizations and were stimulated by fears of racial degeneration.[7] It was preceded by John Beddoes's *Races of Britain* which equated the Cornish (along with the Irish and Welsh) with the 'African Negro' and contrasted them with the blond-haired eastern English.[8] Racist attitudes persisted through the Edwardian period and into the inter-war years. In 1908 William Hudson wrote of a smallholder in west Penwith who 'reminded me an orang-utan and at the same time of a wild Irishman of a very low type'.[9] D. H. Lawrence described the Cornish more than once as 'mindless', while a contemporary of his, Philip Heseltine, concluded in 1917 that the 'average Cornishman is a veritable savage – ignorant, suspicious and quite hysterically ill-tempered'.[10] Cornwall and its Celtic past could be romanticized but this representation had difficulty in accommodating the contemporary Cornish Celt. Here was the beginning of the twentieth-century distinction between Cornish landscape (romantic and 'good') and Cornish people (who were problematic once they ceased to fit romantic stereotypes).

Those few academics who study Cornwall find it difficult to escape a dominant English nationalist discourse of the 'discovery' of the periphery. Within this discourse Cornwall is either routinely dismissed and ignored or, in a violent lurch to the opposite extreme, drooled over as a fascinating 'other'. This results in an over-attention to the moment of 'discovery' and an under-awareness of the role of Cornish people in making their own past. At bottom, the academic visitor is unable to resist the tourist gaze and becomes a rural *flaneur* – a spectator who maintains their distance while at the same containing their own excitement. Furthermore, the cultural historian's focus on the written word and fine art results in a concentration on the articulate and literate 'visitor' and on a small minority of locals, that 'subaltern' class of intelligentsia. The net outcome is a model where the Cornish people become passive recipients of more powerful discourses. Clearly, such discourses were and are very influential. However they are always reproduced in a process of everyday negotiation and during this meanings subtly alter. It is this subtlety that is lacking in the 'discovery school' of writers. Instead, they oversimplify the Cornish past through uncritically accepting a transition when, almost overnight, Cornwall changed from an industrial to a post-industrial society.

The accounts of Dodd and Vernon are also replete with omissions reflecting a superficial reading of Cornwall's history. Dodd for example asserted that the 'recent history' of Cornwall in the 1880s included a 'declining tin industry and 'the decimation of the fishing industry by European competition'.[11] Right in a very general sense but wrong in the details. The tin industry was recovering in the 1880s while the fishing industry was at its peak in the 1880s before being affected by English rather than 'European' competition. Similarly, Vernon's argument that both English imperialists and Cornish revivalists reified a 'pastoral peasantry' completely misses the role of mining in Cornish self-representations.[12] Unsure of the details of Cornish history, the English academic discoverer then grossly oversimplifies the pre-nineteenth-century Cornish past. For instance Korey argues that until the 1860s Cornwall's integration with England had been 'steadily accelerating'.[13] Such a linear view of Cornwall's gradual integration into England has been comprehensively rebutted by Philip Payton.[14] And the argument of this book has been that aspects of Cornish difference endure and new differences are created at the same time as integration occurs. Such historical over-simplification reflects a broader problem that the 'discovery school' has with Cornwall's past. Like all discoverers of 'primitive' cultures, the past of the discovered culture is rendered 'timeless' and its people basically history-less, as history effectively begins at the point of discovery. This foreshortened sense of the past of colonized peoples results in a lack of awareness of continuity. Thus the non-English imaginations and the cross-border exchanges of the late nineteenth century were not, as Korey and Vernon propose, new but yet another manifestation of Cornwall's 'dual' traditions going back to the ninth or tenth centuries.

So how should we treat the growth of romantic representations of Cornwall from the 1880s? Stanhope Forbes, the mouthpiece of the artists who had settled in Newlyn from 1883 onwards, was unarguably

keen to suppress the modernity of Cornwall. In 1900, after almost
two decades of residence, he could write that the 'natives' were a
'simple and harmless folk' who 'dug no ugly mine pits', a view that is
either incredibly localized to Newlyn or amazingly ignorant of how
most people made a living little more than a generation earlier.[15]
What Forbes and his compatriots were seeking was a deep and reas-
suring (though mythical) English rurality. There is no evidence that
the Newlyn painters themselves viewed Cornwall as 'Celtic',
although their representations could be co-opted into discourses of
the Celt. Instead, like many later migrants, they gazed upon
Cornwall, and saw an unspoilt England.[16] 'It is, indeed, melancholy
to contemplate the gradual extinction of so many beautiful features
of our English landscape: the thatched roof, the little latticed
windows, the many characteristic and essentially cottage features
which gave so much style and charm to our English villages' wrote
Forbes.[17] In a similar way, novelists did much to transform 'industrial
failure into an alien place of primitive mystery'.[18] Korey points out
how writers as well as painters redesignated unemployment as peace,
poverty as simplicity, social disorder as primitiveness, misery as
melancholy. This was a Cornwall that was mutating from being the
site of a 'forward-looking, confident masculinity' as in the writings of
Charles Kingsley to one of anti-modernist resistance and feminized
passivity as in the later works of Daphne du Maurier.[19] Around 1900
Cornwall changed gender, while remaining representationally
unchanged as part of England.

However, most of the art and literature upon which acres of print
have been devoted passed the Cornish people by. For them, artistic
colonies inhabited a parallel universe, offering new opportunities for
income as models in the fishing villages but not directly connecting
with their everyday lives. At times relations between artists and locals
could be tense. After a disputed election in St Ives in 1897 it was
reported that

> it is certain no love is lost between the artists and the fishermen . . . some of
> the former, who had pitched their easels on the beach and were quietly
> working, were interfered with by the fishermen, who gathered in threatening
> groups. Fish and other missiles were thrown, and the painters were so much
> annoyed that they were obliged to give up their work, being followed by a
> jeering crowd, throwing herrings etc., as they returned to their studios.[20]

If relations between artistic and native communities were cooler than
they have usually been painted, so the influence of novelists such as

Hardy, Virginia Woolf and D. H. Lawrence on the popular imagination was more indirect. In a perceptive analysis, Alan Kent has
identified three literary groups active in early twentieth-century
Cornwall.[21] First, there was a group of modernists, part of a canon
of 'great' English literature, who viewed Cornwall as (Celtic) primi-
tivism. Then there were other outsiders who synthesized their own
personal identity with Cornwall, such as Daphne du Maurier.
Perhaps the most interesting of this group was Charles Lee, who,
more than any other non-Cornish writer, convincingly portrayed the
Cornish dialect and explicitly brought the idea of a Cornish nation
into the mainstream of the Cornish regional novel.[22] The third group
included the Cornish writers who made up the 'Cornish School'. This
was actually a somewhat more disparate grouping than Kent implies,
ranging from Quiller-Couch, whose work shaded into the romantic
genre and was very acceptable to the English middle-class literary
consumer, to writers such as Herbert Lowry. Lowry's novels and
short stories, and those of Henry Harris, reflected the nostalgia and
sense of loss already present in Cornish working-class culture but
also vividly portrayed the residual cultural distinctiveness of
Cornwall, for example the role of emigration and the forthright
female presence of the Cornish matriarchal figure.[23]

But the Cornish novelists most read by their own people were the
Hockings. This family, two brothers and a sister, from St Stephen in
Brannel, 'collectively put Cornwall on the mental map of more
readers in Britain and America in the late nineteenth and early twentieth century than any other writers during that phase'.[24] This was
partly due to their prodigious output. The eldest brother, Silas Kitto
Hocking (1850–1935) published over ninety novels from 1878; Joseph
Hocking (1860–1937) also wrote over ninety from 1887 and their
sister Salome (1859–1927) nine novels between the mid-1880s and
1905. The Hockings were heavily influenced by Methodism – both
brothers were United Methodist Free Church ministers – and Kent
has described their writing as 'pulp Methodism'. Moreover, brought
up on the edge of the clay district and maintaining their links to
Cornwall throughout long spells up-country, they spoke with an
authentic Cornish voice that found a ready market among Cornish
people both in Cornwall and overseas. Alan Kent's book on the
Hockings has restored their importance but their influence on early
twentieth-century Cornish identity calls for further exploration. For
theirs was the voice of 'traditional' Cornishness, patriotic but by no

means nationalist, Methodist but also writing within a popular romantic genre.

But Cornish popular novelists or their readers had little place in English imaginations of Cornwall. For Cornwall 'had to remain remote yet also become accessible in its remoteness'.[25] Its incorporation into an English romantic representation was an example of the 'domestic exotic',[26] temptingly different yet tamed and unthreatening. The context for this was both the material changes that were producing a common identity in late nineteenth-century Britain, changes that included cheaper and faster rail travel, popular newspapers and mass spectator sports, and the cultural angst that accompanied the 'moment of Englishness' that Krishan Kumar claims occurred in the late nineteenth century. This re-emphasized an English exclusiveness and reasserted Anglo-Saxonism together with a south-country Englishness, rural and timeless.[27]

The Cornish Revival

However, this moment of Englishness also opened up a space for non-English cultural traditions. It is no coincidence that at this time the Gaelic revival in Ireland was looking back to the 'pure' Gaelic roots of Irish culture and the Cymru Fydd movement in Wales was beginning to reassert the value of the Welsh cultural heritage. As England became more 'Saxon' and 'south-country' so the peripheries became more Celtic.

The 'discovery school' tends to view the Cornish revival as another aspect of the broader romanticist gaze. For Korey, revivalists, 'with little ethnic capital left in the bank', merely passively adopted English perceptions of the Celt.[28] Vernon also sees the roots of Cornish nationalism as English imperialism, with revivalists appropriating English folkloric and anti-modernist visions.[29] In contrast Philip Payton interprets the Cornish revival as an integral part of a project to create a post-industrial economy and culture in Cornwall.[30] Payton's analysis is a valuable antidote to the over-structural approach of the 'discovery school'. Nevertheless, the revival in the early twentieth century remained a largely ineffective and feeble movement. It was constrained not just because of its failure to escape English romanticism but because of broader structural constraints inherited from Cornwall's past. But, despite its limitations, it was the result of real local agency and a genuine and ultimately to some extent successful attempt to revalue the non-English tradition in Cornish culture, to restore a role for the Cornish language and recreate Cornwall's 'Celtic' roots.

Roy Green identified three phases in his model of the Cornish revival.[31] First, there was an antiquarian phase from the 1850s to 1914, followed by a period during which the institutions of the revival appeared in the inter-war years, and then a period when cultural nationalism was joined by political nationalism from 1950. While overly simplistic, for example, political nationalism can be observed in the 1930s,[32] this serves as a useful categorization. One of its strengths is that it pushes the origins of the Cornish revival well back into the nineteenth century and stresses the role of Cornish people in its early genesis. Indeed, we can go further. The identity of the Cornish as 'ancient Britons' that occasionally surfaced before the 1850s was the bridge from an industrial to a 'Celtic' identity. Cornwall's place as a Celtic country, affirmed linguistically by Lhuyd around 1700 but then overlain by a confusing mélange of Druidism and theories of racial origin by William Borlase and others, was reappropriated by the mid-century antiquarians. Moreover, this occurred at the height of Cornwall's industrial phase, before the debilitating deindustrialization and its supposed 'semantic vacuum' had transformed things.

Antiquarian Celticism laid the foundations for the Cornish Revival. The latter has conventionally been dated from 1903/4, the years that saw Cornwall's acceptance into the Celtic Association and Henry Jenner's publication of his *Handbook of the Cornish Language*, which held out the opportunity for Cornishmen and women to relearn their former language. But this ignores Jenner's involvement in a brief burst of interest in the Cornish language in the late 1870s.[33] In 1878 a meeting at Paul, near Penzance, to commemorate the centenary of Dolly Pentreath's supposed death attracted a 'larger than anticipated assembly'.[34] Recitals of Cornish numerals and fishermen's cries, and words and even a couple of sentences passed down orally combined with speeches from antiquarians, 'old songs and carols' and a rendering of 'Trelawny', all of which confirmed the possibility of linking the revival with more popular interest in the linguistic heritage. However, this was to come to nothing. One reason was Jenner's withdrawal from the scene, perhaps disillusioned by the lack of interest he had received from Cornwall's 'opinion formers' when he had proposed a committee in 1876 to revise the spelling system of medieval Cornish and bring it closer to English spelling conventions.[35]

While we can thus extend the roots of the revival back into the nineteenth century we might also downplay the Edwardian revival. Jenner's *Handbook* was certainly an achievement but the shadowy Cowethas Kelto-Kernuak, founded around the same time to preserve Cornwall's Celtic heritage and inspire interest in it soon faded away.[36] It was not until the 1920s that the Cornish revival obtained its institutional shape. In 1920 Robert Morton Nance was instrumental in forming the St Ives Old Cornwall Society. His initiative soon spread across west and then east Cornwall and in 1925 the Federation of Old Cornwall Societies was formed. The Old Cornwall movement was not just intended to preserve the fragments of Cornwall's heritage. It was also based on the belief that only by keeping alive these 'Celtic' fragments could 'Cornwall be kept Cornish still'. The revivalist agenda was articulated in the hope that 'future generations will arise, Cornish still, to make good use of [the fragments]. It's for such a "New Cornwall" that we work.'[37] The growth of the Old Cornwall movement, with its regular journal and local meetings, reflected the strength of the Cornish identity. But Nance's hopes for a New Cornwall soon became submerged in a flood tide of local history. Nonetheless, the Old Cornwall Societies did provide a bridge between the revivalists and popular culture. The Cornish Gorseth was less of a bridge. This body, formed in 1928 along the lines of the Breton and Welsh Gorseths, was intended to stimulate the intellectual life of Cornwall by recognizing the work of those active in Cornish organizations and Cornish matters. But its bardic trappings, formalities spoken in stilted Cornish, and mix of Anglican and pagan rituals did not make for easy acceptance. In the 1930s, moreover, the establishment orientation of the Gorseth and the localism of Old Cornwall Societies attracted criticism from more impatient cultural nationalists. These were involved in the formation of Tyr ha Tavas (Land and Language) in 1932. This has tended to be seen as the first political nationalist movement, although its activities, conducted mainly through the Cornish language, were orientated towards language revival. Furthermore, it remained an organization of exiles in London and other English cities with shallow roots in 1930s Cornwall.

The failure of the early twentieth-century revivalists to engage with popular Cornish culture, still dominated by Methodism and industri-

alism, has led to the argument that the Cornish revival was an ideo-
logical project to restore a pre-industrial medieval Cornwall.[38]
Rejecting Cornwall's industrial failures, it looked back to a more
unambiguously Cornish(-speaking) Cornwall. But to do this it also
had to enter a pre-Reformation, Catholic world. The role of Anglo-
Catholics in the early revival is regarded as evidence of the yearning
for a medieval religion to match a medieval language.[39] Anglo-
Catholics were more likely to be interested in the saints and stone
crosses that were a staple of Celtic Cornwall. Individual Anglo-
Catholics, such as Henry Jenner or the Reverend Lach-Szyrma, were
prominent in the early revival. Yet, as Everitt points out, the Anglo-
Catholic influence was waning by the early 1930s, with the death of
Jenner in 1934 and of Bishop Frere in 1935 and his replacement by
the low church Joseph Hunkin.[40] Others have pointed to the early
involvement of nonconformists in the revival. The Methodist writer,
the Reverend Mark Guy Pearce, who died in 1930, was interested in
Cornish, as was Arthur Browning Lyne of the *Cornish Guardian*, who
also gave his support to the Old Cornwall movement. Garry Tregidga
uses this evidence, together with the fact that all the main organizers
of Tyr ha Tavas were nonconformists, to qualify the Anglo-Catholic
aspect of the revival, especially in the inter-war years.[41] More generally, Ronald Perry has challenged the characterization of the early
revivalists as 'a romantic, anti-industrial group intent upon dragging
Cornwall back towards a pre-industrial society'. His empirical survey
of Edwardian revivalists suggests to him that they compartmental-
ized their economic and cultural agendas, pragmatically trying to
modernize Cornwall economically at the same time as being interested in Cornwall's past in an antiquarian way.[42]

Recent research suggests also that the argument that the revivalists
collaborated with the Edwardian tourist industry to construct a
Celtic Cornwall should be played down.[43] The thesis of collusion
between the Great Western Railway and the revivalists before 1914
has been convincingly demolished, again by Perry.[44] He finds no
connection before 1914 between Cornwall's Celtic heritage and
tourism promotion. Indeed, local revivalists, even Duncombe-Jewell
and Lach-Szyrma, did not refer to Cornwall's Celtic heritage in their
tourist guide-book writings. More widely, local tourist leaders failed
to follow the lead proposed by Silvanus Trevail and Sabine Baring-
Gould and adopt a marketing strategy based on Cornwall's Celtic
heritage. Instead, it was left to the Great Western Railway's publicity

office to define Cornwall's collective tourist identity and the connections it made between Cornwall and Celticity before 1914 were indirect, to say the least.

Guide-book Cornwall

If 'collusion' cannot be squared with the empirical evidence before 1914 it can in the 1920s and 1930s. Those decades saw explicit links between the genre of Cornish Riviera guide-book writings, notably the output of S. P. B. Mais, and the revivalists. Perry argues that this produced a hybrid 'Celto-Mediterranean concept' of Cornwall, which involved an emphasis on 'difference' for the tourist gaze.[45] But it was a safe and unthreatening 'difference', domesticated and patronized. The Cornish Celt had ceased to be a 'noble savage' and instead become a 'charming savage'.[46] It was in this period that the guide-book writers reached new heights of romanticism – 'in the Duchy medievalism still exists, the candle lit by the early saints still burns, the age of chivalry is emphatically not dead, and our most remote ancestors still haunt the ancient places'.[47] This was an 'other' that fed off Geoffrey of Monmouth's Arthurian legends rather than memories of older British independence, and that adopted Q's 'delectable Duchy' as the preferred term for describing Cornwall, but a duchy stripped of any connotations of constitutional ambiguity.

It was also a medievalism that appealed to many Cornish revivalists, preferring the term duchy as a means of avoiding the description 'county'. In contrast, Cornish Methodist culture had viewed the medievalism of duchy, Gorseth and Celtic saints and crosses with a degree of suspicion. John Harris, although prepared to use Cornish traditions in his poetry, was critical of 'medievalising tendencies' in writing about Cornwall, preferring the everyday heroism of mid-nineteenth-century Cornwall to the myths of the past.[48] Much later, Jack Clemo, in the 1930s, after a brief flirtation with the Gorseth and the Cornish language, rejected the Cornish revival and its 'infinite remoteness . . . from the world'.[49] Although other Methodists were beginning to overcome their suspicion of the Cornish revival, its collusion in the inter-war decades with tourist representations meant that it diverged even further from the everyday experience of the Cornish people. The unworldliness of the revivalists at a time of deep and chronic economic difficulties, their emphasis on ceremony and ritual and their dabbling in what was by now regarded as a dead language 'failed to win the hearts and minds of the ordinary Cornish-man and woman'.[50] Vernon has pointed out that the 'high cultural tone' of the revival 'seemed to deny the Cornishness of those who failed to meet its exacting standards'.[51] In addition, Alan Kent has argued that the revival's choice of the more 'Celtic' Cornish language as a badge of difference, rather than the Anglo-Cornish dialect of Cornwall, was significant. It limited Cornish working-class expression by repressing their voice and a 'crucial moment for the mobilization of popular Cornish culture was thus lost'.[52] A desire to avoid the English language joined with attitudes to Cornish dialect that were structured by class values and, paradoxically, indistinguish-able from an upper-class English viewpoint.

But the problems of the Cornish revival in the inter-war period lay deeper than class and status insensitivity. For early twentieth-century revivalists were unable to avoid the structural constraints posed by Cornwall's history. The revivalists wished to foster Cornwall's non-English and in particular its 'Celtic' cultural traditions. But they were, nonetheless, enthusiastic imperialists. Jenner stated in 1926 that the Cornish belonged 'to the old British race, and may well be proud to be citizens of the British Empire'.[53] This led him to reject the Irish Celts and their struggle for independence, 'for in that direction pol-itics lie'.[54] While not keen on the politics of self-government Jenner's own politics were extremely conservative, flirting with far-right legit-imism and royalism in the Edwardian period.[55] At bottom the early revivalists could not escape the Cornish royalist tradition. Explicitly rejecting Cornwall's Englishness, they were nonetheless unable to escape the English tradition in Cornwall or the royalism that had shaped it. A hyper-loyalism, magnified by class and status divisions, meant the revival was extremely unlikely to look either to the Anglo-Cornish dialect, to progressive economic and social policies or to nationalist politics as a way out of Cornwall's paralysis.

Far from being a part of a project to rebuild a post-industrial future, the pre-1939 Revival was tethered to Cornwall's past, unable to shake off the shackles of deindustrialization. While revivalists dithered, preferring unworldly romanticism to uncomfortable reality, local Liberal-leaning elites beacame increasingly parochial and conservative. Just as seventeenth-century royalists were prepared to fight anyone in order to display their loyalty to the crown, so did twentieth-century councillors jealously guard their right to be 'independent', although in practice that 'independence' was by now little more than a hollow rhetorical shell, merely masking a lack of imagination. The old conservative rebelliousness of the sixteenth and seventeenth centuries lived on but, now stripped of its rebelliousness, it was merely conservatism.

The Great War and its aftermath: 1914–1921

Independent councillors and Cornish revivalists alike supported the war effort in 1914–18 and the high culture Cornishness of the revival was submerged in a wartime British/English patriotism. Cornwall remained peripheral in the First World War, a supplier of men and material. However, some have noted that the call for volunteers for the army in 1915 was viewed as a 'dismal failure'.[56] Despite major recruiting drives, relatively few signed up outside those rural parishes still dominated by the landed gentry. Young men in the mining and clay communities in particular ignored the call. Stuart Dalley suggests that the reason for the lack of enthusiasm in the older industrial centres was twofold. In the mining west people remembered the Boer War which had led to lost jobs in South Africa, shutting off the flow of remittances back to Cornwall. The Great War similarly was not good for Cornish mining and during its course major mines closed, including Dolcoath, Botallack, Wheal Jane and St Ives Consols. The response of young miners was still to head overseas, for the mines of the south rather than the trenches of the Somme. Meanwhile, in the clay district men were unenthusiastic to sign up for a 'king and country' that had not hesitated to use force to break their strike only a couple of years earlier. But, as Dalley reveals, what looks like indifference or hostility to the war effort in mining and clay districts masks the higher numbers of volunteers for the navy and public enthusiasm on the outbreak of war in seafaring towns like St Ives. Early indifference had given way by 1916 to levels of support similar to elsewhere. D. H. Lawrence and his German wife Freda certainly suffered from this in 1917 when hostility from the local population around Zennor, suspicious that the couple were communicating with German submarines, was one of the reasons leading to their expulsion.[57]

But the war did bring to the surface a simmering sense of class resentment. From 1917 trade union membership rocketed. Virtually confined to skilled crafts in the nineteenth century, it spread to railway workers and dockers in 1910–13. In 1914 the unskilled and semi-skilled general trade union, the Workers' Union, claimed just 400 members in Cornwall; by 1918 its membership was a staggering 15,000, or around 15 per cent of the Cornish male workforce. The Workers' Union channelled the frustration of workers long inured to low wages and poor working conditions into an explosion of indus-trial action in 1918–20. In 1918 there was a three-month lock-out at Levant mine and by February 1919 Joe Harris of the Workers' Union was claiming that 'it was impossible to control the men for any length of time . . . they see no reason why they must live in a state of semi-starvation'.[58] In the first three months of 1919 alone there were strikes by Penzance dockers, South Crofty miners, workers at Harveys coal and timber merchants at Camborne and Truro building workers. Strikes and demands for wage increases continued unabated through that year. In 1920 echoes of Cornwall's older tradition of food rioting were heard in riots at Redruth and Penzance over the price of butter. But this time these were carefully orchestrated demonstrations by the Workers' Union to put pressure on the authorities.[59]

It was not just in the industrial arena that the Cornish working classes at last began to flex their muscles and challenge the comfort-able 'independent tradition', whereby Tories and Liberals colluded in depoliticizing local politics. In the 1918 general election, the fledgling Labour Party in Cornwall, dominated by the Workers Union, mounted a strong challenge to the Liberals. They came within a few hundred votes of defeating the Liberal in the new Camborne constituency and won a respectable 38 per cent of the vote in St Ives.[60] The parliamentary challenge was reinforced by a scattering of victories in the local elections of 1919 and 1920 in Falmouth, St Austell and Camborne–Redruth. Meanwhile, Truro's first socialist councillor, W. A. Phillips, became Truro's first Labour mayor in 1919. In fact, he was the first Labour mayor anywhere in south-west Britain. And yet in the 1923 general election, when the first minority Labour Government was returned to power, the Labour Party fielded just one candidate in Cornwall, winning a dismal 2 per cent of total votes cast. In contrast, Liberals won 56 per cent of the vote, only 4 per cent short of their landslide of 1906. What had happened? As Treve Crago argues, Cornwall saw only a 'red mirage' in the years 1918–21, or a 'proto-alignment', as the change from Liberal-Conservative to Labour–Conservative contests, along with the rest of

industrial Britain, proved to be a chimera.[61] Instead, Cornish politics
reverted to the old order – Liberal–Tory battles at parliamentary level
and the independent consensus at the local level. Philip Payton interprets this as support for his thesis of 'paralysis' as Cornwall became a
'curious anachronism', where older issues more reminiscent of
Gladstone's era dominated political discourse.[62] As the rest of Britain
turned to class politics Cornwall remained stuck firmly in the nineteenth century.

Garry Tregidga has more recently supported this, pointing out how
Cornwall was typical of peripheral regions in Europe, especially
Scandinavia, where a combination of regionalist, rural and religious
discontent offered a conducive environment for an older non-
socialist radicalism to survive. In the short term Tregidga isolates two
factors that prevented Labour building on its 1918–20 successes.
First, Isaac Foot, the charismatic inter-war Liberal leader, won a by-
election in Bodmin in February 1922 that led to a 'great revival' of
Liberalism across Cornwall.[63] Not for the last time, the residual
strength of Liberalism amongst the rural nonconformist population
of farming east Cornwall not only saved Cornish Liberalism but also
acted as a springboard for renewal in the west, which appeared to be
on the brink of embracing a newer, socialist variety of radicalism.
Second, and perhaps more critically, the short-lived post-war
economic boom collapsed in 1921. By January of that year unemployment was rising fast and mining in particular began to enter what
many feared was its final crisis, as one part after another of the trun-
cated Cornish mining industry shut down. Late in the same year the
Camborne, Illogan, Redruth and District Unemployment Relief
Committee was issuing an appeal towards a fund for the 'relief of
distress in the towns' as unemployment hit 36 per cent.[64] Moreover,
this depression was not restricted to the remaining mining districts.
The mayor of Penzance reported that 'there were . . . children practically staving and men and women suffering in secret hunger and
privation without murmuring'.[65] This was the 1870s all over again.
Such conditions, during which a miners' choir of unemployed tin
miners from west Cornwall travelled the length and breadth of
Britain raising money to help their communities, was hardly
conducive to trade unionism and radical politics. The Labour surge
melted away almost as quickly as it had appeared. As the 'red mirage'
receded, the old order was quickly restored.

Paralysis? The 1920s and 1930s

Its restoration was marked in two ways. First, pre-war issues such as temperance or free trade dominated general elections in Cornwall, even in 1929 when the Liberals under Lloyd George were fighting on new policies that prefigured the later welfare state and Keynesianism. Dawson notes the 'uncanny' parallels between the 1906 election and that of 1931, the latter apparently a rerun of the former.[66] The second aspect reminiscent of pre-war times was the Liberal monopoly of parliamentary seats in 1923 and again in 1929, by this time an unusual phenomenon and one that did not occur in any English county. However, conclusions that the old order was simply restored may be premature. For, if we analyse electoral performance in terms of votes rather than seats, there is evidence of change. In 1929, for example, Liberal monopoly of Cornish seats was obtained with just 42 per cent of the votes. This was way below 1906, when they polled 60 per cent. Liberal victories were secured by a poor showing for the Tories, whose 38 per cent was below the 40 per cent they secured in 1906. Meanwhile the Labour Party won a significant 18 per cent, fighting all five seats for the first time. Second, the old order was never exactly restored in that trade unionism, though weakened by the 1921 depression, survived. In the 1926 General Strike Cornish workers joined their up-country colleagues. Even the *West Briton* had to admit that railway workers and dockers were solidly out on strike. Builders, stonemasons and quarrymen in west Cornwall and carpenters at Camborne–Redruth joined them and the government thought it prudent to send HMS *Valhalla*, with 120 men, to Falmouth to protect 'public and property'.[67] Trade unions survived even the difficult circumstances of Cornish mining, where a bitter strike at South Crofty in 1939 divided the local community.

A more qualified analysis might note the greater resilience of the 'old order' in east Cornwall. Trade unionism was weaker in the east and Liberalism, led by Isaac Foot, apparently more dynamic and radical. In the west, in contrast, it had atrophied. Sir Charles Mallett in 1929 claimed that Liberalism in St Ives was a 'slow, mild, timid thing'.[68] There, Liberalism reflected the social conservatism of the small-town middle classes and small farmers. This was shown by the ease with which Liberal voters in 1924 and 1931 turned to Conservatism rather than Labour; the Tory vote even in the 1935 election was at an all-time high of 47 per cent. It was in this context that Labour mounted its second challenge from 1932 onwards. From 1934 it began to win local government seats in Falmouth, Truro and, notably, broke through in the east, at Liskeard and Lostwithiel. At the parliamentary level, the young A. L. Rowse spearheaded a new strategy of 'Cornish socialism', abetted by Claude Berry, the editor of the *Cornish Guardian*. This basically stole Liberalism's clothes by adopting a 'religious and community agenda'. Nonetheless, it helped to propel Rowse into second place in the St Austell constituency in 1935.[69] Only the war and his growing disillusion with both socialism and Cornwall prevented him from becoming Labour's first Cornish MP.[70]

Although the thesis of a paralysis in Cornish politics requires some rethinking, the evidence for economic and socio-cultural paralysis in the inter-war years would seem overwhelming. Here, at last, we meet unadulterated paralysis. As we have seen, the short-lived boom of 1918–20 gave way in 1921 to a disaster in mining, when at its lowest ebb later in that year only 440 miners were at work in Cornwall, a figure only just over 1 per cent of the mine labour force recorded in the 1861 census. Despite the millions of pounds the crown had siphoned away from tin mining since the fourteenth century, the duke of Cornwall, on a visit to Tincroft, regretted that 'I cannot give more help'.[71] The former mining heartlands were left to their own devices as the industry made a slow recovery in the 1920s to employ 3,700 miners at its peak in 1928, a figure that was just 2,000 by 1939.[72]

What began with mining was soon generalized. Farmers were badly hit by low prices for food. Many were also saddled with debts taken on in the good years of 1918 and 1919 when they had bought their farms from their former landlords, as large estates were sold up. Cornish agriculture also had structural problems, with small farms and low levels of capitalization. One obvious solution – cooperation – did not come easily to rural communities that were by this time enmeshed in the culture of parochialism. Fishing experienced even harder times, as the years from the early 1920s to 1938 saw steady decline. What fishing remained was concentrated on Newlyn. Meanwhile, even the pre-1914 success story of clay struggled in the inter-war years. In 1919 the three largest clay companies amalgamated to form English China Clays, dominating the industry and apparently providing a sound foundation for its future. By 1927 the clay industry had recovered from the short-lived slump of 1921 and production was back at pre-war levels. However, the international economic crisis of 1929–32 hit clay very badly because of its dependence on the American market, destination of 40 per cent of clay exports. Output fell by almost a half in just three years as prices plummeted by a third. Some recovery in the mid-1930s was cut short again in 1937/8 by continuing problems in the American economy and on the outbreak of the Second World War clay production was still below the record levels of 1929. Wages had fallen and short-time working was rife.

Unemployment and low wages were now the endemic Cornish problem. Male unemployment rates over the period 1929–38 averaged almost 18 per cent, compared with an English rate of just under 15 per cent. At its worst in 1932 one in four men were out of work; at its best, in 1937, unemployment still ran at 13 per cent. And real levels of unemployment were even worse, as the problem was masked by a resumption of mass migration, now more likely to be to Slough than South Africa or Aylesbury than Adelaide. The 1931 population of 328,000 drifted downwards to 308,000 by 1939. Chronic unemployment and depopulation was exacerbated in these decades by the restructuring problems of the UK more generally, as older staple industries were replaced by newer ones. The problem in Cornwall was that, at the beginning of the 1920s, a quarter of the workforce was employed in declining extractive and farming sectors. The newer growth industries of cars, chemicals and financial and professional services were hardly visible.

The only new industry Cornwall had was tourism. Paul Thornton has argued that mass tourism in Cornwall really arrived in the 1920s and 1930s, relatively late in the British context.[73] This period saw population growth in coastal communities and the rise of new holiday towns such as Bude and Newquay, to some extent bucking the generally stagnating picture elsewhere. But even tourism only grew slowly, with just one new, large hotel built in this period.[74] At this time, tourism was a net job creator in Cornwall and Newquay did enjoy one of the lowest unemployment rates in inter-war Cornwall.[75] Yet tourism was also dependent on unpredictable changes in demand resulting from changes of fashion in metropolitan England. Indeed, it is typical of a contemporary feature of this period – the increase in core-dependency, on both English markets and English capital. London banks had by now taken over independent Cornish banking firms; Cornwall's biggest food-processing company was sold to a Wiltshire producer; Cornwall's major shipping line – Bains – was sold to P&O; and its explosives works were undercut and eventually bought out by a giant chemical combine.[76]

Nevertheless, even in the 1930s there were some signs of dynamism. Cornish engineering companies such as Holmans at Camborne and Stephens & Son of Carn Brea had managed to carve out export markets, Holmans in particular developing new markets for their compressed air tools and machinery.[77] Numbers employed in general engineering, in contrast to the overall trend, doubled between the 1920s and 1940s.[78] A contemporary could still write proudly of local engineering firms in 1932 that 'by adopting the methods of the great works in the Midlands and the North, by the use of the most modern tools, the employment of highly skilled workmen, the manufacture of high class patented specialities for foreign mines and by the great enterprise displayed these firms have built up very successful businesses'.[79] Ship repairing was another bright spot on the economic horizon as an increase in employment at Falmouth Docks continued throughout the inter-war period. Even in the clay industry the 3,900 employed in 1939 were producing about the same output as the 5,000 workers of 1929,[80] evidence of a considerable growth in productivity. The 1930s also saw 'a number of technical innovations of great significance' in clay as well as further structural rationalization in 1932.[81]

The growth of multiple stores in the 1930s was an indication of both modernization and growing core-dependency. Despite chronically high unemployment in parts of Cornwall, firms such as Marks and Spencer (Falmouth 1935) and Woolworths (Camborne and St Austell 1930; Bodmin and Newquay 1935 and Liskeard 1938) opened new stores.[82] This hardly squares with the picture of a totally paralysed society and the presence of stagnation and dynamism, the old and the new, in 1930s Cornwall serves to qualify generalizations about the whole of Cornwall suffering from paralysis. A more nuanced interpretation needs to take into account geographical contrasts. For example, unemployment in 1935 varied from less than 10 per cent in the eastern farming districts of Launceston and Bude, with their high number of self-employed, to as high as 40 per cent in Redruth, 44 per cent in St Columb and a staggering 65 per cent in Gunnislake.[83] Such striking variations within Cornwall suggest that the dominant inter-war theme was one of contrasting subcultures, a pattern established in the 1890s. No doubt the culture of 'making-do', defensive, nostalgic, parochial and inward-looking, was present in various spheres of Cornish society.[84] But it coexisted with contrasts of lifestyle and life-chances, with change and even sparks of dynamism. In a similar way, a stubborn sense of individualism and pride in being Cornish also coexisted with new romanticized representations of Cornwall.

The Second World War and the 1950s

Conservatism was stirred but not shaken by the Second World War. Cornwall, like the rest of Britain, became a part of the mobilized war economy and unemployment melted away. Unlike in the First World War, Cornwall now lay on the frontline of the war effort, hosting thousands of American troops during the preparations for D-Day in early 1944. And, unlike the Great War, it saw a rapid growth of population in the early years of the war. The threat of mass bombing led to large-scale voluntary (and some compulsory) evacuation from the big cities, especially to Cornwall's coastal towns. The population, around 308,000 in 1939, expanded to 371,000 within just two years, although it began to fall again after 1941.

The 1950s were a transitional period between the inter-war years and the social revolution that began in the 1960s. On the surface, the inter-war paralysis continued. Population numbers had fallen from their wartime peak back to 345,000 by 1951, where they stabilized at a level above that of pre-war, before resuming a gentle downwards slide in the 1950s. Out-migration of Cornwall's youngsters, by now a taken-for-granted cultural rite of passage, resumed, a sign both of a relative absence of well-paid work but also of the new opportunities provided by the expanding state sector of post-war welfare Britain. Superficially, this seemed to be a period when Cornwall converged most closely with the rest of Britain, when its English tradition was by far the most important part of its dual identity. Cornish people, along with everyone else, benefited from the new welfare state and its protection 'from cradle to grave' and the benefits of this may have struck people in Cornwall as even greater, given the economic difficulties of pre-war. It would have seemed churlish, surely, to reject the centralized state solutions on offer in post-war 'consensus' Britain. Cornwall seemed to be following, more or less happily, in the wake of mid-century British modernity.

However, under the surface change was coming. Politically, the Labour Party gained its first MP in the 1945 election, in A. L. Rowse's old stamping ground of Falmouth and St Austell. Boundary changes, detaching Falmouth from Truro and St Austell, meant that from 1950 Labour's Cornish representative was Harold Hayman, member for the new Falmouth–Camborne constituency. But Hayman remained the sole Labour voice, the other four MPs throughout the 1950s being Conservatives. The Tory Party in Cornwall retained its core support of just over 40 per cent of the electorate even in the 1945 election and in both the 1950 and 1959 general elections it won a solid 44 per cent: not a majority, but enough in a disproportionate voting system to guarantee it four of the five Cornish seats. Meanwhile the Liberal vote continued its downward trend, falling to 33 per cent in 1945 and just 26 per cent in 1950. By 1950 the Labour Party had finally overtaken it as the main opposition to the Tories, coming second in all three western constituencies. In 1951 and 1955 the Liberals failed to contest first Truro and then Falmouth–Camborne, a symptom of their relative weakness. But Labour's breakthrough was yet another of those twentieth-century Cornish false dawns. Its 33 per cent of the vote in 1951 proved to be its high point. Labour's failure in post-war Cornwall is explained by two factors. First, socio-economically, the small towns, diverse small-scale workplaces and self-employment of Cornwall did not make it a favourable breeding ground for trade unionism or ideal territory for the Labour Party. Second, the Labour Party had failed to kill off Liberalism. Wedded to a centralist agenda, the Labour Party in Cornwall was ill-equipped to react to a discernible anti-metropolitanism that began to assert itself in the later 1950s.

While the political landscape was beginning to change, albeit slowly, so the economic landscape offered new elements which began to have wider implications. The most striking of these was the 'unaccustomed prosperity' of the 1950s.[85] Unemployment was as low as 2 or 3 per cent in Truro, Falmouth, St Austell and north Cornwall in 1948 and what was for Cornwall almost full employment continued through the next decade.[86] The reasons were twofold. First, the restructuring of the Cornish economy away from mining was by now virtually complete. By 1948 only 8 per cent of men were still employed in mining, clay and quarrying combined, by now slightly fewer than in engineering, where new post-war firms had established themselves, especially at Camborne–Redruth. Nevertheless, a large number worked in the low-wage sectors of farming and tourism, while unemployment was masked by the process of out-migration and by a lower than normal proportion of women in paid employment. Moreover, while the 1948 unemployment rate in some places was as low as 2 per cent, in others such as St Columb, Perranporth/St Agnes and Redruth it was five times greater. And unemployment in Cornwall, though historically low, was never as low as in other parts of Britain. For example, at the time of the 1950 election unemployment in Cornwall was 4.9 per cent when it was only 1.9 per cent in Great Britain.[87] The second reason for this new prosperity was that Cornwall was part of a booming post-war economy based on European reconstruction and growing trade. Government spending boosted the building trade, and the growth of jobs in the National Health Service and local government was shared across the UK, centre and periphery alike. However, this accompanied a parallel extension of external control over the Cornish economy in the 1940s, with nationalization and centralization of electricity, water and gas on a 'regional' basis. This could be seen as part of a longer twentieth-century trend whereby outside ownership and control – over banking, communications and retail outlets – steadily grew, thus constraining the options open to Cornwall's industrialists and planners.[88]

The 1950s for some brought a submergence of the idea of a distinct Cornish identity, buried in the avalanche as the Cornish rushed to sign up to a British modernity. At a time when British society belatedly began to take on a more meritocratic and democratic appearance Cornish people had to reconcile their Cornishness with wider identities in order to be educated to degree level, to advance in their professional careers and to join the upwardly socially mobile millions of post-war Britain. Social mobility seemed to entail cultural mobility and Cornishness, because of earlier romanticism, was something to be suppressed, 'something ignorant and primitive'.[89] A whole generation of upwardly mobile Cornishmen and women in the 1950s followed A. L. Rowse and, sometimes reluctantly, sometimes enthusiastically, shed or suppressed their Cornish identity. Rowse himself had publicly and histrionically rejected Cornwall, believing that Cornwall had rejected him in the 1930s:

> And I have
> Out of Cornwall, out of the kingdom of the cliché,
> Out of the region of misunderstanding, out
> Of the dark realm of suspicion and misapprehension[90]

For many, like Rowse, given the social conservatism and narrow small-town parochialism that had fastened on so much of Cornish life, escaping it was blessed relief.

But not all felt this way. Though Exeter academics could, as late as 1969, characterize Cornwall as a place which lacked 'vitality and leadership and common purpose. [It] is still a land of many regions, mutually remote and parochial and very slow to change',[91] the Cornish identity persisted to fuel sparks of creativity even in this most 'English' of decades. In art the St Ives modernists emerged in the late 1940s, soon becoming the leading centre of modernist and abstract art in Britain. And their dynamism contained a considerable though often understated native input. Peter Lanyon fused his deep knowledge of the Cornish landscape with his abstract paintings, providing a more culturally situated modern art, and linking an older Cornish attachment to place to modernistic artistic expression. In the process he created an art that was both new and at the same time manifestly Cornish.[92] The work of local artists Mary Jewels and John Wells also made important contributions to the St Ives 'school'. Similarly in literature, Denys Val Baker's *Cornish Review* (first series 1949–52) corralled an impressive range of literary talent working in and on Cornwall. While Val Baker, not himself Cornish, was a self-confessed romantic, a position that made it difficult for him to reach out to aspects of the Cornish experience, he did much to help promote a vitality in Cornish literature in these years. Meanwhile native authors – Rowse, Jack Clemo and Charles Causley – were at their peak of activity in these years. Clemo's novel *Wilding Graft*, set in an unremittingly bleak pre-war clay country, has been described as Cornwall's first modernist novel.[93] Causley, meanwhile, used his location on the Cornish border to synthesize Cornish and English visions, perhaps best displaying the dual allegiances of these years.[94]

The way Cornish communities contributed to the Festival of Britain in 1951 neatly illustrated Cornwall's continuing hybridity. While they took part in this pageantry of pride in Britishness, this 'British event, telling the story of British contributions', Festival programmes also informed their readers that 'the Cornish people like to regard themselves as a nation apart from the English'. Exhibitions of Cornish books and performances of plays such as 'Tristan of Cornwall' joined Choral Society renderings of 'Merrie England'.[95] In the decade that followed poets, writers and artists kept the embers of Cornish identity glowing, while historians could still refer back to Cornwall's non-English past[96] and Cornish people could still get fired up when the Cornish rugby team threatened to win the county rugby championships, as almost happened in 1958. The Cornish identity survived, but it was cocooned within the framework of domesticated 'otherness' established by the romanticism of the late nineteenth and early twentieth centuries. The Cornish intelligentsia, often forced to look elsewhere for education and career prospects, but also structured by the dual traditions of Cornwall's past, were unable to transcend the patronizing location mapped out for Cornwall in the greater British and English imagination. However, in the 1960s things began to change.

Notes

[1] Ella Westland, 'D. H. Lawrence's Cornwall: dwelling in a precarious age', *Cultural Geographies*, 9 (2002), 266–85.

[2] Jane Korey, 'As we belong to be: the ethnic movement in Cornwall, England', PhD thesis, Brandeis University (1992), pp. 81 and 79.

[3] Philip Dodd, 'Englishness and the national culture', in Robert Colls and Philip Dodd (eds), *Englishness: Politics and Culture 1880–1920* (1986), p. 14.

[4] Philip Dodd, 'Gender and Cornwall: Charles Kingsley to Daphne du Maurier', in Keith Snell (ed.), *The Regional Novel in Britain and Ireland 1800–1990* (1998), pp. 119–35.

[5] Malcolm Chapman, *The Celts: The Construction of a Myth* (1992).

[6] James Vernon, 'Border crossings: Cornwall and the English imagi(nation)', in Geoffrey Cubitt (ed.), *Imagining Nations* (1998), pp. 153–72. Vernon rather condescendingly dismisses work in Cornish Studies as that of 'Cornish nationalist historians'. For the same point see also J. P. D. Cooper, *Propaganda and the Tudor State: Political Culture in the Westcountry* (2003). The work that Vernon and Cooper cite is Cornish nationalist only in that Cornwall is viewed as a unit worthy of study in its own right. Strangely such writers never seem to define approaches that assume that England is a natural unit worthy of similar study as 'English nationalist'. For an explicitly Cornish nationalist history see John Angarrack, *Our Future is History: Identity, Law and the Cornish Question* (2002).

[7] John Urry, 'Englishmen, Celts and Iberians: the ethnographic survey of the United Kingdom, 1892–1899', in George W. Stocking jr, *Functionalism Historicized: Essays on British Social Anthropology* (1984), pp. 83–105.

[8] Cited in Vernon, 'Border crossings', p. 97.

[9] W. H. Hudson, *The Land's End: A Naturalist's Impressions in west Cornwall* (1908), pp. 95–6.

[10] Cited in Westland, 'D. H. Lawrence's Cornwall', pp. 272–3.

[11] Dodd, 'Englishness', p. 14.

[12] Vernon, 'Border crossings'.

[13] Korey, 'As we belong to be', p. 78.

[14] Philip Payton, *The Making of Modern Cornwall: Historical Experience and the Persistence of 'Difference'* (1992), p. 2.

[15] Stanhope Forbes, 'Cornwall from a painter's point of view', *Journal of the Royal Cornwall Polytechnic Society*, 68 (1900), 53.

[16] Bernard Deacon, 'Imagining the fishing: artists and fishermen in late nineteenth century Cornwall', *Rural History*, 12 (2001), 159–78.

[17] Forbes, 'Cornwall', p. 58.

[18] Korey, 'As we belong to be', p. 181.

[19] Dodd, 'Gender and Cornwall', pp. 125–7.

[20] *Cornish Times* (6 Nov. 1897). For more on relations between the two communities see Deacon, 'Imagining the fishing'.

[21] Alan Kent, *The Literature of Cornwall: Continuity, Identity, Difference* (2000), p. 148.

[22] Charles Lee, *Paul Carah, Cornishman* (1898).

[23] H. D. Lowry and Catherine Dawson-Scott, *Wheal Darkness* (1906); Henry Harris, *The Luck of Wheal Vor* (1901).

[24] Alan Kent, *Pulp Methodism* (2002), p. 12.

[25] Keith Robbins, *Nineteenth Century Britain* (1988), p. 25.

[26] Chris Thomas, 'See your own country first: the geography of a railway landscape', in Ella Westland (ed.), *Cornwall: The Cultural Construction of Place* (1997), p. 120.

[27] Krishan Kumar, *The Making of English National Identity* (2003), pp. 207ff.

[28] Korey, 'As we belong to be', p. 183.

[29] Vernon, 'Border crossings'.

[30] See, for example, Philip Payton, 'Paralysis and revival: the reconstruction of Celtic-Catholic Cornwall', in Ella Westland (ed.), *Cornwall: The Cultural Construction of Place* (1997), pp. 25–39.

[31] Roy Green, *The National Question in Cornwall* (1981), pp. 22–3.

[32] See Bernard Deacon, Dick Cole and Garry Tregidga, *Mebyon Kernow and Cornish Nationalism* (2003), chap. 2.

[33] It also ignores Cornwall's reported presence at the 1867 Pan-Celtic Conference. See Amy Hale (1997), 'Rethinking Celtic Cornwall: an ethnographic approach', in Philip Payton (ed.), *Cornish Studies Five* (1997), p. 91.

[34] *West Briton* (24 Aug. 1876 and 3 Jan. 1878).

[35] Henry Jenner, *Prospectus of the Cornish MSS society* (1876).

[36] For the fringe activities of its founder, L. C. Duncombe Jewell, alias Cameron, see Sharon Lowenna, '"Noscitur a sociis": Jenner, Duncombe-Jewell and their milieu', in Philip Payton (ed.), *Cornish Studies Twelve* (2004), pp. 61–87. For a more sympathetic view of Jenner see Derek Williams (ed.), *Henry and Katharine Jenner: A Celebration of Cornwall's Culture, Language and Identity* (2004).

[37] Robert Morton Nance, *Old Cornwall Societies: What they Are and What they are Doing* (1925).

[38] See, for example, Philip Payton and Bernard Deacon, 'The ideology of language revival', in Philip Payton (ed.), *Cornwall since the War: The Contemporary History of a European Region* (1993), p. 273.

[39] See Payton, 'Paralysis and revival'.

[40] David Everett, 'Celtic revival and the Anglican Church in Cornwall', in Philip Payton, *Cornish Studies Eleven* (2003), p. 217.

[41] Garry Tregidga, 'The politics of the Celto-Cornish Revival, 1886–1939', in Philip Payton (ed.), *Cornish Studies Five* (1997), pp. 125–50.

[42] Ronald Perry, 'Celtic revival and economic development in Edwardian Cornwall', in Philip Payton (ed.), *Cornish Studies Five* (1997), pp. 112–24.

[43] Philip Payton and Paul Thornton, 'The Great Western Railway and the Cornish-Celtic revival', in Philip Payton (ed.), *Cornish Studies Three* (1995), pp. 83–103.

[44] Ronald Perry, 'The changing face of Celtic tourism in Cornwall, 1875–1975', in Philip Payton (ed.), *Cornish Studies Seven* (1999), pp. 94–106.

[45] Ibid.

[46] Simon Tresize, 'The Celt, the Saxon and the Cornishman: stereotypes and counter-stereotypes of the Victorian period', in Philip Payton (ed.), *Cornish Studies Eight* (2000), pp. 54–68.

47 S. P. B. Mais, *The Cornish Riviera* (1934).

48 John Hurst, 'Mine, moor and chapel: the poetry of John Harris', in Ella Westland (ed.), *Cornwall: The Cultural Construction of Place* (1997), pp. 40–52.

49 Jack Clemo, *Confession of a Rebel* (1949), p. 90.

50 Perry, 'Changing face of Celtic tourism', p. 101.

51 Vernon, 'Border crossings', p. 108.

52 Kent, *Literature of Cornwall*, pp. 157–8

53 *West Briton* (29 April 1926).

54 Henry Jenner, *Who are the Celts and What has Cornwall to Do with Them?* (1928), p. 42.

55 Lowenna, *Noscitur a sociis*.

56 Stuart Dalley, 'The response in Cornwall to the outbreak of the First World War', in Philip Payton (ed.), *Cornish Studies Eleven* (2003), pp. 85–109.

57 Ella Westland, 'D. H. Lawrence's Cornwall', pp. 266–85.

58 *West Briton* (6 Feb. 1919).

59 Treve Crago, '"Play the game as men play it": women in politics during the era of the "Cornish proto-alignment" 1918–1922', in Philip Payton (ed.), *Cornish Studies Eight* (2000), p. 152.

60 See also Garry Tregidga, 'Party, personality and place: researching the politics of modern Cornwall', in Philip Payton (ed.), *Cornish Studies Ten* (2002), p. 195.

61 Crago, 'Play the game'.

62 Philip Payton, 'Labour failure and Liberal tenacity: radical politics and Cornish political culture, 1880–1939', in Philip Payton (ed.), *Cornish Studies Two* (1994), p. 91.

63 Garry Tregidga, 'Socialism and the old left: the Labour Party in Cornwall during the inter-war period', in Philip Payton (ed.), *Cornish Studies Seven* (1999), pp. 74–93.

64 Frank Michell, *Annals of an Ancient Cornish Town, Being Notes on the History of Redruth* (1978), p. 215.

65 *West Briton* (8 Dec. 1921).

66 Michael Dawson, 'Liberalism in Devon and Cornwall, 1910–1931: "the old-time religion"', *Historical Journal*, 38 (1995), 425–37.

67 *West Briton* (6 May 1926).

68 Cited in Dawson, 'Liberalism in Devon and Cornwall', p. 432.

69 Tregidga, 'Socialism and the old left', pp. 86–9.

70 Philip Payton, *A. L. Rowse and Cornwall: A Paradoxical Patriot* (2005), p. 119.

71 The duke of Cornwall gave a mere £300 to the relief fund (*West Briton*, 25 Aug. 1921).

72 Cornwall County Council, *Development Plan 1952 Report of Survey* (1952), p. 76.

73 Paul Thornton, 'Cornwall and changes in the "tourist gaze"', in Philip Payton (ed.), *Cornish Studies One* (1993), pp. 80–96.

74 Communication from Ronald Perry.

75 Cornwall County Council, *Development Plan*, p. 77.

76 Ronald Perry, 'The making of modern Cornwall, 1800–2000: a geo-economic perspective', in Philip Payton (ed.), *Cornish Studies Ten* (2002), p. 177.

77 Clive Carter, *Cornish Engineering 1801–2001: Two Centuries of Industrial Excellence in Camborne* (2001), pp. 76–7.

78 Cornwall County Council, *Development Plan*, p. 76.

79 Stephen Michell, 'Cornish Foundries – what they have achieved', *Royal Cornwall Polytechnic Society Report*, ns 7 (1932), 193–202.

80 Cornwall County Council, *Development Plan*, p. 76.

81 Kenneth Hudson, *The History of English China Clays: Fifty Years of Pioneering and Growth* (n.d.), pp. 62–4.

82 Gareth Shaw, Andrew Alexander, John Benson and John Jones, 'Structural and spatial trends in British retailing: the importance of firm-level studies', *Business History*, 40 (1998), 79–93.

[83] Cornwall County Council, *Development Plan*, p. 77.

[84] Bernard Deacon and Philip Payton, 'Re-inventing Cornwall: culture change on the European periphery', in Philip Payton (ed.), *Cornish Studies One* (1993), pp. 62–79.

[85] Ronald Perry, 'Cornwall circa 1950', in Philip Payton (ed.), *Cornwall since the War: the Contemporary History of a European Region* (1993), p. 29.

[86] Employment statistics in this paragraph from Cornwall County Council, *Development Plan*, pp. 75–81.

[87] Tregidga, 'Bodmin man', p. 170.

[88] Perry, 'Making of modern Cornwall'.

[89] Kent, *Literature of Cornwall*, p. 208.

[90] Ibid., p. 208. And see Philip Payton, *A. L. Rowse*, pp. 129–48.

[91] Frank Barlow (ed.), *Exeter and its Region* (1969), p. 4.

[92] David Crouch and Mark Toogood, 'Everyday abstraction: geographical knowledge in the art of Peter Lanyon', *Ecumene*, 6 (1999), 72–89.

[93] Kent, *Literature of Cornwall*, p. 211.

[94] Ibid., p. 248.

[95] Borough of Liskeard, *Festival of Britain Programme of Events* (1951).

[96] F. E. Halliday, *A History of Cornwall* (1959).

8

New Cornwall: population flows and policy follies, 1960–2005

In the 1960s something happened that was unpredicted. The County Council, resigned to continuing relative poverty, had assumed in 1952 that there would be a rise in population to 1971 of just 5,500, or 1.7 per cent of the 1951 figure.[1] The actual rise, of 36,200 or 10.5 per cent, caught everyone by surprise. And this was only the start. Population continued to jump by leaps and bounds to over 500,000 by 2001, almost 50 per cent above that of 1961. Only nine English counties grew faster than Cornwall in this same period. Six were spread in an arc north and west of London, from Berkshire through to Cambridgeshire. In addition West Sussex grew slightly faster, as did the more rural, less densely populated counties of Shropshire and Herefordshire on the Welsh borders.[2] In Cornwall, this massive growth was almost entirely the result of in-migration. Many more people came to live than left to work or study elsewhere. Cornwall's culture of out-migration was now joined by a culture of mass in-migration. This final chapter traces the economic context and cultural consequences of this demographic revolution. While there has been dynamism in the cultural sphere, in the political the difficulties of shaking off the legacy of royalist and 'independent' traditions resulted in the magnetism of the 'big idea' in late twentieth-century Cornwall. Lost opportunities and policy follies are highlighted while the potential of enhanced European aid to kick-start a twenty-first-century economic and cultural renaissance is critically assessed. Finally, the chapter concludes by reflecting again on Cornwall's dual traditions.

Industry-led growth 1960–1975

Despite stubborn myths of retirement migration, the bulk of migrants were people of working age. By the late 1960s Cornwall was seeing a net gain of young adults, in stark contrast to the previous century of net loss. At first, it appeared that the inflow of younger, better-off, more educated people was both symptom and cause of an economic rejuvenation. Employment grew strongly in the 1960s, with a particular rise in light engineering factories, boosted by regional development policies. The number of manufacturing units rose by sixty-four in just five years from 1966 to 1970 and factory workers by 7,300 from 1960 to 1975. This was equivalent to a gain of over 10,000 jobs, or around 8 per cent of the total Cornish workforce, if we include the jobs created by the wages spent by these factory workers.[3] Given the depressing history of the previous century, this was little short of an economic miracle. The effect of the manufacturing boom was felt even more by women. Doreen Massey has pointed out how firms were attracted to Cornwall by the availability of a cheap, under-employed reserve labour force of women.[4] Women in Cornwall's coastal communities also gained the lion's share of the economic advantages of tourism. Mass tourism had come of age in the 1950s as car ownership spread into the lower middle classes and skilled working classes. Tourist numbers then grew massively, by 50 per cent from 1964 to 1973, to peak at just over three million visitors.[5] Tourism at first was of net economic benefit, even if its cultural and social effects were more debatable.[6] Locally owned guesthouses and hotels made money and local people were employed.

Enthused by this westwards surge of capital, planners became transfixed by the idea of 'growth poles', centres of investment and economic activity that would regenerate their surrounding hinter-lands. But in Cornwall there was no obvious urban 'growth pole' around which the growing population would congregate, spinning off consumer demand. Unlike Finistere in Brittany, where Brest in the north and Quimper in the south acted in this way in the 1970s and 1980s, the lack of cities in Cornwall threatened to lead to Home-Counties sprawl rather than dynamic growth.[7] The answer for the planners looking at what they saw as the south-west of England was Plymouth. This place, with over 200,000 people, stood out as the obvious 'growth pole'. The inexorable logic was that Plymouth would be the growth centre for an economic region comprising Cornwall and Devon and would attract high-tech industry, the benefits of which would filter down the A38 into Cornwall.

The impact of Cornwall's 'second industrial revolution'

Unemployment had been reduced and the hope was that earnings would rise. Indeed, for a short time in 1973 the rate of male jobs in relation to male unemployment was better in Cornwall than in the UK as a whole. Some overexcited economists went so far as to argue that Cornwall was well on its way to becoming part of the prosperous south-east of England.[8] However, this investment also had a territorial aspect. Much of it was in the form of 'screwdriver plants', factories involved in relatively low-level assembly of goods. These were often branches of firms with headquarters located many hundreds, if not thousands, of miles away. Perry calculated that as much as 50 per cent of the new manufacturing factories were branch plants.[9] This was only the start. Potter showed that while only 39 per cent of manufacturing employment in Cornwall *and* Devon in 1966/7 was in branch factories, by 1989/90 this proportion was 64 per cent, and it was even higher in the strategically important large firms.[10] Economic growth and the 'second industrial revolution' therefore accompanied a deepening dependence on external capital, for some dangerously perpetuating Cornwall's peripheral status.[11]

Furthermore, Plymouth's role was turning out to be less of a growth pole for the Cornish economy and more a drain on it. Plymouth's main industry – its naval dockyard – was itself another example of a 'branch plant', subject to changing defence policies and political manoeuvrings in Whitehall. Meanwhile, tourism brought in its wake seasonal unemployment, observable in St Ives as early as 1948 when a summer unemployment rate of just 2 per cent soared to 10 per cent in winter.[12] As holidaymakers, especially from the wealthier south-east of England, came and enjoyed their holidays, some decided to buy into the guesthouse trade themselves. By the end of the 1950s the ownership and control of tourism slowly began to slip away from the Cornish. In places like Padstow, as the locals were consigned to new council estates on the edges of the town, they began to contrast their economic and social powerlessness with that of better-off newcomers.[13]

Culturally, dissatisfaction with the urban-led consensus began to mount in the peripheries of Britain in the later 1950s. In Scotland and Wales, this took the form of increased support for Scottish and Welsh nationalism. In Cornwall, cultural nationalism had taken a political turn in 1951, with the formation of Mebyon Kernow (Sons of Cornwall). However, its early emphasis on economic matters gave way to a more cultural nationalist approach after the mid-1950s. Remaining a small pressure group into the 1960s, MK experienced a sudden growth of membership in 1966 and 1967, triggered by its opposition to plans to accommodate an overspill population from Greater London. These schemes had attracted many councillors still fighting the 1950s battle against population decline, although at the end of the day only Bodmin accepted the overspill 'solution'. But the campaign against overspill did what almost two decades of quiet lobbying had failed to do; it catapulted MK, almost accidentally, into both the public gaze and electoral politics in the late 1960s.[14] It also led to MK devising its own economic and social manifesto for Cornwall's future in 1968, *What Cornishmen Can Do*. In many ways this was a ground-breaking document, anticipating later 'mainstream' policies such as renewable energy, more emphasis on value-added industries such as food processing rather than the primary industry of farming, a diversification of the economy, higher quality 'cultural' tourism and a University of Cornwall. But it was to take many years for these ideas to seep into wider consciousness.

For MK had missed the boat. The absence of political electoral nationalism in the 1950s meant that the only home for anti-metropolitanism in Cornwall was the Liberal Party. The Liberal revival of the late 1950s was confined to east Cornwall. Here, traditional Liberalism survived the dark years of the late 1940s and early 1950s and provided a bridge to the more community-orientated politics of the 1960s and 1970s. The Liberal surge of the late 1950s, displacing Labour as the second party in Cornwall in 1959, was at first part of a broader 'Tamarside Liberalism' shared with rural west Devon. It was Peter Bessell, candidate in Bodmin in the late 1950s, who began to develop a clearer Cornish agenda on the back of this traditional Tamarside Liberalism, calling in 1958 for a 'measure of devolution' and seeking to develop Cornwall's marketing image 'as a county apart, rather than as just a county'.[15] Cornish Liberalism then consolidated its electoral strength in the east Cornish constituencies of Bodmin and North Cornwall and from there moved west. John Pardoe from North Cornwall joined Bessel in the House of Commons in 1966 and both of these signed up with Mebyon Kernow in its 1960s pressure group phase. By 1974 Bessel had gone, embroiled in financial problems and pursued by colourful stories about CIA links. But he was more than replaced by David Penhaligon, MP for Truro from 1974 to 1986. Penhaligon was the embodiment of

Cornish Liberalism, direct, populist and using his Cornishness to full effect. Yet he also shared the ambiguities of the popular Cornish identity. As a result he was somewhat ambivalent on regionalization, at times supporting a Devon and Cornwall framework in opposition to what he saw as a 'bastardised form of regionalism' based on the seven-county South West.[16] His tragic death in a road accident robbed Cornish Liberalism of its leader but his presence had put in place the foundations for growing local electoral success in the 1980s. By this time, however, the basis of Cornwall's population growth had shifted, making local political 'power' something of an illusion.

Economic recession and population-led growth 1973–1995

The two oil shocks of 1973 and 1980/1 effectively put paid to Cornwall's manufacturing-led growth and ruthlessly exposed the shallowness of its 1960s boom. After the first crisis of 1973 inward investment slowed to a trickle. In addition, unemployment rose rapidly from 1976 to 1981, although the total number of jobs in the Cornish economy was stable. It was the second oil crisis of 1980/1, coupled with Thatcherite politics of global competitiveness, that devastated Cornwall's manufacturing economy. Cornwall's older industries felt the bracing breeze of global competition. And wilted. Major firms such as Rank Bush Murphy on the post-war industrial estate at Pool, between Camborne and Redruth, closed down, with a loss of 2,500 jobs. Meanwhile, Holmans engineering at Camborne, which had survived and even prospered during a century of structural readjustment, was absorbed into a larger group with up-country headquarters, as was Silly Cox ship repairers at Falmouth. Even the clay industry shed labour and at the end of the 1980s English China Clays moved its headquarters to Reading. In the 1960s tin mining enjoyed its last boom as prices doubled and new mines opened at Mount Wellington, Wheal Jane and Wheal Concord, the first since the Edwardian mini-boom half a century previously. But by 1985 only one mine – South Crofty – survived as tin prices plummeted to a third of their peak. While manufacturing and traditional industries reeled, even tourism growth slowed down in the ten years after 1973, although visitor numbers were stabilized at a high level.

And yet, despite all this, inward migration continued and in fact grew strongly as the 1970s experienced levels of population growth not seen since the 1830s. A number of factors contributed to this process. First, the expanding public sector in Cornwall, operating within a UK-wide labour market, drew in people to fill the new jobs in education, health and local government. This happened at the same time as managerial and executive level jobs in the private sector were being exported as a result of the concentration of ownership on the south-east of England. Second, while surveys of in-migrants in the 1980s suggested they were seeking a better 'quality of life',[17] the detailed peaks and troughs of migration implied that it was in fact heavily structured by more mundane economic factors. Peaks of in-migration in the early 1970s and again in the late 1980s coincided with house price booms. During these periods people living in the south-east of England could cash in the equity on rapidly rising property values, buy a home in Cornwall and often have money left over to cushion the transition. But the principal mechanism attracting people to Cornwall was, directly and indirectly, tourism. Holiday experiences triggered later moves west, increasingly in the 1970s via a second home that could be rented out as a holiday home prior to movement. A study in the 1980s found that 55 per cent of all new entrants into the tourist industry were simultaneously moving to Cornwall.[18]

The result was that, by the 1980s, the Cornish economy was controlled from the outside by multinational and other companies and run to a large extent on the inside by a new population of in-migrants.[19] Furthermore, what Cornish nationalists termed 'Devonwall' was given its institutional kiss of life in 1974, when Cornwall County Council quietly joined with Plymouth City Council and Devon County Council to set up a Devon and Cornwall Joint Committee. One of the aims of this was to 'establish a regional identity for Devon and Cornwall'.[20] The fact that Cornwall already had an identity and the implications of Devonwall for that identity apparently did not trouble the County Council. Devonwall was uncritically embraced by councillors, irrespective of party label.

Jeffrey Stanyer has observed that the apparently rational arguments accompanying regionalization in Britain actually 'dissolve into contradiction, moralising and pious moralising' on closer inspection.[21] Regions do not come ready-made; they are created by power. The Devonwall discourse, or way of thinking about regions, gained its strength in the later 1980s and the 1990s not just from the geographical centrality of Plymouth but also from the economic weakness of Cornwall and the power and influence of Plymouth-based media, the privatized utilities and the 'great and the good'. 'Devon and Cornwall' development institutions proliferated to service the optimum marketing areas of the large media and utility companies. As a result, Devonwall was actively and constantly promulgated by the media and accepted unthinkingly by local political actors. Cornwall County Council's occasional rhetoric against Cornwall's loss of institutions was fatally compromised by a less noisy practice of active collaboration. For example, in 1988 it called for a joint Devon and Cornwall planning body.[22] Later, in 1996, the Council's Economic Development and European Committee, dominated by Liberal Democrats, voted against a resolution to call for a Cornish Development Agency.[23]

The impact of population-led growth

After the 1970s, as other possibilities evaporated in the economic desert of neo-liberalism, policy-makers turned with relief to the holiday trade. Here was something they could all understand. Instead of the thankless task of evolving policies to diversify the Cornish economy, attention turned to the holiday and leisure industry and to population-led growth as the panacea for chronic economic decline. Maybe more people would provide more jobs and dynamise the Cornish economy with new ideas and attitudes. But these hopes were dashed. Economically, by the 1990s it was becoming clear that population-led growth and dependence on tourism had 'failed miserably ... migrants most certainly did not stimulate economic growth'.[24] For population growth to work, it needed to create more jobs than job-seekers. It failed to do this. As Malcolm Williams puts it 'Cornwall got the population without the growth'. The number of in-migrants of people of working age after the 1960s always outstripped the creation of jobs, thus embedding chronic unemployment and driving wage levels down in the more 'competitive' labour market of the 1980s. Migration, far from being the solution to Cornwall's ills, became part of its problems.

Indeed, studies suggested that in-migrants slid down the economic scale after a decade or two. Rather than dynamizing a backward economy, they were dragged down by it. Despite their initial advantages, they became economically less active after their move and contributed to Cornwall's relatively low proportion of economically active people.[25] The reasons for this lay in the dominance of tourism and its close relationship with in-migration. Most new tourist businesses were family concerns, employing few people. And when they did take on staff, they were badly paid. Dunkerley and Faerden described tourism as an industry of 'low wages' with 'minimal security'.[26] Tourist businesses were not led by the dynamic profit-maximizers of myth. Instead, they turned out to be 'satisficers', seeking a reasonable living rather than maximizing efficiency. Instead of regenerating Cornwall's economy, tourist-led population growth merely reproduced the 'low economic dynamism' of its dominant small-business sector.[27]

If the economic effects of tourism were less than inspiring the cultural effects seemed little short of catastrophic. For mass tourism structured the expectations of both in-migrants and non-migrants. Only familiar with Cornwall as a place of leisure, migrants at first viewed it as such. Ominously, everyday life in Cornwall became increasingly to be seen through the prism of the tourist industry. The media focused on tourist-related stories as other aspects of life were crowded out. In the 1990s a survey of a thousand executives of UK companies asked them how they rated six regions as locations for business and industry. The six included Cornwall, which was ranked resoundingly at the bottom, putting it below such regions as east Norfolk, west Cumbria and north Wales.[28] Michael Galsworthy, initiator of the In Pursuit of Excellence campaign complained that 'It is quite wrong for Cornwall to be promoted solely as a tourism centre'.[29] By the late twentieth century the consequences of an economy overdependent on tourism were all too plain.

The 'end of Cornwall'

In the 1980s some commentators began to point to the broader effects of population-led growth. For them it involved a process whereby Cornwall was 'swamped by a flood of middle class, middle aged, middle browed city-dwellers who effectively imposed their standards upon local society. Integration and assimilation was a one-way process – of "urbanisation" rather than "ruralisation"'.[30] And not just academics worried about this. Cornish revivalists sank into deep despair in the early 1970s. MK's first foray into parliamentary elections had brought little success – around 2 per cent of the vote – and weakened the movement by forcing out Liberal Party supporters. Moreover, the victory over overspill was soon to turn to ashes as it dawned on people that unplanned in-migration was running at levels far higher than the planned overspill of the 1960s. A sense of despair became palpable as an 'end of Cornwall' rhetoric dominated. Professor Charles Thomas, director of the newly formed Institute of Cornish Studies, claimed in 1973 that there was a 'siege mentality' and concluded that there were 'not many real Cornish left, and not all that much left of real Cornwall'.[31] The notion of 'real' Cornish and by implication 'less real' Cornish reflected a turn towards what became an inconclusive but heated debate about who the 'real' Cornish were.

This underpinned the formation of the revived Stannary Parliament in 1975, supporters of which claimed that Cornwall's Stannary Convocation had never been abolished and that the constitutional rights it rested on could still be exercised. It was a convenient position for those attracted to the idea of a Cornish independence still linked somehow to duchy and crown. It was also a convenient bolthole for those dispirited by the growing realization that the electoral road to Cornish political institutions was going to be a long and weary one. For a moment in the mid-1970s it looked as if MK was going to reject the electoral route altogether for a more romantic appeal to ancient rights and ethnic certainties. But it did not, a decision that carried the possibility of evolving a more inclusive civic nationalism in Cornwall. But initiatives such as the Stannary Parliament reflected a heightened sense of difference between Cornish and non-Cornish in the brittle 1970s. Some of this had material foundations. Industrial changes were producing a clear ethnic division of labour as branch factories brought skilled workers and managers with them. Meanwhile, the proportion of local men and women in the top jobs of local government, the health service and education was falling. Mass tourism had its class and ethnic dimensions as well. Research on Sennen concluded that former relations of deference between hosts and visitors, lived out in the shared space of guesthouses, were replaced after the 1950s by greater social and physical distance as self-catering and holiday homes grew in popularity. As the class composition of locals and visitors converged, their social contact actually diminished.[32] For some, this social separation was evidence of colonialism, reflected in the housing geography of

Cornwall as coastal communities and inland villages saw their property rapidly change hands whereas council estates and the older
industrial areas remained more obviously Cornish.[33]

Population growth levels from 1961 to 2001, ranging from 28 per
cent in the west in Penwith to 63 per cent in Caradon in the east, were
not solving Cornwall's endemic problems of low wages, low incomes
and high unemployment. But they did create growing environmental
problems. The number of houses in Cornwall doubled from 1961 to
2001. Growing demand for road space, leisure facilities, shops and
workplaces added to pressure on resources and land. Although hard
facts are difficult to acquire, it would be reasonable to assume that
since 1961 the built-up area of Cornwall has at least doubled and
perhaps trebled. Clearly, such growth was unsustainable. Traffic
congestion, rising CO_2 emissions and extreme weather associated
with global warming, as well as the lower level but more visible litter
footprints around supermarkets, schools and main roads were all
evidence of an emerging environmental crisis. A green critique
merged in the 1970s and 1980s with that from Cornish nationalist
groups to produce a recognizably Cornish 'oppositional economics'.
This called for a range of alternative policies, including a slowdown
in population growth, greater focus on Cornwall's maritime tradition, an end to overdependence on tourism and more investment in
higher education in Cornwall.[34]

Cultural renaissance

However, while Stannary revivalists and environmentalists alike
despaired, neither could predict the cultural outcome of this social
revolution. For, despite the dire warnings and apocalyptic rhetoric of
the later 1960s and 1970s, the following decades saw a resurgence of
cultural Cornishness. As in other peripheral and rural European
regions, where communities have closed ranks and asserted their
identities in the face of an invasion of outsiders, 'Cornish identity is
being expressed and performed more vigorously in a number of
arenas'.[35] As early as 1977 it was observed that a revival of interest in
Cornish history and the Cornish language was contributing to 'a new
sense of Cornish national consciousness'.[36] One of the more visible
symbols of this was the black and white St Piran's flag, originally seen
as 'MK's flag'. It now symbolizes Cornwall and is found on car

stickers, in advertising and business logos and is even used by local government as well as being vigorously waved at sporting events and demonstrations of all kinds. The widespread acceptance and recognition of the flag is a perfect example of what Michael Billig calls 'banal nationalism', the taken for granted expression of nationalism through everyday symbols and images.[37] St Piran's flag does not have to be waved any more – it is accepted in Cornwall and outside as a statement of Cornwall and Cornish identity.

The cultural renaissance expressed itself across a number of genres. For example, in literature the writings of N. R. Phillips and Myrna Combellack in the 1980s established, tentatively, a new school of Cornish realism, explicitly rejecting the romanticism that gripped writing about Cornwall.[38] Alan Kent responded to this in his novel *Clay* (1991) and called for the smashing of the romantic sandcastles by a new generation of Cornish writers.[39] However, the development of this literature has been slow. More energy has gone into Cornish music and dance. The first Cornish dance group – Cam Kernewek – emerged in the 1970s, to be followed in 1980 by Ros Keltek. From these modest beginnings Cornish dance grew to include a number of groups across Cornwall, tied together by the Cornish Dance Society. Some of the organizers of Ros Keltek were involved in setting up the annual Lowender Peran festival at Perranporth, which quickly took its place in the round of pan-Celtic cultural festivals. Such events consolidated a sense of inter-Celtic connection, something reinforced by a rash of town twinnings with communities in Brittany and by the appearance in the late 1970s of ferry links between Plymouth and Roscoff in Finistere.

Meanwhile, Cornish music expanded its repertoire far beyond male voice choirs and brass bands. The Kesson Cornish music website includes Camborne Town Band and the Four Lanes and Holman Climax male voice choirs.[40] But these artefacts of nineteenth-century Cornish popular culture are now far outnumbered by the Cornish folk, folk-jazz and other artists who dominate the forty-two groups and artists listed. Cumpas, the Cornish Music Project, began in the twenty-first century to popularize Cornish music amongst a wider audience, especially schoolchildren, under the logo 'know your past, understand your present, create your future'.[41] This project was typical of a music scene that combined a strong participatory ethos with raw energy and a willingness to experiment. Dalla was a band which, perhaps more than any other, displayed an eclectic blend of traditional and new, receiving much critical acclaim in the early years of the new millennium, beyond Cornwall as well as within. Like many of the other Cornish artists, its first two CDs, *A Richer Vein* and *Hollan Mouy/More Salt*, included tracks sung in Cornish.

In areas outside music and dance the language made less impact. Nonetheless, signs in Cornish began to sprout in the 1980s and even some businesses used Cornish in their activities, examples ranging from a washing machine repair firm in Redruth to Ottakers bookshop, Tesco and Asda. Cornish was, after much hesitation, at last accepted by the British government as a recognized minority language under the Council of Europe Charter for Regional and Minority Languages in 2003. However, it was only classed as a Part 2 language, in contrast to Welsh and Scots Gaelic, and much effort will be required to find the resources to fund the proposed language strategy. Even more difficult is the task of rebuilding trust within the Cornish-language movement, which split three ways in the mid-1980s. The debate between supporters of these three groups was and is heated and intense, although a mite arcane to the non-Cornish speaker in the street.[42] Yet, despite differences between graphemes and phonemes, spelling and pronunciation, the disputing groups perhaps say more than they intend about Cornish culture and identity. All three share a desperate quest for authenticity.[43] But this constantly eludes them, given the ambiguity of the original Cornish-language sources and the margin of error involved in restoring written evidence in order to build a spoken language. In this, the Cornish-language movement shares the uncertainties of postmodern society more generally, a society which seeks certainty only to be confronted by risk and doubt. And in its heterogeneity the modern Cornish-language movement reflects more closely the reality of modern Cornwall, one where many 'Cornwalls' compete for attention.

Despite its internecine difficulties, the Cornish language played its part in the emergence of a Cornish short film industry in the 1990s, and in 2002 even a full-length feature film in Cornish appeared with English subtitles. The infant Cornish film and TV industry was aided by Cornwall's inclusion in the Celtic Film and Television Festival in the 1990s. However, it suffers from both material and cultural constraints. Materially, Cornwall has no television company of its own so output is dominated by the Plymouth-based Westcountry

Television and the BBC. Culturally, it is bedevilled by the romantic or patronizing stereotypes that appear to be deeply embedded in agencies such as the BBC.[44]

Not only links to other Celtic countries underpinned late twentieth-century cultural energies but wider overseas connections to areas of nineteenth-century Cornish migration. The first wave of Cornish transnational identity, succoured by occupationally homogeneous mining communities, had dissolved after the First World War as second- and third-generation immigrants assimilated into American and Australian society. However, in the 1970s, growing interests in family roots and heritage triggered a turn to a hyphenated identity, to self-identification as Cornish-Australian or Cornish-American. This occurred first and went deepest in South Australia, location of the intensely Cornish nineteenth-century communities of the Yorke peninsula. Here, the Kernewek Lowender (*sic*) festival was begun in 1993 and soon became a high spot of the Cornish-Australian calendar. It was followed by the Gathering of Cornish Cousins in North America, which drew together Cornish-Americans in a similar way. This second wave of transnationalism utilized the internet to foster communications. It has also fed back into Cornwall itself. As Payton argues, 'the very existence of [new Cornish] identities was enormously supportive of attempts in Cornwall to assert separate identity, the international flavour of contemporary Cornishness a firm rebuttal for those claiming to detect parochialism in Cornish perspectives'.[45] The Cornish overseas adopted with gusto the symbols of Celtic revivalism: St Piran's flag, the Cornish tartan and even kilts, and shamelessly synthesized these with a more familiar 'traditional' industrial culture associated with mining and with 'Cousin Jack', the Cornish international mining migrant.

The support of the transnational Cornish was evident in one of the most visible public manifestations of renewed late twentieth-century confidence and pride in Cornish identity – the re-enactment in 1997 of the trek from St Keverne to Blackheath in 1497. A core of thirty or so walkers were joined by thousands more when they set off at St Keverne, when they crossed the Tamar into Devon at Launceston and again at the end of the walk at Blackheath. In the process they garnered much publicity for Cornwall and its identity.[46] A second public demonstration of Cornishness involved even more people. In the late 1980s the Cornish rugby team began to experience another one of its periodic phases of success. Although the English county rugby championships was by now a watered down and devalued event from which the best players were excluded, this gave Cornwall more chance to succeed and in any case made little difference to the thousands who supported their team in 1989–91. Just as they had in 1908, 1928 and 1958, large crowds flocked to the spiritual home of Cornish rugby at Redruth. There, they did some of the same things as their fathers and grandfathers, and even great grandfathers, had done, singing 'Trelawny' and cheering the ritual of hanging a pasty on the crossbar of the goal. But they were also very different. Women were present, the black and white St Piran's flag was everywhere and a band dressed in Cornish kilts – the Falmouth Marine Band – entertained the crowd. This spontaneously formed collection of amateur musicians nicely appealed to the self-parodying ironic twentieth-century Cornish sense of humour.

The rugby phenomenon illustrated how Cousin Jack and the Cornish bard were coming together after two or three generations of mutual incomprehension. In the process a new self-representation was in the making – one of the Cornish as 'industrial Celts', proud of both 'Celtic' and industrial traditions.[47] Other blends were noticeable. In 2002 Amy Hale claimed to observe a traversing of the boundaries between spiritual Celts and industrial Celts, while Alan Kent argued that youth surf culture in Cornwall was co-opting Celtic revivalist motifs and symbols in tattoos, jewellery and surfing logos, generating 'new notions of Cornish Celticity' in the 1990s.[48] Breaking down cultural borders was the name of the game as Cornish culture eclectically stitched new cultural practices onto old traditions, adopting and borrowing elements from other cultures and ransacking its past indiscriminately for cultural referents. This more relaxed attitude to Cornishness heralded a real qualitative change in the late twentieth century, a more innovative, dynamic experimentation that took place in widely divergent aspects of Cornish culture and culture in Cornwall, from 'Cornish' music to sport to poetry to surf culture and beyond.

Nonetheless, we should not get too excited by all this. Cultural novelty coexisted with stubbornly entrenched residual stereotypes. The TV comedy genre of the sleepy Cornish coastal village populated by a variety of 'characters' is particularly deeply rooted in media culture.[49] And hybridity is still structured by the twin traditions of Cornish history – its non-English and English influences. Thousands of Cornish men and women rushed to enlist in 'Trelawny's Army' when Cornwall were playing (and winning) rugby matches in the early 1990s. But equally, many thousands (perhaps even some of the same people) could also support the England football team when it was playing (and losing) in the 2004 European championships. Without too many contradictions, they flew the St George's flag from cars that also sometimes sported a St Piran's badge. For Cornish nationalists, immured in an oppositional world where Cornwall is not England, this could be frustrating at best, deeply depressing at worst. But what is to the Cornish nationalist false consciousness is perhaps better described as split consciousness, a reflection of the past millennium. In the light of that history it surely comes as small surprise that the Cornish can be intensely 'Cornish' but also unthinkingly 'English'. This Janus-faced aspect of the Cornish identity is a part of its heritage. It gives rise to an identity unique within the British Isles, simultaneously, and some might say schizophrenically, county or regionalist on the one hand and nationalist on the other. This crops up in many guises. For instance in 1991 the presidents of the Yorkshire and Cornwall Rugby Football Unions both provided pre-match messages before the county championship final. The Yorkshireman saw 'county' rugby as a stepping-stone to English rugby success. But the Cornishman felt moved to refer to Bishop Trelawny's imprisonment in the 1600s, arguing that 'the Cornish have the additional motivation of a Celtic people striving to preserve an identity'.[50]

Although Cornwall has been to varying degrees 'of England' since the early medieval period, culturally its people appeared to be imagining themselves after the 1970s as gradually more 'not of England'. Celtic revivalist influence strongly implanted itself and injected a major creative impulse into Cornish culture. However, dependence and lack of confidence were more profoundly embedded in the political sphere, where the legacy of the Cornish royalist tradition continued to cast a baleful shadow.

The 'big idea' and policy follies

After the 1970s Cornwall continued to slide inexorably down the league tables of wages and income. In the mid-1970s male wages were around 15 per cent lower than the British average, while female wages were just over 10 per cent adrift. However, by 2001, male earnings were a full 28 per cent and female earnings 18 per cent lower. Yet there was no real debate within Cornwall about how to challenge this decline. A deeply ingrained deference over-estimated the ability of external experts and undermined confidence in local solutions. This was institutionalized in the twentieth century by the 'Cornish consensus' in local government, where cross-party independent politics merely reinforced parochialism. Councillors looked to their own patch and no further. Parochialism in local government was reinforced by the lack of indigenous business or intellectual classes. The former was weakened in the inter-war years by the chronic problems of economic restructuring and then snuffed out by post-war company mergers and economic 'rationalization'. In parallel, the absence of a university and the out-migration of the best educated robbed Cornwall of an intellectual class who might have engendered a critical debate about the future.

Irrespective of party label, councillors embraced an approach we might characterize as the 'big idea'. This involved a 'reductionist simplification of conventional dogma . . . quick and easy solutions to extremely complex problems'.[51] Once the oil crisis of 1973 put paid to Cornwall's short-lived 'second industrial revolution', local government and media elites in Cornwall and the south-west lurched from one 'big idea' to another. Inward manufacturing investment was an early one, soon to be displaced by population growth and tourism. These were followed in the 1980s by road building, the title of a 1983 Cornwall County Council document – *Roads to Prosperity* – summing up the facile connection between dual carriageways and economic growth. In the later 1980s there was a short-lived infatuation with the idea of an external saviour, the developer who would dispense his millions on some benighted spot such as Hayle with the benefits flowing like honey through the land. Occasionally big ideas overlapped, as in the example of the Eden Project in the late 1990s, where tourism, an individual saviour and population growth appeared to combine.

Little strategic thought or independent research ever went into these big ideas. Their beauty lay in their simplicity, easy to grasp and promote as the answer to all Cornwall's problems. But the problem with the big idea was that most were classic 'policy follies', actually compounding the problems rather than solving them. For example, road building in a peripheral and dependent rural economy may temporarily reduce travel times. But faster roads also encourage suppliers to move warehouses and depots out of Cornwall, which can then be serviced from elsewhere. In addition, shorter travel times encourage people to drive further to work and shop, thus quickly pushing traffic levels back to where they were before the new road was built. In consequence, rapid population growth and growing car ownership meant that traffic in Cornwall increased by a massive 91 per cent from 1990 to 2005,[52] bringing unacceptable financial and environmental costs. Indeed, all of the big ideas shared one charac-teristic; they added to the long-term deterioration of environmental quality in Cornwall and did their bit to stoke up global warming.

But why did local 'opinion-formers' in the last quarter of the twen-tieth century act in such an apparently irrational fashion? First, the onset of neo-liberal Thatcherite policies in the later 1970s and their continuation by New Labour prioritized the market and profit-making above democracy and planning. Manufacturing investment and competitiveness were lauded. But, in regional economies like Cornwall, the role of the despised public sector was actually much more critical as an engine of growth.[53] Interestingly, in the later 1990s, when unemployment in Cornwall began to decline, it was education, health and social work that expanded their share of the 'gross value' of the Cornish economy – from 15.3 per cent in 1995 to 17.8 per cent in 2000. Conversely, manufacturing was stuck on 12–13 per cent while hotels and restaurants declined slightly from 7.1 to 6.9 per cent. Contrary to the received wisdom, government rather than private investment was the key to the health of the Cornish economy. Secondly, even if elements within local government in Cornwall real-ized this, they were hamstrung by institutional weakness. After the 1970s there was a progressive curtailing of local government autonomy in Britain. And since 2000 even the vestiges of strategic planning powers were stripped away. Key decisions about the number of houses to be built are now taken in Taunton by an unelected and unaccountable South West Regional Assembly. Growing institutional weakness compounded the historical legacy of deference to central-ized decision-making and the latest big idea. After all, the latter sometimes seemed to work in English counties. So why shouldn't they work in what both local councillors and local government officers assumed was just another English county? However, just cutting and pasting policies from other areas, without factoring in the unique Cornish combination of geography and economic history, was not a guarantee of success. In fact it was more of a recipe for disaster.

The final factor that militated against seizing those opportunities that did present themselves, for example the possibility of a Cornish Polytechnic in the late 1960s or establishing Cornwall as a European region in the 1980s, was the lack of a civil society where such issues could be raised and debated. The flight of institutions out of Cornwall had produced an institutional vacuum. This was no recent phenomenon. The takeover of Cornish businesses and banks began in the late nineteenth century. The nationalization of the 1940s centralized decision-making away from Cornwall as did the public sector 'rationalizations' of the 1960s, when institutions such as the Cornwall Police Force were amalgamated with those of Devon. Finally, the market-orientated policies of the 1980s and 1990s gave greater power to utilities such as South West Water, based at Exeter. With no TV or daily newspaper produced in and responsible to Cornwall as a unit, decisions were increasingly weighted towards institutions and elites based outside Cornwall and answerable to other masters, whether political or shareholding. The way such decisions were made became opaque when viewed from Cornwall. There was thus no forum outside the emasculated corridors of local government where a vibrant civil society could flourish. And local government was too heavily influenced by the parochial 'city-state' mentality produced in the Edwardian era to take on a wider strategic leadership role.

Objective One – the only game in town

By the early 1990s it was depressingly clear that one of Cornwall's strengths was its relative economic deprivation. Low gross domestic product (GDP) per head now made it eligible for European Regional Development Fund Objective One money, the highest level of grant aid available. The only problem was that, under the rules of European funding, only Level 2 regions qualified for this money. And Cornwall was in the mid-1980s lumped in with Devon as part of a larger Level 2 region. It is likely that pressure from the small but vociferous Devonwall lobby steamrollered the Devon and Cornwall region through with few people being aware of the negative consequences of this action. Devon's higher GDP per head meant that a combined Devon and Cornwall region was nowhere near eligible for Objective One funding.

Cornish pressure groups began to campaign in the early 1990s for a redrawing of the regional map. But at the time the MEP for Cornwall and Plymouth, Christopher Beazley, assured campaigners confidently that Cornwall 'on its own can never hope to obtain European regional grants'.[54] It was just too small. Despite the presence of many other smaller Level 2 regions in Europe, Cornwall County Council meekly followed the MEP's lead and refused to call for Cornwall to be reassigned as a Level 2 region. The Devonwall policy folly stood in the way of European funding. However, the Devonwall lobby was less powerful than it appeared. In reality it was driven by a small and unrepresentative minority of big businesses (just 235 out of 11,000 businesses in Devon and Cornwall were members of South West Enterprise, the Westcountry Development Corporation's private sector arm).[55] In 1997 the incoming Labour government made clear its preference for regionalization based on a seven not two 'county' template and the Devonwall lobby promptly melted away in the face of the central government-sponsored Bristol based Regional Development Agency. From a Cornish perspective Devonwall was an unmitigated policy folly, entered into with no open public debate, dominated by a small, unrepresentative group of business and media interests and Plymouth-based academics whilst wilfully throwing away the strengths that Cornwall possessed.

As the Devonwall ship ran onto the rocks, central government in 1996 asked the Office for National Statistics (ONS) to investigate redrawing the European regional map. In the ONS consultation by far the greatest number of submissions calling for revised boundaries came from Cornwall, the vast majority of these from supporters of some measure of devolution. By 1998 local Devonwall supporters had realized that time was running out, their project squeezed on the one side by mounting calls in Cornwall for it to become a Level 2 region and on the other by central government's preference for Bristol over Plymouth. There was only way to jump – onto the bandwagon. That year witnessed the unedifying spectacle of a host of county councillors and other 'opinion-formers', together with the local media, scrambling desperately onto a 'Campaign for Cornwall', which called for the separation of Cornwall from Devon for European funding purposes. People who only a few months previously had been vehement supporters of Devonwall were now fiercely demanding that Cornwall become a European region. Once the South West Regional Development Agency (SWRDA) was set up that too threw its weight behind calls for a redrawing of the map, by now virtually a *fait accompli*.[56]

Objective One was the latest 'big idea', although using the full potential of EU recognition to rebrand Cornwall as a coherent European region was hastily rejected. Cornwall's Objective One programme became the only one in Britain to be administered from outside the territory receiving the aid. The presence of the new RDA and the government's top–down regionalization ensured that the programme was managed at a south-west regional level. Moreover, in reality, like population-led growth or road building or tourism, Objective One cannot be the panacea for all Cornwall's ills. It brings with it both opportunities and threats. The latest 'big idea' is the 'knowledge economy'. If this entails grasping the opportunities to fill strategic gaps in Cornwall, seeking to generate an economy that is not overdependent on tourism and unsustainable growth, and empowering local communities and adding to their confidence then it might chart a route away from the policy follies of the past half-century, On the other hand, if Objective One stokes up the same old unsustainable trends, merely drawing in more in-migrants while failing to transform Cornwall's underlying problems of peripherality it might reverse the more promising economic trends of the late 1990s and undermine the growing cultural confidence of the past twenty years. Ironically, there was evidence that things were improving, albeit slowly, in the late 1990s, before Objective One funding was in place. Though wage levels were still very low, unemployment was to some extent converging with the general UK level. Culturally, there were signs that fatalism and defeatism were at last being dispelled.

More fundamental and unresolved ambiguities remain around Cornwall's Objective One de facto regional status and its de jure marginal status as a part of an English region. Furthermore, lack of local control, the institutional vacuum in Cornwall and the weakness of its intellectual infrastructure have resulted in the emergence of a peripatetic 'project class', enticed to Cornwall by the well-paid jobs that Objective One and other regeneration initiatives bring and attracted by perceived quality of life factors. We will have to wait and see whether this project class is able to transcend deeply ingrained English stereotypes of Cornwall or understand the socio-cultural context of Cornish economic problems. Ominously, in the corridors of regional government, a stubbornly 'traditional' image of Cornwall still holds sway, one that rests on stereotypes of rurality and leisure/

tourism imagery. Cornwall still acts as the purest foil to dynamic urban metropolitanism, more rural, more sleepy, more remote, more 'tribal', more of a holiday and leisure zone, more romantic, than the 'rest' of the south-west.[57] This strongly embedded discourse of Cornwall takes on even more importance as the peak regional institutions and regeneration quangos engage in increasingly frenetic image politics. As democratic accountability wanes so, in the twenty-first century, the importance of rhetoric waxes. The emphasis of the regeneration industry on 'quality housing', 'office space, 'retail units' and 'leisure complexes' confirms the limited range of what is included within 'development', the staple mantra of 'regeneration' since the 1980s.[58] The main difference in the 2000s is a discernable emphasis on gentrification, or selling Cornwall as an arts and gourmet centre.

The danger of this 'Quality Cornwall' strategy is that it merely consolidates another round of in-migration, adds to pressures on the housing market and undermines employment growth in classic late twentieth-century fashion. In addition, gentrification widens the social divisions of Cornwall's new two-tier society, exacerbating problems of social exclusion. On the one hand we have lifestyle Cornwall, the Cornwall of Rick Stein's restaurants, the Tate, the Maritime Museum, the St Endellion and du Maurier Festivals, the Cornwall of high incomes, four-wheel drives and selfish greed. On the other we have life-struggle Cornwall, estates sunk into a spiral of despair and scarred by poor health, vandalism, drugs and petty crime, places where low incomes and deprivation are the norm. This hidden social crisis may be illustrated by the relatively high number of households headed by a lone parent in west Cornwall in the 2001 Census.

The Cornish identity in the early twenty-first century

As Cornwall enters the third millennium, the contradictions and tensions created by its dual traditions are still visible. In the imagination of the majority of British people Cornwall is England's first and last county. In Cornish imaginations, its place can be more ambivalent. Some people still think of Cornwall as England's last county in more than a geographical sense. In fact in 2004 a survey by the financial services company Morgan Stanley found that 44 per cent of

Cornish residents felt more Cornish than English or British or European, the highest 'local' identification in Britain.[59] Cornwall is the only territory administered as an English county yet which contains a people with a distinct ethnic identity. Memories of Cornwall's non-English origins still inspire non-English identifications. Cornwall's recognition during the twentieth century as a Celtic country portends other possibilities. Meanwhile a renewed Cornish transnationalism reminds the Cornish of a past that looked outwards, to the edges of the British Empire and beyond, rather than inwards to its core. Cornwall is still, to the puzzlement of some, the despair of others, both 'of' England and 'not of' England.

Moreover, a higher proportion of Cornish men and women are prepared to define themselves as Cornish rather than English instead of Cornish *and* English. The end of the twentieth century witnessed a new assertiveness as pent-up frustration over successive denials of their rights spilt over onto anger. This was best illustrated in the enthusiasm which met John Angarrack's book *Our Future is History* in 2002. This was the first explicitly Cornish nationalist interpretation of Cornwall's past, resolutely reconstructing a history of former independence ruthlessly crushed by centuries of English colonialism. Angarrack's book heralded a new breed of Cornish activist, more forthright, more confident and less likely to be appeased or overawed. As well as his historical writings, Angarrack spearheaded a series of campaigns on behalf of the Cornish right to be recognized as an ethnic group. These campaigns were often successful as inconsistencies and illegalities in the bureaucratic treatment of the Cornish were exposed.

Nonetheless, this new human rights activism was still of marginal importance to the majority. And Cornwall's relatively small size still led to its invisibility in official circles and stereotyping in the media. Whereas the north of England received the serious and sympathetic treatment of 'Our Friends in the North' Cornwall still got sniggering sitcoms such as 'Wild West'.[60] Yet even the twin peaks of New Labour began to go out of their way to mention Cornwall. In 2000 Tony Blair said 'we can comfortably be Scottish and British or Cornish and British or Geordie and British or Pakistani and British'.[61] This was uncannily echoed four years later by Gordon Brown who 'suggested it is possible to be Scots or Cornish, Muslim or English and still celebrate a British identity which is bigger than the sum of the parts'. In the cultural sphere the twenty-first-century

Cornish identity is allowed to take its place in the tapestry of British multiculturalism. But in the political sphere the government of Messrs Blair and Brown set its face stubbornly against the arguments of the Cornish campaign for a Cornish Assembly. This campaign was the only one able to demonstrate any degree of popular enthusiasm for devolution through a petition of 50,000 signatures collected in 2000/1. But the 2002 White Paper *Your Region, your Choice* specifically excluded any possibility of basing regional assemblies on other than government-decreed administrative planning regions and showed little wish to recognize Cornwall's distinct position or the strength of its cultural identity. Seen from Westminster, the Cornish were intermittently appearing on the cultural radar screen but politically they were well below the horizon of visibility, a mere irritant in the stately progress of British realpolitik.

In 1993 we pointed to the way a more hybrid identity was synthesizing the hitherto separate strands of twentieth-century Cornish culture.[62] Since that time this has become the received wisdom. Culturally, runs the accepted opinion, things in Cornwall are changing. Kennedy and Kingcome pointed to the many interwoven narratives of Cornwall, where an eclectic mix of DIY subcultures has mushroomed in recent decades.[63] Amy Hale noted the refashioned heritage narratives of Cornwall.[64] The demise of Cornish mining means that it can now join the Cornish language as an aspect of heritage to be preserved, with a symbolic application as an icon of Cornishness rather than a part of everyday life. Thus the two strands of the non-English tradition in Cornwall effectively merge: the Celtic, with its roots deep in Cornwall's British origins although owing its revival to much more recent events, and the industrial, more recent but with traditions running deeply into Cornwall's medieval past. Nevertheless, these now share the social terrain with other ideas and stereotypes from mainstream English culture, directly plugged into Cornish life via the process of mass in-migration.

The future

The challenge for this society is how to foster its cultural energies and extend them into the political and economic spheres. How do we guarantee the right of the Cornish to be Cornish and yet also expand that so it can embrace and include others? For this to happen

Cornishness has to have a civic as well as ethnic aspect. Civic identities require civic cultures to thrive. Peter Wills has pointed out how
civic culture, including history and identity, tends to be passed over
by the regeneration experts as they cluster around the quick fixes
offered by bricks and mortar.[65] Wills called for a civic culture that
recognizes Cornwall's uniqueness, regards Cornwall as a region in its
own right, reinvents a Cornish enterprise culture and recreates a
Cornish institutional framework. In the current over-centralized
political environment, it is difficult to discern Wills's civic culture.
Furthermore, in its absence, and given the institutional vacuum in
Cornwall, other forces are given free rein. Market forces go
unchecked and unchallenged, offering taken-for-granted truisms and
appealing to the tradition of the 'big idea' that has since the 1960s
replaced strategic policy discussion. Whatever 'vision' is on offer
turns out in practice to be more shops, increasing road congestion,
mounting pollution and public squalor as the consumer–citizen stag-
gers from one shallow consumption fix to the next. Similarly, a
politics that hands over decision-making to technocratic bureaucrats
in Bristol or Brussels or to local quangos and where political parties
are obsessed by the narrow world of Westminster merely produces
cynicism with the political process and disturbing levels of alienation
from democracy. In the 2004 Euro-elections the UK Independence
Party, supported heavily by the *Western Morning News*, won the
highest number of votes in four of the six Cornish districts, its success
indicating a level of alienation that suggests new policy solutions may
get a more sympathetic hearing. But, to be heard, they require an
institutional forum, where the future of Cornwall can be properly
debated and shaped. A regional assembly could do much to inspire
government in Cornwall, providing a democratic strategic leadership
but remaining human-scale and accountable, unlike the large
centrally imposed regions of government-engineered English devolution. However, Cornwall's institutional vacuum also means that any
regional assembly must have considerably more powers than the
feeble institutions envisaged in the 2004 Regional Assemblies Act.[66]

Tom Nairn, in supporting more independence for Scotland, rejects
Britishness, which he powerfully argues has lost its way since the
disappearance of empire and offers only an increasingly hollow
appeal to past 'greatness' and long-gone traditions.[67] But just as
Britishness is problematic for Scotland, so is Englishness for
Cornwall. We cannot easily reject our Englishness, because to do that

we would have to reject an important part of our heritage. Culturally, the Cornish are obviously intimately affected by centuries of English influence. Nonetheless, we can reject Cornwall's location as the unthinking tail of the English dog. Being merely English offers dismal and unexciting prospects when the English are themselves wracked by self-doubt and uncertainty. However, unlike English regions, Cornwall's past gives it another card to play.[68] With the proper institutional framework, Cornwall could become a progressive European region, utilizing existing cultural links with Brittany to expand its networks with other European partners, making full use of its maritime location, generating the spin-offs from its considerable cultural capital and evolving its own small-scale policy solutions. Control over the decisions that shape its future would extend existing cultural confidence. Such a future, with a sense of direction led by democratic and inclusive Cornish institutions and empowered Cornish communities, could even finally knit together the sometimes schizophrenic dual traditions of the Cornish past, using its tensions creatively to construct, at last, that 'new Cornwall' many have sought.

Cornwall has never possessed more than 2 per cent of the people of the British Isles yet it has contributed more than its fair share to Britain's history. It is unique in that it looks both to the English core and outwards to other 'Celtic' societies and further overseas to the 'transnational' communities created by its industrial history. Cornwall is not another Celtic country writ small, nor is it just another English county. In the cultural sphere its maritime connections played a stronger role; in the political sphere landward influences predominated. At times such as the twelfth, sixteenth and twentieth centuries, the latter were in the ascendancy; at others, such as the seventh, the fifteenth and late eighteenth/early nineteenth, overseas influences came to the fore. But just as contemporary Cornwall suffers from the imposition of the all-encompassing 'big idea', so its past has suffered from the imposition of grand, overarching narratives, whether of independence/integration, industrialization/ deindustrialization or centre/periphery. To understand Cornwall's past properly we need to be sensitive to differences within Cornwall and recognize the existence of Cornwalls, existing and potential, in the past and in the future.

Notes

[1] Cornwall County Council, *Development Plan 1952 Report of Survey* (1952), p. 107.

[2] Calculated from published *Census*.

[3] Perry et al, *Counterurbanisation*, pp. 55 and 67–68.

[4] Doreen Massey, 'Industrial restructuring as class restructuring: production decentralization and local uniqueness', *Regional Studies* (1983), 73–89.

[5] Allan Williams and Gareth Shaw, 'The age of mass tourism', in Philip Payton (ed.), *Cornwall Since the War; The Contemporary History of a European region* (1993), pp. 84–97.

[6] See Arthur Quiller-Couch, 'How to develop Cornwall as a holiday resort' *Cornish Magazine* 1 (1898), 237–38 for an early expression of the native distrust of tourism.

[7] Ronald Perry, 'Self-image, external perceptions and development strategy in Cornwall', in Michael Havinden, Jean Queniart and Jeffrey Stanyer (eds), *Centre and Periphery: Brittany and Cornwall and Devon Compared* (1991), pp. 230–2.

[8] D. J. Spooner, 'Some qualitative aspects of industrial movement in a problem region of the UK', *Town Planning Review*, 45 (1974), 63–88.

[9] Ronald Perry, 'The role of small manufacturing business in Cornwall's economic development', in Gareth Shaw and Allan Williams (eds), *Economic Policy and Development in Cornwall* (1982), p. 30.

[10] Jonathan Potter, 'External manufacturing investment in a peripheral rural region: the case of Devon and Cornwall', *Regional Studies*, 27 (1992), 193–206.

[11] Philip Payton, 'Socio-economic change in post-war Cornwall: the dynamics of the centre–periphery relationship', *Journal of Interdisciplinary Economics*, 4 (1992), 241–8.

[12] Cornwall County Council, *Development Plan*, p. 81.

[13] J. Herman Gilligan , 'Padstow: economic and social change in a Cornish town', in C. C. Harris (ed.), *Family, Economy and Community* (1990), pp. 165–85.

[14] Bernard Deacon, Dick Cole and Garry Tregidga, *Mebyon Kernow and Cornish Nationalism* (2003), pp. 49–52.

[15] Garry Tregidga, '"Bodmin Man": Peter Bessell and Cornish politics in the 1950s and 1960s', in Philip Payton (ed.), *Cornish Studies Eight* (2000), pp. 161–81.

[16] Annette Penhaligon, *Penhaligon* (1989), p. 110.

[17] Peter Mitchell, 'The demographic revolution', in Philip Payton (ed.), *Cornwall since the War; The Contemporary History of a European Region* (1993), pp. 135–56.

[18] Gareth Shaw, Allan Williams and J. Greenwood, *Tourism and the Economy of Cornwall* (1987).

[19] Perry et al., *Counterurbanisation*, pp. 56–65.

[20] Cornwall County Council, Planning Committee Agenda, 6 Sept. 1988.

[21] Jeffrey Stanyer, 'The Janus-faced periphery: Cornwall and Devon in the twentieth century', *Policy and Politics*, 25 (1997), 85–97.

[22] Cornwall County Council, Planning and Employment Committee minutes, 29 June 1988.

[23] *West Briton* (18 Jan. 1996).

[24] Malcolm Williams, 'Why is Cornwall poor? Poverty and in-migration since the 1960s', *Contemporary British History*, 17 (2003), 55–70.

[25] Malcolm Williams and Tony Chapman, 'Cornwall, poverty and in-migration', in Philip Payton (ed.), *Cornish Studies Six* (1998), pp. 118–26. Carol Williams, 'Housing in Cornwall: a two-tier system?', in Philip Payton (ed.), *Cornish Studies Three* (1995), pp. 194–206.

[26] David Dunkerley and Ian Faerden, 'Aspects of seasonal employment in Devon and Cornwall', in Peter Gripaios, *The South West Economy* (1985), p. 22.

[27] Ronald Perry, 'Economic change and "opposition" economics', in Philip Payton

(ed.), *Cornwall since the War: The Contemporary History of a European Region* (1993), p. 74.

[28] *Western Morning News* (3 Aug. 1995).

[29] *Western Morning News* (21 Oct. 1998).

[30] Perry et al., *Counterurbanisation*, p. 129.

[31] Charles Thomas, *The Importance of Being Cornish in Cornwall* (1973), p. 21.

[32] Michael Ireland, 'Gender and class relations in tourism employment', *Annals of Tourism Research*, 20 (1993), 666–84.

[33] Bernard Deacon, 'Is Cornwall an internal colony?', in Cathal O Luain (ed.), *For a Celtic Future: A Tribute to Alan Heusaff* (1983), pp. 259–72.

[34] Bernard Deacon, Andrew George and Ronald Perry, *Cornwall at the Crossroads: Living Communities or Leisure Zone?* (1988).

[35] Amy Hale, 'Representing the Cornish: contesting heritage interpretation in Cornwall', *Tourist Studies*, 1 (2001), 185–96.

[36] Colin Rallings and Adrian Lee, 'Politics of the periphery – the case of Cornwall', paper presented to the 'Politics of the United Kingdom' Conference, Aberystwyth (1977).

[37] Michael Billig, *Banal Nationalism* (1995).

[38] N. R. Phillips, *The Saffron Eaters* (1987) and Myrna Combellack, *The Playing Place* (1989). These have been followed by N. R. Phillips, *Horn of Strangers* (1996) and *Apocalypse Dreckly* (2005); Myrna Combellack, *A Fine Place: The Cornish Estate* (2002) and *The Permanent History of Penaluna's Van* (2003). See also Alan Kent, *Proper Job, Charlie Curnow!* (2005).

[39] Alan Kent, 'Smashing the sandcastles: realism in contemporary Cornish fiction', in Ian Bell (ed.), *Peripheral Visions: Images of Nationhood in Contemporary British Fiction* (1995), pp. 173–80.

[40] www.kesson.com/kesson, accessed 9 Sept. 2004.

[41] www.cumpas.co.uk, accessed 9 Sept. 2004.

[42] For a flavour of the debate of the 1980s see P. A. S. Pool, 'A plea for Unified Cornish', *Old Cornwall*, 10 (1989), 431–5; Wella Brown, 'The reform of revived Cornish', *Old Cornish*, 10 (1989), 436–40; Richard Gendall, 'The language of the Cornish people', *Old Cornwall*, 10 1990), 531–5.

[43] Bernard Deacon, 'Language revival and language debate: modernity and post-modernity', in Philip Payton (ed.), *Cornish Studies Four* (1996), pp. 88–106.

[44] For an excellent review see Alan Kent, 'Screening Kernow: authenticity, heritage and the representation of Cornwall in film and television, 1913–2003', in Philip Payton (ed.), *Cornish Studies Eleven* (2003), pp. 110–41.

[45] Philip Payton, *The Cornish Overseas* (1999), p. 396. See also Bernard Deacon and Sharron Schwartz, 'Cornish identities and migration: a multi-scalar approach', *Global Networks* 7 (2007), 289–306.

[46] Simon Parker (ed.) *Cornwall Marches on! Keskerdh Kernow 500* (1998).

[47] Hale, 'Representing the Cornish'.

[48] Amy Hale, 'Whose Celtic Cornwall? The ethnic Cornish meet Celtic spirituality' and Alan Kent, 'Celtic nirvanas: constructions of Celtic in contemporary British youth culture', in David C. Harvey, Rhys Jones, Neil McInroy and Christine Milligan (eds.), *Celtic Geographies: Old Culture, New Times* (2002), pp. 157–70 and 208–26.

[49] BBC TV, *Wild West* (2003); ITV, *Doc Martin* (2004).

[50] *Camborne Packet* (13 April 1991).

[51] Perry, 'Economic change', p. 78.

[52] BBC Radio Cornwall news report, 24 Feb. 2005.

[53] Lovering argues this is the case for Wales in John Lovering, 'Theory led by policy: the inadequacies of the "new regionalism" illustrated from the case of Wales', *International Journal of Urban and Regional Research*, 23 (1999), 379–95.

[54] *West Briton* (4 March 1993). This was echoed by academic commentators, for example, Peter Gripaios ('Review of *Cornwall Since the War*', *Regional Studies*, 28 (1994), 766) stated 'Given its small size in population and workforce terms, it may not get (a lot of money)'. Both were proved wrong.

[55] *Western Morning News* (10 July 1995).

[56] For the role of the SWRDA in this and the way they airbrushed the earlier role of Cornish activists out of the story see Bernard Deacon, 'Under construction: culture and regional formation in south-west England', *European Urban and Regional Studies* (2004), 213–25.

[57] Ibid.

[58] See CPR Regeneration, *How to Regenerate Camborne, Pool and Redruth* (2004).

[59] *Daily Telegraph* (18 March 2004).

[60] Mark Sandford, 'A Cornish Assembly? Prospects for devolution in the Duchy', in Philip Payton (ed.), *Cornish Studies Eleven* (2003), pp. 40–56.

[61] *The Times* (11 Feb. 2000); *Guardian* (8 July 2004).

[62] Bernard Deacon and Philip Payton, 'Re-inventing Cornwall: culture change on the European periphery', in Philip Payton (ed.), *Cornish Studies One* (1993), pp. 62–79.

[63] Neil Kennedy and Nigel Kingcome, 'Disneyfication of Cornwall – developing a Poldark heritage complex', *International Journal of Heritage Studies*, 4 (1998), 45–59.

[64] Hale, 'Representing the Cornish' (2001), p. 192 and 'Whose Celtic Cornwall' (2002), p. 164.

[65] Peter Wills, 'Cornish regional development: evaluation, Europe and evolution', in Philip Payton (ed.), *Cornish Studies Six* (1998), pp. 143–62.

[66] Sandford, 'Cornish Assembly', p. 50.

[67] Tom Nairn, *After Britain: New Labour and the Return of Scotland* (2001).

[68] Eric Hobsbawm, *Nations and Nationalism since 1780* (1992), p. 178.

Index